Lecture Notes in Computer Science 13865

Founding Editors

Gerhard Goos
Juris Hartmanis

Editorial Board Members

The series Lecture Notes in Computer Science (LNCS), including its subseries Lecture Notes in Artificial Intelligence (LNAI) and Lecture Notes in Bioinformatics (LNBI), has established itself as a medium for the publication of new developments in computer science and information technology research, teaching, and education.

LNCS enjoys close cooperation with the computer science R & D community, the series counts many renowned academics among its volume editors and paper authors, and collaborates with prestigious societies. Its mission is to serve this international community by providing an invaluable service, mainly focused on the publication of conference and workshop proceedings and postproceedings. LNCS commenced publication in 1973.

Cameron Browne · Akihiro Kishimoto ·
Jonathan Schaeffer

Editors

Computers and Games

International Conference, CG 2022
Virtual Event, November 22–24, 2022
Revised Selected Papers

Springer

Editors
Cameron Browne 🆔
Maastricht University
Maastricht, The Netherlands

Akihiro Kishimoto 🆔
IBM Research - Tokyo
Tokyo, Japan

Jonathan Schaeffer
University of Alberta
Edmonton, AB, Canada

ISSN 0302-9743   ISSN 1611-3349 (electronic)
Lecture Notes in Computer Science
ISBN 978-3-031-34016-1   ISBN 978-3-031-34017-8 (eBook)
https://doi.org/10.1007/978-3-031-34017-8

Preface

This volume collects the papers presented at the 11th *Computers and Games* conference (CG 2022) which took place during 22–24 November 2022. This conference was held online in 2022 and coordinated from Maastricht University (the Netherlands), the University of Alberta (Canada) who provided the Zoom stream on which the conference was conducted, and IBM Research, Tokyo (Japan).

The bi-annual *Computer and Games* conference series is a major international forum for researchers and developers interested in all aspects of artificial intelligence and computer game playing. Earlier conferences took place in Japan (1998 and 2000), Canada (2002), Israel (2004), Italy (2006), China (2008), Japan (2010 and 2013), and Taiwan (2018). The previously scheduled occurrence of this event, planned for 2020, was cancelled due to the COVID epidemic, and the 2022 event was held online for the first time.

The themes for this year's CG conference were widened to include games research beyond the usual traditional/mathematical games research. This is reflected in the greater number of papers on multi-player and simulation games.

The CG 2022 programme consisted of four keynote talks and five regular paper sessions, as listed below. All papers and presentation videos can be accessed at the CG 2022 web site.[1]

Session 1: Classic Games

The opening session, chaired by Jos Uterwijk, collected three papers focussed on analyses of classic board games. These included "FairKalah: Towards Fair Mancala Play" by Todd Neller and Taylor Neller, "Improving Search in Go Using Bounded Static Safety" by Owen Randall, Ting-Han Wei, Ryan Hayward, and Martin Müller, and "Chinese Checkers Bitboards for Move Generation and Ranking Using Bitboards" by Nathan Sturtevant.

Keynote: Matt Ginsberg *What I Learned from Dr Fill*
The first keynote speaker was Matt Ginsberg (Google X), introduced by Martin Müller. For more than a decade Dr Ginsberg has been developing technology for solving crossword puzzles. His talk showcased his program's superhuman performance in the 2021 American Crossword Puzzle Tournament – the technologies used, the challenges faced, and the areas for improvement.

Session 2: Multi-Player and Multi-Action Games

This session, chaired by Todd Neller, presented new results in a variety of multi-player, multi-action, and simulation games. The papers presented were "Solving Chainmail

---

[1] https://icga.org/?page_id=3434

Jousting" by Daniel Collins, "An Algorithm for Multiplayer Games Exploiting Opponents' Interactions with the Player" by Kyle Sacks and Brayden Hollis, and "Incentivizing Information Gain in Hidden Information Multi-Action Games" by Nathan Lervold, Gilbert L. Peterson, and David W. King.

Keynote: Murray Campbell *The Evolving Role of Games in AI*
The second keynote speech was by Murray Campbell (IBM T.J. Watson Research Centre), introduced by Jonathan Schaeffer. Dr Campbell talked about the past, present, and future research challenges posed by trying to develop strong game-playing AIs. Contrary to those who think that working on game AI is a thing of the past, a convincing argument was given that there are many interesting and important Game AI challenges for our community to work on.

Session 3: Solving Games

Michael Hartisch chaired this session on solving, or at least providing more complete complexity analyses, of some classic and modern games. This session included the papers "QBF Solving Using Best First Search" by Yifan He and Abdallah Saffidine, "Oware is Strongly Solved" by Xavier Blanvillain, and "Solving Impartial SET Using Knowledge and Combinatorial Game Theory" by Jos Uiterwijk and Lianne Hufkens.

Keynote: Tao Qin *Deep Reinforcement Learning for Game Playing and Testing*
The third keynote speech was by Tao Quin (Microsoft Research AI4Science), introduced by Akihiro Kishimoto. His talk covered two topics on deep reinforcement learning and games: The world-best Mahjong-playing program Suphx which has achieved the level of 10 dan for the first time, and the automated game-testing agent Inspector, which is based on game pixels or screenshots and which is applicable to a variety of video games.

Session 4: Measuring Games

This session on *Measuring Games*, chaired by Reijer Grimbergen, explored ways of computationally measuring games for their potential to interest human players. The papers included "Which Rules for Mu Torere?" by Cameron Browne and "Measuring Board Game Distance" by Matthew Stephenson, Dennis J.N.J. Soemers, Éric Piette, and Cameron Browne.

Keynote: Olivier Teytaud *AI and Games: New Directions*
The fourth and final keynote was by Olivier Teytaud (Meta AI Research), introduced by Cameron Browne. Dr Teytaud gave a high level overview of recent developments in AI for playing and analysing games, and new lines of research that might be pursued. It nicely complemented Dr Campbell's keynote talk.

Session 5: Decision Making in Games and Puzzles

Matthew Stephenson chaired Session 5 on *Decision Making in Games and Puzzles*, which focused on the decision-making process in terms of playing games, cheat detection, and new content generation. The papers included "Improving Computer Play in Skat with Hope Cards" by Stefan Edelkamp, "Batch Monte Carlo Tree Search" by Tristan Cazenave, "Human and Computer Decision-Making in Chess with Applications to Online Cheat Detection" by Thijs Laarhoven and Aditya Ponukumati, and "Procedural Generation of Rush Hour Levels" by Gaspard de Batz de Trenquelleon, Ahmed Choukarah, Milo Roucairol, Maël Addoum, and Tristan Cazenave.

Acknowledgements

The organisation of CG 2022 was partly supported by the European Research Council as part of the Digital Ludeme Project (ERC CoG #771292). The online technology was provided by the University of Alberta's AI4Society. Thanks to Nicolás Arnácz and Eleni Stroulia for their tremendous support.

November 2022

Cameron Browne
Akihiro Kishimoto
Jonathan Schaeffer

Organization

Organizing Committee

Cameron Browne   Maastricht University, The Netherlands
Akihiro Kishimoto   IBM Research, Japan
Jonathan Schaeffer   University of Alberta, Canada

ICGA Executive

Tristan Cazenave   LAMSADE Université Paris Dauphine PSL
                                      CNRS, France
Hiroyuki Iida   Japan Advanced Institute of Science and
                                      Technology, Japan
David Levy   Independent, UK
Jonathan Schaeffer   University of Alberta, Canada
Jaap van den Herik   University of Leiden, The Netherlands
Mark Winands   Maastricht University, The Netherlands
I-Chen Wu   National Yang Ming Chiao Tung University,
                                      Taiwan

Program Committee

Bruno Bouzy   Paris Descartes University, France
Cameron Browne   Maastricht University, The Netherlands
Tristan Cazenave   LAMSADE Université Paris Dauphine PSL
                                      CNRS, France
Lung-Pin Chen   Tunghai University, Taiwan
Reijer Grimbergen   Tokyo University of Technology, Japan
Michael Hartisch   University of Siegen, Germany
Ryan Hayward   University of Alberta, Canada
Chu-Hsuan Hsueh   Japan Advanced Institute of Science and
                                      Technology, Japan
Hiroyuki Iida   Japan Advanced Institute of Science and
                                      Technology, Japan
Nicolas Jouandeau   Paris 8 University, France
Tomoyuki Kaneko   University of Tokyo, Japan

Contents

Decision Making in Games and Puzzles

Classic Games

FairKalah: Towards Fair Mancala Play

Todd W. Neller[⊠] and Taylor C. Neller

Gettysburg College, Gettysburg, PA 17325, USA
tneller@gettysburg.edu
http://cs.gettysburg.edu/~tneller/

Abstract. Kalah (a.k.a. Mancala) is a two-player game of perfect information that has been a popular game for over half a century despite a strong first player advantage. In this paper, we present initial game states that are fair, as well as optimal play insights from analysis of optimal and suboptimal states.

1 Introduction

Kalah (a.k.a. Kalaha), usually called "Mancala" in the United States, is a Mancala game variant invented in 1940 by William Julius Champion and patented in 1955 as US Patent 2,720,362 [3]. In the Mancala games family, it is most closely related to Dakon [10, p. 75] from Java. Despite being a perfect information game with a strong first player advantage [5], Kalah has enjoyed popularity in the United States and Germany through its history. In this paper, we share initial game states that are fair[1] and provide insights to game play from analysis of optimal and suboptimal states.

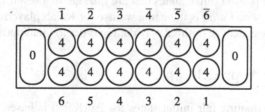

Fig. 1. Kalah initial board state with 4 pieces per play pit

Kalah (a.k.a. Mancala) is played on a rectangular board as depicted in Fig. 1 with 6 play pits for each player along the long side and 1 score pit ("Kalah") for each player on the player's right-hand end of the board. In the standard initial board state, each of the play pits starts with 4 pieces (a.k.a. seeds, counters) per pit. In constrast to prior rules, we label play pits by the number of pits they are clockwise from that player's score

---

[1] In this paper, we use "fair" in the sense that two perfect players would draw the game. There is no game-theoretic advantage for either player.

© The Author(s), under exclusive license to Springer Nature Switzerland AG 2023
C. Browne et al. (Eds.): CG 2022, LNCS 13865, pp. 3–13, 2023.
https://doi.org/10.1007/978-3-031-34017-8_1

pit. Pits of the second player (a.k.a. "north player") are notated with overbars. Numbers depicted within pits indicate the number of pieces in that pit[2].

On a player's turn, the player selects one of their play pits containing pieces, removes all pieces from that play pit, and redistributes ("sows") them counterclock-wise, one piece per play/score pit, and skipping their opponent's score pit. If the last piece redistributed lands in their score pit, the player takes another turn, i.e. gets a free move; otherwise, it becomes the opponent's turn. If the last piece redistributed lands in an empty play pit of the player (including after having redistributed pieces to all oppo-nent play pits), then that piece captures: both that piece and any pieces in the opponent's opposite play pit are removed from the pits and placed into the player's score pit[3].

The game ends when, at the end of a turn, there are no pieces left in one player's play pits. Their opponent scores any remaining pieces in play pits. The player with more pieces in their score pit wins. If the number of pieces in the score pits are the same, the players draw (i.e. tie) the game.

While boards and pieces are readily available commercially, this game has often been played with egg cartons and bowls as play and score pits, respectively. Glass beads, beans, stones, and shells are just some of the materials used throughout the world to play Mancala games.

Featuring simple rules and accessibility of materials, Kalah has been successfully popular, but with a little play, one can easily discern that opening with plays 4 and 1 put the second player at a significant advantage. Irving, Donkers, and Uiterwijk computed that optimal play for the standard initial board results in a first player win by 10 points (39–19). In our notation, one line of optimal play of Fig. 1 is as follows: 41, $\overline{56}$, 3, $\overline{3}$, 1513, $\overline{5}$, 2, $\overline{1}$, 621, $\overline{2}$, 131214, $\overline{13}$, 2, $\overline{5}$, 3, $\overline{4}$, 6, $\overline{12}$, 5, $\overline{3}$. Using this notation has the convenience that when there are free moves on a turn (e.g. 131214), the number of pieces moved is the same as the pit label for all except the final move.

In this paper, we present initial states that are *fair*, i.e. that result in a draw between two optimal players. *FairKalah* is the name we use for Kalah played from a fair initial state. Additionally, we analyze optimal play data in order to yield optimal play insights.

2 Algorithmic Approach

Our approach to computing fair initial states for FairKalah is based on Java code we ported from Irving's original C code used for the results of [5]. We computed a 24-piece endgame database (1.16 GB), so search could terminate when half of the pieces had been scored. The standard initial board has 48 pieces with 4 pieces per play pit. At the top level of our algorithm, we enumerated all possible ways that one could move one or two of these pieces to different pits, including score pits[4] (e.g. Sect. 7 boards).

---

[2] Thus, a potential free move is easily seen where the number of pieces matches our numeric label for that pit.

[3] There is some controversy over whether "empty captures" were intended, as they were disal-lowed in Dakon. However, a strict reading of the patent makes no requirement for the number of opponent pieces opposite. Our interpretation is consistent with [5] and most printed rules.

[4] When we have a fair game with piece(s) in the score pit, we have essentially created a fair game with fewer piece(s) and a perfect komi compensation for fairness.

For each candidate initial game state, we evaluate the game value using the MTD(f) algorithm [4,9]. "Game value" here has more information than win/lose/draw; it is the score difference at game end with optimal play. Search was highly optimized with the MTD(f) algorithm, our large endgame database, and Irving's node ordering: transposition table move, free moves right-to-left, captures right-to-left, and remaining moves right-to-left. For MTD(f), we used an initial game value guess of 0, with Plaat's "next" choice being that of Van Horssen's Algorithm 2, and using Van Horssen's "SAFE" choice for storing the new best move in the transposition table.

After computing all 3 fair boards needing one piece movement and all 251 fair boards needing two piece movements (Sect. 7 Appendix), we computed and stored all non-terminal states along all possible optimal lines of play for these 254 fair initial positions.

3 Analysis of Fair Optimal Game Trees

A *fair optimal game tree* (FOGT) is a subtree of a game tree where the root game state of the subtree has game value 0 (i.e. results in a draw with perfect play), and each state node retains only successor-state children with game value 0. That is, a fair optimal play tree contains best plays of a drawn (sub)game.

There are pros and cons of analyzing data for optimal decisions from all game tree nodes, which we do later in the paper. On the positive side, one gains a complete picture of optimal play for any game states. On the negative side, the distribution of states includes mainly states that optimal players would not allow. That is, the distribution of states is skewed towards irrelevance in optimal game play.

In contrast, FOGTs provide the opportunity for focused insight on optimal play. We can ask questions of a state distribution where *both* players are playing optimally, gaining insight to what the highest level of Kalah play looks like. In the following subsections, we share raw and derived features of our collected game states as well as insights from the data.

3.1 Features

Of special interest are statistical and machine learning insights on the choice of optimal plays themselves. For this exploration, we define features that we conjecture may be relevant to optimal play decision-making and/or node game value prediction. These include both raw state variables and derived variables.

depth the number of plays made so far in the game (not included in model input)

player the current player p, either 0 or 1 for first/"s"/south player or second/"n"/north player, respectively (not included in model input)

pit_6, ..., pit_1, score, pit_6o, ..., pit_1o, score_o the number of pieces in each pit starting with the current player's leftmost play pit and proceeding counter clockwise around the board

counters, counters_o the sum of pieces in the current player's and opponent's play pits, respectively

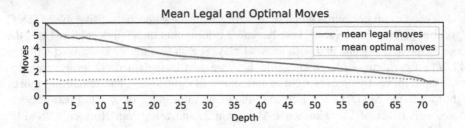

Fig. 2. Branching factor and optimal moves by depth.

free_moves, free_moves_o the number of current player and opponent play pits, respectively with pit index n containing n pieces

is_free_move_n whether or not pit n has n pieces

is_closest_free_move_n whether or not a pit n is the closest free move to the score pit

capture_move_n number of pieces captured by playing pit n

move_count number of non-empty pits on the current player's side of the board

move_count_o number of non-empty pits on the opponent's side of the board

relative_mobility move_count minus move_count_o

is_closest_move_n whether or not a pit n move is the closest move to the score pit

score_gain_n the number of pieces scored after pit n is moved

is_largest_capture_move_n whether or not a pit n move captures the largest number of pieces among all capture moves

largest_capture the largest number of pieces that the current player could capture

score_diff the current player's scored counters minus their opponent's scored counters

counter_diff the current player's in-play counters minus their opponent's in-play counters

is_exposed_n whether or not pit n has no pieces across from it

piece_threat_n number of pieces in pit n under immediate threat of capture

game_val The current player score minus the opponent score if the game was played to completion with perfect play (0 for fair game states)

optimal_n whether or not pit n of the current player is an optimal move

3.2 Optimal Play Branching Factors and Tension

From the 9,991,466 unique nonterminal optimal play states of these MTD(f) searches (including optimal endgame database states), there are 28,366,064 total plays and 15,828,178 optimal plays, yielding average play and optimal play branching factors of approximately 2.839 and 1.584, respectively. The number of states with 1–6 optimal moves are, respectively: 5,619,419, 3,188,759, 933,219, 219,859, 29,112, and 1,098. Thus, 88.16% of states have 1 or 2 optimal plays. Most states with 6 optimal plays avoid playing into the opponent play pits with the opponent having a forced emptying of their pits on the next turn (e.g. 1 piece adjacent to their score pit).

For FOGT states, there is a decreasing trend in both branching factor and number of optimal moves with increasing depth, as shown in Fig. 2. Whereas the branching factor is always 6 at the root, the mean branching factor non-monotonically decreases to 1 as the number of pieces on the board decreases with depth. However, the mean number of optimal moves remains relatively steady, between 1 and 2 throughout play, slightly increasing for moderate depths.

As a result FOGT game tension, defined as the fraction of game-losing moves, is shown in Fig. 3. This derives from Cameron Browne's measure of puzzle tension [2], i.e. the fraction of losing plays. Here, we observe that tension is close to $\frac{5}{6}$ for root nodes, indicating that most but not all FairKalah roots have a unique optimal first play. This then non-monotonically decreases with depth down to 0.

A significant implication of this is that real-time management of play should favor computation distributed more towards early decisions. We would expect a precomputed opening book with a time-management policy such as OPEN [1] to be advisable for blunder avoidance when using limited memory and time, respectively.

3.3 Strategic Insights

Recall that a player gets a free move, i.e. another turn, when playing n pieces from pit n and having the last piece redistributed to the player's score pit. Of the 9,991,466 unique nonterminal optimal play states, 5,558,640 (55.63%) offer free moves. Of these, 5,326,495 (95.82%) have the closest free move to one's score pit as an optimal move. Thus, if one has one or more free moves, one should most likely play the closest free move to one's score pit.

In the remaining 232,145 (4.18%) states, the strategic considerations are diverse. In some states, taking the free move would force one to then play a closer pit that would spill one more pieces onto the opponent's side. In others, it is preferable to accumulate pieces in low index pits for endgame scoring. And, of course, some free moves spoil capture opportunities.

Captures are another important strategic consideration. Given that taking the closest free move is a frequent optimal play, we will now restrict our attention to states without free moves. There are 4,432,826 (44.37%) non-free-move states. Of these, 3,777,047 (85.21%) offer capture move(s). Of these non-free-move states with potential capture(s), 3,212,373 (85.05%) have an optimal capture move. Thus, if there is no free move, there is a 72.47% chance that a capture move is optimal.

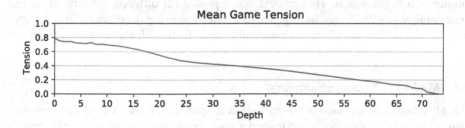

Fig. 3. Game tension by depth.

This brings us to consideration of the frequencies with which play pits are found to be optimal:

Pit	States Optimal	Percent
1	3568534	35.72%
2	2945674	29.48%
3	2640664	26.43%
4	2527830	25.30%
5	2333925	23.36%
6	1811551	18.13%

As we can see, pits closer to a player's score pit are indeed more likely to be optimal plays. The probability of optimality of the closest pit is highest and that probability decreases monotonically with each farther pit to slightly over half of the probability in the farthest pit. This is to be expected as close free moves are the most frequent and easy to set up, and one often clears the farthest pits in response to capture threats.

Note that our FOGT data fully supports the wisdom of the node-ordering heuristic of [5]: After a stored transposition table move (if available), consider free moves, then captures, then other moves, preferring moves closer to the score pit within each category. This should, in turn, guide our strategic prioritization of move considerations in play.

4   Modeling Optimal Play for Diverse States

We are interested in using such data to build predictors of expected game value as well as optimal move prediction by pit. While examining optimal game states of Kalah led to some interesting results, predictive power of models trained on only FOGT data did not generalize well to non-fair states. Thus, to better model optimal play, we generated a different training data set that included unfair (non-0 value) Kalah states.

In order to efficiently generate diverse state data, we randomly generated distinct starting nodes by randomly scoring 5 pieces from different pits. We then analyzed optimal play for each node using a breadth-first-traversal limited to 100 nodes per depth, similar to a beam search. This process was repeated for different randomized initial states until 9,449,283 states were generated. After removing depth and player number features and adding the aforementioned engineered features from the point of view of the current player, the number of unique states was 6,151,746.

4.1   Model Performance Summary

For all prediction, we used a 50–50 train-test split. For prediction of the negamax state game value `game_val`, we trained a number of different models: scikit-learn's `LinearRegression`, `DecisionTreeRegressor`, and `RandomForest-Re-gressor`, as well as the CatBoost `CatBoostRegressor`. `DecisionTree-Regressor` had a `min_samples_split=500000`, `RandomForestRegress-or` had hyperparameters `n_estimators=100`, and `CatBoostRegressor` had

Model	MSE	R^2
Linear regression	23.69	0.81
Decision tree	43.84	0.63
Random forest	5.70	0.95
CatBoost	4.37	0.96

Fig. 4. Regression model performance summary

`iterations=30`, `learning_rate=0.9`, and `depth=16`. A performance summary is given in Fig. 4.

Similarly, we built classification models for each play pit predicting `optimal_n`, i.e. whether the pit is an optimal play using scikit-learn's `LogisticRegression` and `RandomForestClassifier`, as well as the `CatBoostClassifier`.

Since empty play pits are illegal for play and trivial to predict as not optimal, our performance measurements per pit are for only states where those pits are not empty. Accuracy and log loss performance results are given per pit number in Figs. 5 and 6, respectively. We also include a "Base predictor" row for a probabilistic prediction based on the frequency of non-empty pit states for which that pit is optimal.

Model	6	5	4	3	2	1
Base predictor	.68	.68	.67	.65	.57	.58
Logistic regression	.80	.80	.78	.77	.77	.86
Random forest	.87	.86	.86	.85	.86	.89
CatBoost	.89	.88	.88	.87	.87	.92

Fig. 5. Classification accuracies per non-empty pit model

Model	6	5	4	3	2	1
Base predictor	.63	.63	.63	.65	.68	.68
Logistic regression	.43	.44	.47	.48	.46	.31
Random forest	.31	.32	.33	.33	.32	.23
CatBoost	.27	.28	.28	.29	.29	.21

Fig. 6. Classification log loss per non-empty pit model

4.2 SHAP Beeswarm Figure Interpretation

Using the `shap` package, we generated beeswarm plots in Figs. 7 and 8, to visualize SHapley Additive exPlanation (SHAP) values [7] for our CatBoost `game_val` and `optimal_1` prediction models, respectively. SHAP values "assign each feature an importance value for a particular prediction." [6] Each instance in our dataset represents one point for each horizontally visualized feature. The subset of features included are the most significant to the model prediction according to SHAP values, with higher features being most significant. The horizontal position of each point is determined by

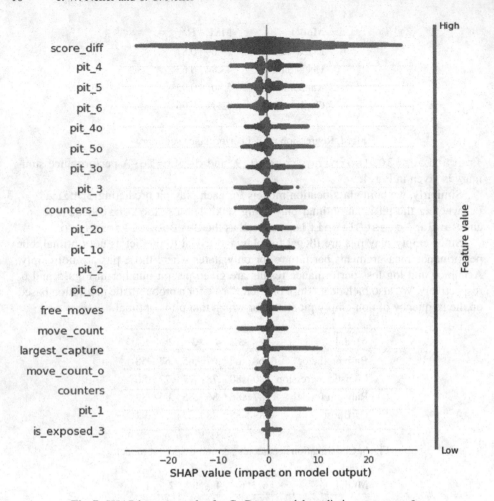

Fig. 7. SHAP beeswarm plot for CatBoost model predicting `game_val`

its SHAP value for that feature, and points are bunched more thickly along each feature row to show density. Color of a dot represent the original feature value for that instance, with red/blue indicating high/low values, respectively.

For example, Fig. 7 shows us first and foremost that `score_diff`, i.e. the current score difference is the strongest positively correlating predictor for the final score different, i.e. the game value. Looking at the next five most significant features, we see that number of pieces in pits 4, 5, 6, $\overline{4}$, $\overline{5}$, $\overline{3}$, and 3 are all strong predictors of game value, with more pieces in those pits tending to positively correlate with higher game values with the exceptions of pits 4 and 3. More pieces in opponent pits (`counters_o`) negatively correlate with game value.

Turning our attention to Fig. 8, we see that the single most significant predictor for pit 1 being an optimal play is the fact that it is the closest free move, i.e. a free move. The number of pieces in pit 1 is the next most significant feature, with more pieces negatively correlating with optimality. Higher numbers of free moves positively correlate, as taking a farther free move first would add a piece to pit 1, ruining the free

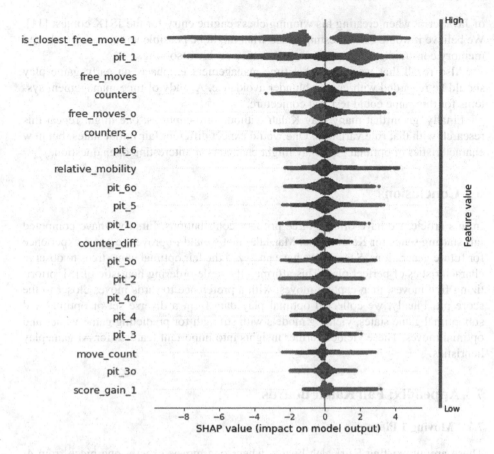

Fig. 8. SHAP beeswarm plot for CatBoost model predicting `optimal_1`

move option. A greater number of counters for either player negatively contributes to prediction of optimality, but the number of opponent free moves positively contributes.

We lack space here to share all of the insights that can be drawn from such plots, but such explanatory visualizations can be helpful for forming hypotheses of strategic significance in play.

5 Future Work

We believe there are interesting future work possibilities in seeking to approximate optimal play under computational constraints. Whereas one can easily compute any optimal play on current retail computers within half a minute using our 1.16 GB endgame database and search optimization, we are interested in what is possible for web and mobile apps with limited computational resources.

Our best predictive models of optimal play are memory intensive, yet we believe the necessity of strict memory and time limitations can spur further insight to Kalah AI strategy. It was surprising what Óscar Toledo Gutiérrez was able to accomplish in 1 KB of JavaScript when creating his winning chess engine entry for the JS1K contest [11]. We believe it would be interesting to see what might be possible with various code and memory constraints. Limitations breed creative problem-solving.

Also recall that we expect that time-management emphasis on early game play should be rewarded with greater blunder avoidance. A study of time-management systems for this game could test that conjecture.

Finally, given that many play Kalah without zero-captures, one might repeat this research with that rule variation. One would expect different fair initial states, but how characteristics of optimal gameplay might change is an interesting open question.

6   Conclusions

In this article, we have offered three primary contributions. First, we have computed fair starting states for Kalah (a.k.a. Mancala) that should improve the game experience for future generations. Second, we have analyzed the fair optimal game trees to observe characteristics of perfect play. This affirmed the node-ordering heuristic of [5], prioritizing free moves, then capture moves, with a preference towards moves closer to the score pit. Finally, we collected optimal play data from a diverse set of optimal and suboptimal game states, yielding models with strength for predicting game values and optimal moves. These yielded further insights into important features for AI gameplay heuristics.

7   Appendix: FairKalah Boards

7.1   Moving 1 Piece

These are all existing FairKalah boards where one moves exactly one piece from 4-pieces-per-pit initial conditions.

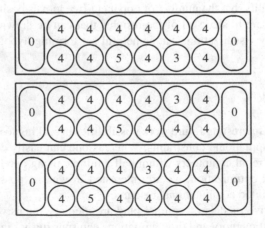

7.2 Moving 2 Pieces

All 251 existing FairKalah boards where one moves exactly two pieces from 4-pieces-per-pit initial conditions are available in SVG image form and as CSV data from the FairKalah website [8]. In the CSV data, comma-separated integers on each line indicate the number of pieces in each pit (including scoring pits) starting from the first (i.e. "south") player's leftmost play pit and proceeding counterclockwise.

References

1. Baier, H., Winands, M.H.M.: Time management for Monte-Carlo tree search in go. In: van den Herik, H.J., Plaat, A. (eds.) ACG 2011. LNCS, vol. 7168, pp. 39–51. Springer, Heidelberg (2012). https://doi.org/10.1007/978-3-642-31866-5_4
2. Browne, C.: Tension in puzzles. Game Puzzle Design J. **3**(2), 71–78 (2017)
3. Champion, W.J.: Game counter (US Patent US2720362A, 1955–10-11). https://patents.google.com/patent/US2720362A/en
4. van Horssen, J.J.: Move selection in MTD(f). ICGA J. **41**, 1–9 (2019). https://doi.org/10.3233/ICG-190096
5. Irving, G., Donkers, J., Uiterwijk, J.: Solving Kalah. ICGA J. **23**(3), 139–147 (2000). http://citeseerx.ist.psu.edu/viewdoc/summary?doi=10.1.1.4.7870
6. Lundberg, S.: beeswarm plot - SHAP latest documentation (2022). https://shap.readthedocs.io/en/latest/example_notebooks/api_examples/plots/beeswarm.html. Accessed: 2022-09-03
7. Lundberg, S.M., Lee, S.I.: A unified approach to interpreting model predictions. In: Guyon, I., et. al. (eds.) Advances in Neural Information Processing Systems, vol. 30. Curran Associates, Inc. (2017). https://proceedings.neurips.cc/paper/2017/file/8a20a8621978632d76c43dfd28b67767-Paper.pdf
8. Neller, T.W., Neller, T.C.: FairKalah: Fair Mancala. http://cs.gettysburg.edu/~tneller/games/fairkalah/. Accessed: 2022-08-29
9. Plaat, A., Schaeffer, J., Pijls, W., de Bruin, A.: Best-first fixed-depth minimax algorithms. Artif. Intell. **87**(1), 255–293 (1996). https://doi.org/10.1016/0004-3702(95)00126-3
10. Russ, L.: The Complete Mancala Games Book: How To Play the World's Oldest Board Games. Marlowe & Company (2000). https://books.google.com/books?id=BA9yHQAACAAJ
11. Toledo Gutiérrez, O.: Chess programs (2022). https://nanochess.org/chess.html. Accessed: 2022-09-03

Improving Search in Go Using Bounded Static Safety

Owen Randall[1,2]([✉]), Ting-Han Wei[1,2], Ryan Hayward[1], and Martin Müller[1,2]

[1] Computing Science, University of Alberta, Edmonton, AB, Canada
{davidowe,tinghan,hayward,mmueller}@ualberta.ca
[2] Amii, University of Alberta, Edmonton, AB, Canada

Abstract. Finding the winner of a game of Go is difficult even on small boards due to the game's complexity. Static safety detection algorithms can find a winner long before the end of a game, thereby reducing the number of board positions that must be searched. These static algorithms find safe points for each player and so help prove the outcome for positions that would otherwise require a deep search. Our board evaluation algorithm Bounded Static Safety (BSS) introduces two new methods for finding valid lower bounds on the number of safe points: *extending liberties* and *intersecting play*. These methods define statically evaluated greedy playing strategies to raise the lower bound of a player's guaranteed score. BSS can solve positions from a test set of 6×6 games at an average of 27.29 plies, a significant improvement over the previous best static safety method of locally alternating play (31.56 plies), and far surpassing Benson's unconditional safety (42.67 plies).

Keywords: Go game · Safety under alternating play · Game solving · Game tree search · Static evaluation

1 Introduction

Go is a classic test bed for computing science research. Much previous work on board evaluation has focused on heuristic estimates. For example, AlphaGo [13] and its successors [12,14,15] train a value network, a deep neural network that predicts the winning probability in an arbitrary Go game state. While these heuristics led to superhuman strength Go programs, they do not find the game-theoretic value of a Go state: exact board evaluation methods are required for this task [11,16,17]. Exact game solvers can also be used to find mistakes in the play of strong game playing programs [4], and exact board evaluation in Go has been used to provide the ground truth for training neural networks which predict point ownership: this auxiliary task improved the accuracy of the open source program KataGo [18,20]. Therefore there is practical value in pursuing and improving exact board evaluation methods. We focus on static analysis of safe points: we give a strategy that guarantees a minimum number of points for

© The Author(s), under exclusive license to Springer Nature Switzerland AG 2023
C. Browne et al. (Eds.): CG 2022, LNCS 13865, pp. 14–23, 2023.
https://doi.org/10.1007/978-3-031-34017-8_2

a player. If this number is above a threshold which depends on board size and *komi*, then the player is guaranteed a win.

Bounded Static Safety (BSS) improves upon previous algorithms for static safety [2,6]: after first using such algorithms to find a core set of safe points, it uses new greedy strategies to find higher guaranteed scores for each player. Our experiments show that BSS typically solves game positions much earlier than previously possible. This improves the efficiency of search-based solvers for Go, enabling more difficult positions to be solved in the same amount of time.

2   Related Work

Benson's static algorithm [2] finds *blocks* of stones that are *unconditionally safe*: they cannot be captured, even when the defender always passes. *Safety by local alternating play* (LAP) finds a larger set of of safe stones and surrounded regions by allowing simple local defender responses, based on concepts such as *miai strategies* and *chains* [6]. We use the Benson and LAP implementations in the open-source program Fuego [3] as baselines for evaluating BSS. Work by Niu et al. applies static safety analysis based on LAP within a specialized local search framework [8], with extensions to finding safety in open regions [9,10], and resolving seki [7]. Those algorithms are designed for large-scale searches on 19×19 boards, while our BSS algorithm focuses on fast static analysis which can be used within a small board solver.

3   Background

3.1   Rules of Go

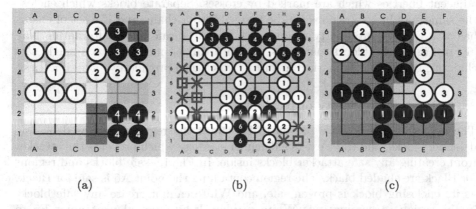

(a)   (b)   (c)

Fig. 1. Example Go positions. (a) With block numbers and shaded liberties (b) Sure liberty regions (c) Safe regions.

This section provides a very brief summary of the rules of Go; see [1] for full details. In Go, two players take turns placing a stone of their color on a point on the board. A *block* is a group of adjacently connected stones of the same color. A *liberty* is an empty point adjacent to a block. Figure 1a shows an example position with labeled blocks and their liberties. A play on the last liberty of a block captures it, and it is removed from the board. A no-suicide rule forbids players from killing their own blocks.

3.2 Sure Liberty Regions

Let $A_{\neg c}$ be all of the points which are not of color c, then a basic *region* of color c is a maximally connected subset of $A_{\neg c}$; see [8] for full details. Regions are enclosed by blocks of their color, e.g. in Fig. 1b, the points marked Y make up a region enclosed by the black blocks marked 3 and 4. If a defender block B is an enclosing block for region R, and there exists a strategy such that B always has a liberty in R when it is the attacker's turn, then R is a *sure liberty region* for B. This concept is closely related to, but more narrowly defined than the popular notion of an *eye*. For example, in Fig. 1a, A4 is a trivial sure liberty region for block 1. A block with at least two sure liberties is safe under local alternating play (LAP).

Miai strategies help to identify sure liberty regions. An *interior point* of a region is a point which is not adjacent to an enclosing block. A region is a sure liberty region if every empty interior point is adjacent to at least two unique adjacent defender liberties. A miai strategy on such liberty pairs ensures that there is always a liberty available to the enclosing block, even if it is the attacker's turn, as the attacker must leave at least one empty point in the region due to the no-suicide rule. For example in Fig. 1b, the region containing point A9 enclosed by block 1 is a sure liberty region for block 1 using the miai strategy. The points in the region marked by squares are interior points and each require a pair of adjacent liberties which are marked by crosses. Separate blocks which enclose the same sure liberty regions can be merged into a chain, and if a set of chains has at least two sure liberty regions each then it is safe under alternating play [6]. In Fig. 1b the blocks marked 3, 4, and 5 can be merged into a single safe chain using the regions marked Y and Z, which also provide two sure liberties.

3.3 Proving the Safety of Regions

The points of a region are proven to be safe if the region is enclosed by safe defender blocks, and there exists a defender strategy which prevents the attacker from creating any safe attacker blocks inside. In Fig. 1c, safe blocks and regions for Black are shaded black. The region containing the point A6 is safe for Black, as its enclosing block is proven safe, and White cannot create any safe blocks in the region. Assuming it is White to play, White can play at point F5 to make the block marked 3 safe, making this an unsafe region for Black. A region which contains two non-adjacent points which could become attacker eye points is considered unsafe.

4 Improving Lower Bounds for the Number of Safe Points

We propose two novel static techniques, *extending liberties* and *intersecting play*. In LAP safety, lower bounds on player scores are calculated by simply counting the number of safe points on the board. We develop defender strategies which greedily occupy nearly empty points, in order to increase the defender lower bound. To compute the bound, the attacker plays an optimal response to each greedy strategy. Evaluating the score resulting from these strategies *does not require search*. Defender scores are initialized by using LAP safety analysis, before additional safe points are counted using the new techniques. The resulting lower bound is at least as good as the underlying baseline method.

4.1 Technique 1: Extending Liberties

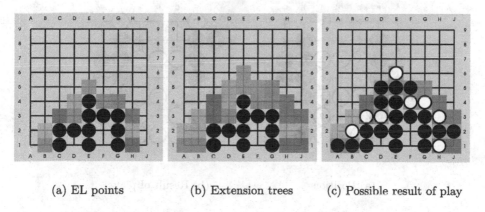

(a) EL points   (b) Extension trees   (c) Possible result of play

Fig. 2. Example position with extension trees colored. Empty points of the same color belong to the same extension tree. (Color figure online)

The extending liberties strategy has the defender greedily play on *Extending Liberties (EL) points* which are empty points in unsafe regions that are adjacent to safe defender blocks. Any defender stones placed adjacent to a safe defender block will also become safe, improving the lower bound of their score. Figure 2a shows every EL point for Black as a different shaded color. Playing on an EL point could create new EL points, e.g. in Fig. 2a if Black plays C3, points B3 and C4 become EL points. We define an *extension tree* as a set of an EL point and any empty adjacent points. Extension trees must be non-overlapping to avoid over-counting. Figure 2b shows a valid extension tree layout where the points in each extension tree are shaded the same color. There can be multiple valid extension tree layouts. In practice a valid layout is chosen arbitrarily.

The value of an EL point is equivalent to the size of the extension tree it belongs to. In Fig. 2b EL point B2 is more valuable than EL point B1, because its extension tree has more points. If the defender plays on an EL point, any points in the same extension tree become EL points themselves, however their respective extension trees do not grow. If the attacker plays on an EL point, any points in the same extension tree are removed from play. The defender plays greedily with respect to the value of EL points. Thus the optimal attacker strategy is to also play greedily with respect to the value of EL points. Figure 2c shows a possible line of play if Black is following the extending liberties strategy and White is responding optimally. The lower bound on the defender's score is increased by the number of safe points they would gain by playing this strategy. For the example position in Fig. 2 the lower bound for Black's score would increase from 14 to 22 using the extending liberties technique.

4.2   Technique 2: Intersecting Play

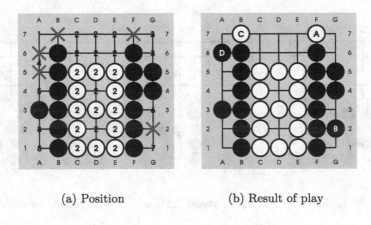

(a) Position   (b) Result of play

Fig. 3. An example 7 × 7 position.

Intersection points are empty points such that placing a stone on that point subdivides the region it was placed in. In an *intersecting play strategy*, the defender only plays on their intersection points which create new safe points. The optimal attacker responses are therefore also on the same points to prevent defender safety. Similar to the extending liberties strategy, we define a value for each intersection point, and the defender plays greedily with respect to these values.

We introduce the following terminology to describe this technique:

- *Intersection node*: holds information corresponding to an intersection point; connected to region nodes.
- *Region node*: holds information corresponding to a region that is enclosed by defender blocks and intersection points; connected to intersection nodes.

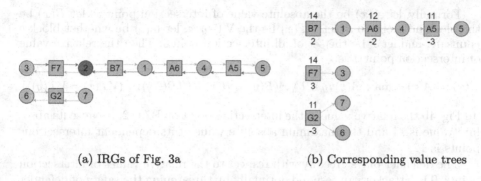

(a) IRGs of Fig. 3a   (b) Corresponding value trees

Fig. 4. Example position for intersecting play. (Color figure online)

- *Intersection-region graph* (IRG): a bipartite graph containing intersection and region nodes. Holds relevant information on the positioning of intersection points and regions.
- *Value tree* (VT): a tree derived from an IRG, which only contains nodes with the potential to be safe.

Figure 3a shows Black's intersection points marked as crosses and the regions associated with region nodes marked as numbers. Note that region nodes are distinct from basic regions as they can be enclosed by intersection points. Region nodes of size zero can exist between adjacent intersection points, e.g. region node 4. Figure 4a shows the IRGs corresponding to the example position. Green nodes are potentially safe, red nodes cannot be safe. E.g. region 2 already contains safe attacker points, so the defender cannot be safe there. Connections are unsafe if they can belong to a trail which includes an unsafe node, in Fig. 4a unsafe connections are colored red.

VTs are constructed from the safe trees which exist in each IRG. The root of each VT is the intersection node adjacent to an unsafe region in its corresponding IRG. If an IRG has no unsafe nodes an arbitrary intersection node is chosen for the root of a VT. Figure 4b shows the value trees derived from the IRGs in Fig. 4a. The numbers above each intersection node are their absolute values, and the numbers below are their relative values. Absolute values represent the number of safe points the defender will gain if they play at this point. In Fig. 3a if Black plays A6, the adjacent block becomes safe, earning Black 12 safe points, therefore the intersection point's absolute value is 12.

A defender move which creates a safe block will affect the value of every intersection point adjacent to that block. In Fig. 3a if the defender plays G2, the adjacent block will become safe which will change the absolute value of intersection point F7 from 14 to 3. The absolute values of intersection points are dependent if they are adjacent to the same unsafe defender block, or are in the same VT. The relative value of an intersection point is the increase in the number of safe points the defender will gain by playing on this point compared to playing on any other dependent intersection point.

Formally, let $A(x)$ be the absolute value of intersection point x, let $B(x)$ be the block adjacent to x, let $VT(x)$ be the VT of x, let $U(b)$ be whether block b is unsafe, and let I be the set of all intersection points. Then the relative value of intersection point x is:

$$R(x) := A(x) - \mathbf{max}\{A(y) \forall y \in I \setminus x | (B(y) = B(x) \wedge U(B(X))) \vee (VT(x) = VT(y))\}$$

In Fig. 4b the relative value of the intersection point on B7 is 2, because its absolute value is 14 and the maximum absolute value of its dependent intersections points is 12.

The defender plays greedily with respect to the relative values of intersection points. The attacker can respond optimally by threatening the safety of defender blocks if possible, or by playing greedily with respect to relative values otherwise. If an unsafe defender block only has two adjacent intersection points, the attacker can threaten the safety of the block by playing on one of these points. In Fig. 3a intersection point B7 initially has a larger relative value than point G2. However, when White plays F7 the safety of the block is threatened, forcing Black to play G2. This allows White to play B7 on their next turn. Figure 3b shows the result of play when following the intersecting play strategy.

5   Results

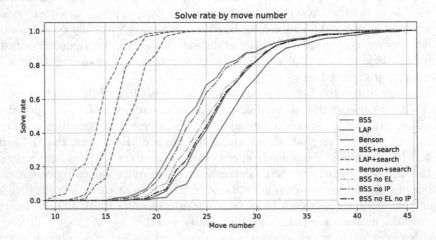

Fig. 5. Solve rate of the positions in 600 6×6 games by the move number of each position for each safety evaluation type. (Color figure online)

We evaluate BSS on a test set of 600 6×6 games. We chose 6×6 as it is the smallest unsolved square board size. The games in the test set last between 29 and 124 moves, with a median of 40, for a total of 26,885 positions. We generate

Table 1. The average number of moves each safety evaluation type required to be played before they were able to solve the position.

Type	BSS	LAP	Benson	BSS +search	LAP +search	Benson +search	BSS no EL	BSS no IP	BSS no EL no IP
Av. first solve	**27.29**	31.56	42.67	**14.89**	16.35	17.79	30.83	27.73	31.28

these games by sampling lines of play which are expected to be similar to states that must be covered by a proof tree. One player is a strong heuristics-guided agent, while the opponent plays randomly. The heuristic player represents strong move choices in the OR nodes of a proof tree (moves by the winning side), while the random player creates a random sample from all the legal moves that must be analyzed in an AND node (the losing side). The heuristic player uses one of six Proof Cost Networks (PCN) [19], which are trained similarly to AlphaZero [14], but with the altered training target of minimizing proof size instead of maximizing the win rate. We use 6 PCNs with different training parameters and generate 100 games each to create a dataset with diverse lines of play.

We compare BSS against the static safety implementations for LAP safety [6] and Benson safety [2] in the open-source program Fuego [3]. A position is statically solved when the safety evaluation finds enough safe points for a win. For a 6 × 6 board with a komi of 3.5, Black must have at least 20 points to win with a score of 20:16 or better, and White must have at least 17 points to win by 19:17. This disregards rare cases of seki where some points remain neutral at the end. A position is solved by search when a proof tree is constructed showing that one player can always win. We evaluate the strength of a safety evaluation function by the earliest point in a game when it is first statically solved - earlier generally indicates a stronger safety evaluation.

Figure 5 shows the *solve rate* - the percentage of positions solved - for each move number, with solid lines for BSS (red), LAP (blue) and Benson (green). The average number of moves required to first solve the games in the test set are shown in Table 1. BSS succeeds more than 4 moves earlier than LAP on average, and more than 15 moves earlier than Benson.

The next experiment uses static safety evaluation within a 30 s (wall-clock time) iterative-deepening alpha-beta search with the distance-to-eye heuristic move ordering [5] and hand-tuned positional evaluation function [17]. Static safety is called in two places: 1) to prune moves inside opponent safe regions, and 2) to determine whether the position is statically solved.

The results are shown using the dashed lines of Fig. 5. BSS improves search efficiency over LAP and Benson. The gap between methods is considerably smaller when using search since many early board states are still beyond the reach of all these static methods.

The remaining dashed-dotted lines in Fig. 5 summarize an ablation study of the two techniques extending liberties and intersecting play. Without those techniques, our static safety implementation has performance similar to LAP, as expected. Intersecting play and extending liberties each contribute to the performance of BSS, with extending liberties being more important. We conjecture that the number of intersection points present is often low, and intersection points are often strong moves, so the strong player may often play these points early.

6 Concluding Remarks

BSS is the new state of the art algorithm for exact static safety evaluation. By using the lower bounds found by the extending liberties and intersecting play techniques, we can statically solve Go positions early than previously possible in many cases. Our experiments show that games can be solved by BSS earlier than previous works, that BSS can improve the efficiency of searches, and that our extending liberty technique is the most important for solving early positions. We believe that this work allows for improvement in various Go problems, such as finding game theoretical values, creating ground truths for auxiliary neural network training tasks, and for evaluating Go playing programs.

Acknowledgements. The authors acknowledge financial support from NSERC, the Natural Sciences and Engineering Research Council of Canada, Alberta Innovates, DeepMind, and the Canada CIFAR AI Chair program.

References

1. Sensei's Library. https://senseis.xmp.net/
2. Benson, D.: Life in the Game of Go. Information Sciences 10, 17–29 (1976). Reprinted in Computer Games, Levy, D.N.L. (ed.), vol. II, pp. 203–213, Springer, New York (1988)
3. Enzenberger, M., Müller, M., Arneson, B., Segal, R.: Fuego-an open-source framework for board games and go engine based on Monte Carlo tree search. IEEE Trans. Comput. Intell. AI Games **2**(4), 259–270 (2010)
4. Haque, R., Wei, T.H., Müller, M.: On the road to perfection? Evaluating Leela chess zero against endgame tablebases. In: ACG 2021. LNCS, vol. 13262, pp. 142–152. Springer, Cham (2021). https://doi.org/10.1007/978-3-031-11488-5_13
5. Kishimoto, A.: Correct and efficient search algorithms in the presence of repetitions. Ph.D. thesis, University of Alberta (2005)
6. Müller, M.: Playing it safe: recognizing secure territories in computer go by using static rules and search. In: Game Programming Workshop in Japan '97, pp. 80–86. Computer Shogi Association, Tokyo, Japan (1997)
7. Niu, X., Kishimoto, A., Müller, M.: Recognizing Seki in computer go. In: van den Herik, H.J., Hsu, S.-C., Hsu, T., Donkers, H.H.L.M.J. (eds.) ACG 2005. LNCS, vol. 4250, pp. 88–103. Springer, Heidelberg (2006). https://doi.org/10.1007/11922155_7
8. Niu, X., Müller, M.: An improved safety solver for computer go. In: van den Herik, H.J., Björnsson, Y., Netanyahu, N.S. (eds.) CG 2004. LNCS, vol. 3846, pp. 97–112. Springer, Heidelberg (2006). https://doi.org/10.1007/11674399_7
9. Niu, X., Müller, M.: An open boundary safety-of-territory solver for the game of go. In: van den Herik, H.J., Ciancarini, P., Donkers, H.H.L.M.J. (eds.) CG 2006. LNCS, vol. 4630, pp. 37–49. Springer, Heidelberg (2007). https://doi.org/10.1007/978-3-540-75538-8_4

10. Niu, X., Müller, M.: An improved safety solver in go using partial regions. In: van den Herik, H.J., Xu, X., Ma, Z., Winands, M.H.M. (eds.) CG 2008. LNCS, vol. 5131, pp. 102–112. Springer, Heidelberg (2008). https://doi.org/10.1007/978-3-540-87608-3_10

11. Schaeffer, J., et al.: Checkers is Solved. Science **317**(5844), 1518–1522 (2007)

12. Schrittwieser, J., et al.: Mastering atari, go, chess and shogi by planning with a learned model. CoRR abs/1911.08265 (2019). http://arxiv.org/abs/1911.08265

13. Silver, D., et al.: Mastering the game of go with deep neural networks and tree search. Nature **529**, 484–489 (2016)

14. Silver, D., et al.: Mastering chess and shogi by self-play with a general reinforcement learning algorithm. CoRR abs/1712.01815 (2017). http://arxiv.org/abs/1712.01815

15. Silver, D., et al.: Mastering the game of go without human knowledge. Nature **550**, 354–359 (2017). https://doi.org/10.1038/nature24270

16. van der Werf, E., Winands, M.: Solving go for rectangular boards. ICGA J. **32**(2), 77–88 (2009). https://doi.org/10.3233/ICG-2009-32203

17. van der Werf, E., Herik, H., Uiterwijk, J.: Solving go on small boards. ICGA J. **26** (2003). https://doi.org/10.3233/ICG-2003-26205

18. Wu, D.J.: Accelerating self-play learning in go. CoRR abs/1902.10565 (2019). http://arxiv.org/abs/1902.10565

19. Wu, T.R., Shih, C.C., Wei, T.H., Tsai, M.Y., Hsu, W.Y., Wu, I.C.: AlphaZero-based proof cost network to aid game solving. In: International Conference on Learning Representations (2022). https://openreview.net/forum?id=nKWjE4QF1hB

20. Wu, T.R., et al.: Multi-labelled value networks for computer go. CoRR abs/1705.10701 (2017). http://arxiv.org/abs/1705.10701

An Efficient Chinese Checkers Implementation: Ranking, Bitboards, and BMI2 pext and pdep Instructions

Nathan R. Sturtevant[1,2]([✉]) [iD]

[1] Department Computing Science, University of Alberta, Edmonton, Canada
nathanst@ualberta.ca
[2] Canada CIFAR Chair, Alberta Machine Intelligence Institute, Edmonton, Canada

Abstract. The game of Chinese Checkers has a computationally expensive move generation function. Finding legal moves dominates the performance of a Chinese Checkers program. This paper describes a bitboard representation of the Chinese Checkers board, how to efficiently generate and apply moves to the board, and how to rank and unrank states. When available, the BMI2 PDEP (parallel bits deposit) and PEXT (parallel bit extract) instructions offer significant efficiency gains, especially over a non-bitboard based implementation.

1 Introduction

One important feature of top-performance game playing programs is the ability to search the game tree efficiently. In many games this has meant using efficient bitwise operations on bitboards for the game state [1–3, 5–7].

Thus, while bitboard representations are common, there is, to our knowledge, no bitboard description for Chinese Checkers found in the literature. Chinese Checkers has received research for many years [9, 10], but has received less attention than other games.

This paper describes how bitboards can be implemented for Chinese Checkers. In particular, beyond the more routine bitwise operations that have commonly been used in other games, this paper describes how the BMI2 `pext` and `pdep` operations can be used to extract and deposit bits to allow for efficient move generation in Chinese Checkers.

In addition to describing our efficient implementation, we provide experimental results showing the performance of the approach. For most operations it is 2–3x faster than our baseline implementation. But, for generating and applying/undoing legal moves, it is approximately 9 times faster than the baseline. When used as part of a program that strongly solves Chinese Checkers, a 2x improvement is seen on a small game with 63 billion states. Further experiments show that using the bitboard implementation without native `pext` and `pdep` support degrades performance to be slower than the original implementation for operations that rely heavily on these instructions.

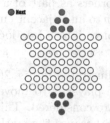

Fig. 1. 7 × 7 Chinese Checkers board

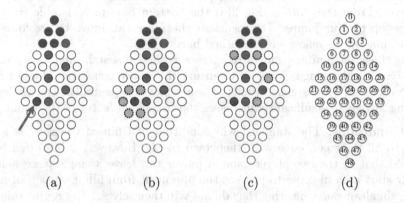

Fig. 2. Legal moves for the piece marked with an arrow in (a). Step moves are marked in yellow with a dashed circle in part (b), and jump moves are marked similarly in part (c). Numbering used for board locations is found in part (d). (Color figure online)

2   Chinese Checkers Rules

Chinese Checkers is a game for 2–6 players that can be played on odd-sized boards, where we indicate the board size by the main playing area in a 2-player game. The most typical board is 9 × 9 with 10 pieces per player, but a 7 × 7 board with 6 pieces per player, as shown in Fig. 1, is also common. The goal of the game is for players to move their pieces to the opposite side of the board from where they started. The winner is the first player to reach a goal state. Although pieces may jump over other pieces, but there are no captures.

Legal Actions: The four 'corners' on the sides the board are reserved as start and end locations for players in a game with more than two players. The rules do not allow players to place their pieces in these locations, although they are allowed to move through the corners as part of a longer action. There are two possible actions: moves that *step* to an adjacent empty location, and moves that *hop* or *jump* over an adjacent piece into a free location. Jumps can be chained together to move a piece far across the board in a single action.

Step Moves: Step moves are illustrated in Fig. 2(a) and (b). Figure 2(a) shows the initial state where the blue player is to move; moves for the bottom blue piece, marked with an arrow, are considered. This piece is allowed to move to five of its neighboring locations, because the sixth location is blocked by a red piece, as shown in Fig. 2(b) by the yellow locations with a dashed border.

Jump Moves: Jumping moves are allowed when a piece can move in a single direction, jumping over a neighboring piece, and landing in a free location on the board. From the state in Fig. 2(a) the bottom blue piece is able to chain together up to four jumps. The locations the piece can move to are found in Fig. 2(c) marked in yellow with a dashed border.

The choice of jumping moves requires a recursive search, and thus can be expensive. Bookkeeping is required to ensure that move generation doesn't continue to loop in circles generating the same moves repeatedly. The choice of stopping anywhere significantly increases the branching factor of the game.[1]

Win Conditions. The standard win condition of Chinese Checkers is for a player to fill their goal area with their own pieces. However, it has often been observed that in the two-player game a player can leave a single piece behind in their start area in order to prevent the opponent from filling their goal area. (While simultaneously insuring they do not win themselves.) To prevent this, we expand the win condition, only requiring that a player have at least one piece in the goal when it is filled with pieces. Thus if a single piece is left in the goal, it can just be surrounded to achieve a victory. Along with this rule, we do not allow a player to move backwards into their own goal to lose the game. This means that, for a player to win the game, they must make the last move. We have described further win conditions, illegal moves, and draws elsewhere [10], but these do not play a significant role in the implementation details described here.

3   Chinese Checkers Bitboard Representation

This paper describes a 7×7 bitboard implementation here that uses 64-bits to represent the board. In particular, the set bits in one 64-bit integer are used to represent the locations of a single player's pieces on the board. When allowing players to temporarily jump into unused corners, 61 bits are required: 49 bits

---

[1] At least 50 actions in 3-player Chinese Checkers [9], and 99 in single-player Chinese Checkers on the 9×9 board [12].

for the main 7×7 diamond, and 3 bits for each of the four unused corners. Our 9×9 implementation uses two 64-bit states to represent the board, but is fundamentally the same as the 7×7 representation. For simplicity we only describe operations in terms of the central 7×7 board.

Operations on the board require a numbering system that map locations on the board to bits. There are many possible numberings that can be used on a board; our implementation just numbers states starting from 0 at the top of the board, as shown in Fig. 2(d). While other mappings can be used, there are certain properties needed by the numbering to ensure that it can be used efficiently for some bit operations.

Our implementation has a separate board representation for the first and second player. Applying an or to these boards would result in a map of all occupied locations. In the pseudo-code below we refer to the occupancy representation of all pieces in a state as s.board. When referring to a particular player we use s.p1Board and s.p2Board. In practice s.board is not stored, but is generated when needed. The state contains an additional variable s.p1Move which indicates whether player 1 is to move in the current state.

There are five basic operations we want to support in our implementation. These are: *GetMoves*, which returns the legal moves, *Apply/Undo Moves* which applies a single move to the game board, *GetWinner* which returns the winner of the game, if any, and *Rank* and *Unrank*, which compute a perfect hash from a state, and a state from a hash. We cover these operations in order from simplest to most complex.

3.1 Get Winner

The game is won when a player fills their goal area with pieces. We precompute a mask containing the goal area for each player. We use this mask to test (1) if the goal area is filled and (2) if a player has at least one piece in the goal. The code for testing if player 1 wins is as follows:

```
// p1 goal area filled
if ((((s.board)&p1Goal) == p1Goal) &&
// p1 has at least 1 piece in goal
(s.p1Board&p1Goal) != 0 &&
// p2 to move
s.p1Move == false)
return 0; // p1 wins
```

The code for player 2 is analogous. The bitboard representation means that we can test all pieces in one operation instead of using a for loop to iterate through all of the locations in the goal.

3.2 Get, Apply, and Undo Moves

Because the number of legal moves in a state can be variable and large, but the number of pieces which can be moved is small, we describe an initial move representation that is more compact.

In particular, we have an array of 6 64-bit integers that represent the legal moves for each of the six pieces on the board for a player. The bits set in each 64-bit integer represent the locations that piece can legally move. For instance, looking at Fig. 2(b) we can see that the piece in location 29 has five step moves and in Fig. 2(c) we can see that it has four jump moves. Thus, the 6th integer (because this is the piece in the largest location) would have bits 22, 23, 28, 34, and 35 set for the step actions, and bits 6, 8, 19, and 31 set for each of the jump actions. Given this representation, we can discuss how we set these bits.

Step Moves: Getting legal step moves is straightforward using standard bit operations. For each location on the board we create a mask which contains the neighboring states. A piece can only move to a neighboring state if it is unoccupied. Thus we can get the legal moves for a piece in location pieceLoc with the following operation:

```
legalMoves |= (˜s.board)&neighborMask[pieceLoc]
```

In one operation this provides **all** steps that can be performed by a single piece, and these can be added to the legal moves for that piece using a bitwise **or**. This is significantly more efficient than a sequential implementation that loops over each possible action, checking to see if a location is free.

Jump Moves. Unfortunately, using standard bitwise operations it isn't possible to simultaneously compute all jump actions. As a start, consider that we have two arrays representing the location jumped over, and the location jumped to, for a given start position. That is, for a piece in location 29 on the board, we would have a first array with values 22, 23, 30, and 35 indicating the locations to be jumped over, and a second array with values 15, 17, 31, and 40 indicating the locations where a piece would land after jumping. Note that the relative orderings of the state jumped over and the final location of the jump are maintained in the two arrays; these also happen to be sorted.

Assuming that these arrays are called jumpOver and jumpTo, the ith move can be tested with the following pseudo-code:

```
legalMoves |=(((s.board>>jumpOver[pieceLoc][i])&((˜s.board)>>
    jumpTo[pieceLoc][i])&0$\,\times\,$1)<<jumpTo[pieceLoc][i]
```

With this approach we could store an array of jumpOver and jumpTo locations for each location on the board. Each location has a maximum of six jump actions, but because some jump actions near the edge of the board are not legal, there will not always be six actions to consider.

Note that the array used for this version can get large, and thus it might be better to store the jumpOver and jumpTo locations more efficiently. In particular, we can have one 64-bit integer from all jumpOver locations and one 64-bit integer for all jumpTo locations. This works because the board numbering preserves the relative sorting of jumpOver and jumpTo locations. Thus, the ith bit in the jumpOver integer and the ith bit in the jumpTo location will both correspond to the same jumping action. Then the question becomes one of extracting out each of the bits and testing their values to see if the jump actions are legal. While this can be done by repeatedly counting trailing zeros and then clearing the low bit, the Intel BMI2 instruction set offers more efficient instructions.

Instead, we can use the pdep (parallel deposit) and pext (parallel extract) operations. pext uses a mask to extract bits from the input into the low-order bits of the output. pdep deposits these bits back into the locations indicated by the mask. These can be used to extract the locations that are jumped over and to simultaneously test for legal jumps.

With this approach, just three lines of code are required:

```
jumpOver = pext(s.board, jumpOverMasks[pieceLoc]);
jumpTo = pext(~s.board, jumpToMasks[pieceLoc]);
moves = pdep(jumpTo&jumpOver, jumpToMasks[pieceLoc]);
```

The first line extracts the bits for the locations that are jumped over. These will be 1 if they are occupied. The second line extracts the locations that are being jumped to. Because the board is inverted, these will be 1 if they are unoccupied. By computing the bitwise and of these locations, we simultaneously test all directions to see if a jump move is possible. The last line deposits any legal moves back into the location that the piece is jumping to.

After jumps for a single pieces at a single location have been computed, they must be recursively computed for all new locations that a piece has arrived at in the previous calculation. This process continues until no new moves are discovered. The whole process is then repeated for all pieces.

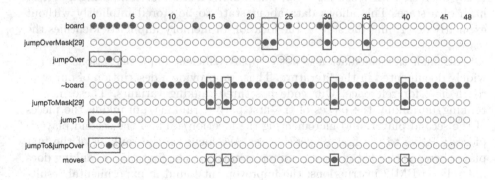

Fig. 3. Operations for computing jump moves

To make this more concrete, we fully illustrate this process for the piece in location 29 in Fig. 2 using Fig. 3. There are four possible locations that this piece can jump over while remaining on the board. These bits are set in jumpOver-Mask[29]. The pext extracts the corresponding bits from the board and places them in the low bits of jumpOver. In order to perform a jump, there must be a piece in one of these locations to jump over. Corresponding to these locations are the locations that the piece would land after jumping, shown in jumpToMask[29].

These bits are extracted from the inverted board bits into the low bits of jumpTo. Doing a bitwise and on jumpTo and jumpOver results in one set bit for every possible jump. Using pdep, these bits are then deposited back into the original locations. The final result indicates that a piece in location 29 can jump to location 31.

This computes all jumps for a single piece in one step, instead of requiring a for loop over the 6 possible directions that a piece can move.

Apply and Undo Moves. The results of finding all moves is a set of bits, one per location that a single piece can move. Each piece has its own set of legal move locations. This cannot be used directly to apply and undo moves. However, it is simple to extract the bits from this set and combine them with the bit for the piece that is moving. Thus, a move action is represented by a 64-bit integer with two bits set, one for the initial piece location and one for the final location. The initial and final locations do not need to be distinguished.

Applying a xor to a player's board representation can be used to toggle both the bit for the current location of the piece as well as the location to which the piece is moving in one step. This process works regardless of whether a move results from a step or a jump. Undoing a move as part of a depth-first search is identical to applying a move.

3.3   Ranking and Unranking States

A key operation when solving a game, is ranking a state, or computing a perfect hash of a state. This allows data about state to be stored implicitly without explicitly describing the state – the location in memory implicitly identifies the state.

Although this calculation is not complex, efficient implementations are not widely documented in the literature. Thus, we provide a description of our approach here for reference. Our code has three ranking variants. These include ranking/unranking the pieces of the first player, ranking/unranking the pieces of the second player, and incrementing the location/rank of the second player's pieces relative to the first player's pieces. We focus on the ranking of the first player here, as this is the most common operation. The first player ranking does not rely on BMI2 instructions; the improvement found in experimental results comes from the improved ranking algorithm. The second player ranking is nearly identical to the first player ranking, except that the pext operation is used to get the board without the first player's pieces. The use of this instruction is important for overall efficiency.

Because the pieces on the board are not distinguished from each other, the ranking problem is related to the combinatorial ways the pieces can be placed on the board. Consider a board with 49 locations and 6 pieces, where the pieces are in locations $\ell_1 \cdots \ell_6$. There are $\binom{49}{6}$ total ways to place these pieces on the board. To compute the rank of an arbitrary state, we need to look at the gap between each pair of pieces to see how many possible ranks are skipped. That is, if the first piece is in location 0 on the board, we can decided to place the second piece anywhere from location 1 to location 44. If the second piece is placed in location 2, we can ask how many possible ranks of all pieces were skipped by that decision. Given the first piece is in location 0, and the second is in location 1, there are $\binom{47}{4}$ ways that the remaining pieces could be placed on the board. Thus, putting the second piece in location 2 increments the rank of the state by exactly $\binom{47}{4}$.

Generalizing this logic and starting with the first piece, when the first piece is put in location ℓ_1 there are

$$\sum_{i=\ell_1}^{49} \binom{i}{5} = \sum_{i=5}^{49} \binom{i}{5} - \sum_{i=5}^{\ell_1-1} \binom{i}{5} = \binom{49}{6} - \binom{\ell_1-1}{6}$$

possible rankings that have been skipped. Note that $\sum_{i=k}^{j} \binom{i}{k}$ is equivalent to computing the sum of the jth diagonal in Pascal's triangle, which is also equivalent to $\binom{j}{k+1}$. This justifies the last simplification of the formula.

In this case a state has a rank of 0 if no ranks are skipped; that is, all pieces are compactly placed at the top of the board in locations 0–5. Generalizing and counting all skips across all pieces we derive:

$$\left[\binom{49}{6} - \binom{\ell_1}{6}\right] + \left[\binom{\ell_1-1}{5} - \binom{\ell_2}{5}\right] + \left[\binom{\ell_2-1}{4} - \binom{\ell_3}{4}\right] \cdots \left[\binom{\ell_5-1}{1} - \binom{\ell_6}{1}\right]$$

By re-arranging terms, this can be re-written as:

$$\left[\binom{49}{6}\right] + \left[-\binom{\ell_1}{6} + \binom{\ell_1-1}{5}\right] + \left[-\binom{\ell_2}{5} + \binom{\ell_2-1}{4}\right] + \cdots \right] - \binom{\ell_6}{1}$$

Since $-\binom{n-1}{k} = -\binom{n}{k} + \binom{n-1}{k-1}$, we can further simplify this to:

$$\binom{49}{6} - \binom{\ell_1-1}{5} - \binom{\ell_2-1}{4} - \binom{\ell_3-1}{3} - \binom{\ell_4-1}{2} - \binom{\ell_5-1}{1} - \binom{\ell_6}{1}$$

This provides a simple formula that can directly compute the rank of a state. When generalizing for a board with n locations and k pieces, the time required to compute the rank is $O(k)$, which contrasts with a similar ranking function described in previous work [4], which runs in time $O(n)$, and is the basis of the ranking we used for our previous work on solving single-agent Chinese Checkers variants [8, 12].

Note that our implementation pre-computes and caches the result of $\binom{n}{k}$ for all n and k that will be encountered in a given run. This cached result is returned from the binom function, which looks up the binomial coefficient for the given n and k. Other functions used in our code include blsr, which clears the lowest bit and tzcnt, which counts the trailing zeros.

```
int RankPlayer1(State s)
{
```

```
int value = s.p1Board;
result = kMaxRank;
for (int x = 0; x < numPieces−1; x++)
{
    result −= binom(boardSize−tzcnt(value)−1, numPieces−x+1)
    value = blsr(value); // clear low bit
}
result −= (boardSize−tzcnt(value));
return result;
}
```

Unranking is the opposite process of ranking, but our code uses a simple $O(n)$ time algorithm, instead of $O(k)$ required for ranking. This could be made more efficient, but unranking is used far less often than ranking, so it is less important to perform these optimizations in the code. The unranking algorithm loops over each possible location, testing whether the next piece should be placed in that location. When a valid location is found, a piece is placed, and the remaining pieces are iteratively placed in the same manner.

```
State UnrankPlayer1(int rank)
{
    State s;
    s.p1Board = 0;
    int nextLoc = boardSize;
    for (int x = numPieces; x > 1; x−−)
    {
        do {
            nextLoc−−;
        } while (binom(nextLoc, x) >= rank);

        s.p1Board |= 1<<(boardSize−1−nextLoc);
        rank −= binom(nextLoc, x);
    }
    s.p1Board |= 1<<(boardSize−1−(rank−1));
}
```

Note that a few details have been omitted from the code for simplicity of presentation; we are able to provide complete code upon request.

4   Experimental Results

We now evaluate our bitboard representations in comparison to the representation that was used for all of our previous published results on Chinese Checkers. The previous implementation is reasonably well optimized after 20 years of use. The original board is represented using three arrays: one containing the contents of the board, and two containing the pieces for each player. A DFS is used to find legal jump moves, with a bitboard used as a hash table for finding duplicates during the DFS. The move data structure contains which pieces is moving, as well as where it moves, which allows for efficient updating of the board. Ranking and unranking are performed using a variant of a previously published implementation [4]. Functions like Get Winner are implemented with for loops.

Experiments are run on a laptop with an 8-Core 2.3 GHz Intel Core i9, 32 GB of 2667 MHz MHz DDR4 RAM, and MacOS Monterey. The code is in C++ and compiled with -O3. The Intel intrinsic headers are used for efficient bit operations. For comparison purposes a custom implementation of the `pext` and `pdep` functions was written using general bitwise operators. We call this implementation non-BMI2. We test each of the major game operations as follows, with timing results reported in microseconds.

Table 1. Board with 49 locations and 3 pieces

Call	Original	BitBoard	non-BMI2
GetWinner	3,611	2,127	2,123
Get+Apply/Undo Succ	235,388	25,555	345,085
RankP1	5,455	3,095	3,097
RankP2	20,744	3,508	77,082
Unrank1	1,052	450	460
Unrank2	1,035	383	1,245
Increment	241	78	2,016

For testing the GetWinner function, we make 1,000,000 GetWinner calls and report the total time averaged over 100 runs. For testing GetMoves, we get the legal moves of a given state 1,000,000 times and then apply and undo all actions that were returned, reporting the total time. For the ranking test we rank the first 1,000,000 states for each player, reporting total time. For unranking and incremental ranking functions we fix one player and then unrank all possible states for the other player. The incremental unranking is only implemented for the second player.

The results in Table 1 show the results on the board with 49 locations and 3 pieces. For the GetWinner function the bitboard implementation is 1.7x faster than the old implementation. The non-BMI implementation does not have any significant overhead. For getting, applying, and undoing actions, the bitboard implementation is 9.2x faster than the old implementation with BMI2. Without the BMI2 instructions the new implementation is 1.5x slower. This is because of the extensive use of BMI2 functions. These trends continue across the ranking operations. There is little overhead for ranking player 1 without BMI2, but the same operations for player 2 are significantly more expensive.

The results on the board with 49 locations and 6 pieces, found in Table 2 follow the same trends as the smaller board, with the most significant gain being an 8.9x improvement in getting, applying, and undoing actions.

Table 2. Board with 49 locations and 6 pieces

Call	Original	BitBoard	non-BMI2
GetWinner	5,825	2,125	2,132
Get+Apply/Undo Succ	677,089	76,144	760,751
RankP1	7,957	5,171	5,868
RankP2	30,798	6,174	74,781
Unrank1	1,264,854	510,715	525,706
Unrank2	457,833	221,845	545,526
Increment	69,968	31,032	759,960

Table 3. Time in seconds to strongly solve games on board with 49 locations.

Pieces	Total States	Symmetric States	Original	BitBoard	Speedup
3	559,352,640	141,219,540	204.51	74.12	2.8
4	63,136,929,240	15,822,357,347	43,187.58	21,597.82	2.0

4.1 Solving Time

Finally, we take a sequential in-memory solver and use it to strongly solve boards with 49 locations and both 3 and 4 pieces. The solver uses both left/right symmetry on the board and symmetry between the players to reduce the total number of states that must be solved. The search uses retrograde analysis backwards from terminal states along with optimizations from previous work [10,11]. In Table 3 we report the total solving time in seconds. The only difference in the code is the representation used for the game. Overall, the BitBoard representation leads to a 2x speedup in total solving time on the 7×7 board with 4 pieces, and a 2.8x speedup on the 7×7 board with 3 pieces. The reduction in speedup is likely due to memory overheads in the solver, as the entire game is stored in memory at the same time in this solver.

5 Conclusions

This paper has described an efficient bitboard representation for Chinese Checkers. This implementation provides a 9x speedup in the common operations of getting and applying successors, and a 2x speedup in strongly solving small Chinese Checkers boards. Future work will investigate faster bitboard methods for when BMI2 operations are not available, such as is the case on Apple's M1 processors.

Acknowledgements. This work was funded by the Canada CIFAR AI Chairs Program. We acknowledge the support of the Natural Sciences and Engineering Research Council of Canada (NSERC).

References

1. Adel'son-Vel'skii, G.M., Arlazarov, V.L., Bitman, A.R., Zhivotovskii, A.A., Uskov, A.V.: Programming a computer to play chess. Russ. Math. Surv. **25**(2), 221–262 (1970)
2. Browne, C.: Bitboard methods for games. ICGA J. **37**(2), 67–84 (2014)
3. Carlini, S., Bergamaschi, S.: Arimaa: from rules to bitboard analysis. Knowledge Representation thesis, University of Modena and Reggio Emilia (2008)
4. Edelkamp, S., Sulewski, D., Yücel, C.: GPU exploration of two-player games with perfect hash functions. In: International Symposium on Combinatorial Search, vol. 1 (2010)
5. Frey, P.W.: An introduction to computer chess. In: Frey, P.W. (eds.) Chess Skill in Man and Machine, pp. 54–81. Springer, New York (1983). https://doi.org/10.1007/978-1-4612-5515-4_3
6. Grimbergen, R.: Using bitboards for move generation in shogi. ICGA J. **30**(1), 25–34 (2007)
7. Heinz, E.A.: How darkthought plays chess. ICGA J. **20**(3), 166–176 (1997)
8. Hu, S., Sturtevant, N.R.: Direction-optimizing breadth first search with external memory storage. In: International Joint Conference on Artificial Intelligence (IJCAI), pp. 1258–1264 (2019). https://webdocs.cs.ualberta.ca/nathanst/papers/DEBFS.pdf
9. Sturtevant, N.: A comparison of algorithms for multi-player games. In: Schaeffer, J., Müller, M., Björnsson, Y. (eds.) CG 2002. LNCS, vol. 2883, pp. 108–122. Springer, Heidelberg (2003). https://doi.org/10.1007/978-3-540-40031-8_8
10. Sturtevant, N.R.: On strongly solving Chinese checkers. In: Cazenave, T., van den Herik, J., Saffidine, A., Wu, IC. (eds.) ACG 2019. LNCS, vol. 12516. Springer, Cham (2019). https://doi.org/10.1007/978-3-030-65883-0_13
11. Sturtevant, N.R., Saffidine, A.: A study of forward versus backwards endgame solvers with results in Chinese checkers. In: Computer Game Workshop at IJCAI, pp. 121–136 (2017). http://www.cs.ualberta.ca/nathanst/papers/sturtevant2017ccsolve.pdf
12. Sturtevant, N., Rutherford, M.: Minimizing writes in parallel external memory search. In: International Joint Conference on Artificial Intelligence (IJCAI), pp. 666–673 (2013)

Multi-Player and Multi-Action Games

Solving Chainmail Jousting

Daniel R. Collins[✉] [iD]

Kingsborough Community College, Brooklyn, NY 11235, USA
dcollins@kbcc.cuny.edu

Abstract. We consider the Chainmail Jousting game by Gygax and Perren (1971), a symmetric game of pure skill for two players. Preliminary analysis produces a payoff matrix with only zero and unit values. We find that this matrix is too large to be solved by existing software tools, such that IEDS of weakly-dominated strategies is needed to find solutions. We then apply the *lrs* solver by Avis et. al. (2010), and find a trio of critical mixed strategies which form the Nash equilibria for the game, including one composed of a simple coin flip between two of the permitted moves. We further consider ways to distinguish the various Nash equilibria, and also some variants of the game.

Keywords: Nash equilibria · IEDS · Chainmail

1 Introduction

The wargame *Chainmail: rules for medieval miniatures* was first published in 1971, by Gary Gygax and Jeff Perren [1]. Gygax would, a few years later, go on to co-author the popular fantasy role-playing game *Dungeons & Dragons* (D&D) – which initially used the rules of *Chainmail* as the foundation for its mechanics [2].

Among the various sub-systems in *Chainmail* was a mini-game for "Jousting". This is a symmetric game of pure skill with complete information for two players, in which the players simultaneously pick an attack and defense mode for their knights, and consult a matrix of results with the consequences of the ride for both players. The Chainmail Jousting game has been played by enthusiasts for over 50 years, and still serves as the marquee tournament event at the annual GaryCon game convention in Lake Geneva, Wisconsin (held in memory of Gary Gygax).

Due to its nature as a symmetric game, with complete information and lack of random chance, and with sufficient complexity to make finding optimal strategies difficult for human players, Chainmail Jousting serves as an excellent example of the application of game theory principles such as iterated elimination of dominated strategies (IEDS) and the search for Nash equilibria. In this paper we present the game rules, offer preliminary simplifying analysis, and find simple mixed strategies which form Nash equilibria for the game (i.e., implementable by a human with polyhedral dice). At the end we briefly consider certain variants of the game seen in the wild.

C. Browne et al. (Eds.): CG 2022, LNCS 13865, pp. 39–48, 2023.
https://doi.org/10.1007/978-3-031-34017-8_4

2 Rules of the Game

The essence of Chainmail Jousting is for each of two players to take the role of knights, "armed with lance and shield, and mounted upon mighty destriers" [1]. On every "ride", each player picks an "aiming point" (attack) from one of 8 options, jointly with a "position in the saddle" (defense) from among 6 options. The matrix in Fig. 1 is then consulted for each attack-vs-defense selection, giving the results of the ride for each player.

JOUSTING MATRIX

Aiming Point	Possible Defensive Positions						PDP - PDP /AP
	1. Lower Helm	2. Lean Right	3. Lean Left	4. Steady Seat	5. Shield High	6. Shield Low	
Helm	M	M	M	H	U	M	4-6
DC	U	B	M	B	B	M	3-6
CP	B/U/I	U	G	B	B/U	U/I	Any
SC	G	M	B	G	G	U	2, 4-6
DF	B	B/U	M	B	M	B	4-6
FP	B/U	G	B	B/U	B/U/I	B	Any
SF	G	M	B/U	G	G	G	4-6
Base	B	G	U	B	B/U/I	B	1, 4-6

B – Breaks Lance *

G – Glances Off

H – Helm Knocked Off *

I – Injured

M – Miss

U – Unhorsed

* Any Knight who breaks his lance or has his Helm knocked off must assume position 4 during the next ride.

Fig. 1. The Jousting Matrix from [1]

Given the 8 attack and 6 defense options, at first glance this would give 8 × 6 = 48 combined options available to each player on any ride. But certain combinations are not allowed, as given in the rightmost column labeled "PDP/AP" ("Possible Defensive Positions Considering Aiming Point"). When we count up the permitted PDPs for each attack option, we get 33 different combined options for each player – formally, these constitute the *pure strategies* for any single ride in the Chainmail Jousting game. For brevity in the rest of this paper, we will call one such combined option a "move" in the game. We will denote any such move with the aiming point code, a slash, and the defensive position number, e.g., "Helm/3" indicates aiming at the opponent's Helm, while taking the Lean Left defensive posture.

Letter codes for results are given at the bottom of the table above: for example, "B" for "Breaks Lance", up to "U" for "Unhorsed". Fundamentally, the goal of the game is to score a "U" result and thereby unhorse the opponent; when this happens the joust is over and the person doing the unhorsing is the winner. Up to 3 rides are attempted if no one is yet unhorsed. For the specific case of breaking a tie (either both knights unhorsed simultaneously, or 3 rides taken with no conclusion), then the schedule of points shown in Fig. 2 is consulted.

RESULT	Attacker	Defender
Breaks lance	−1	0
Helm knocked off	+3	0
Injured	0	−10
Unhorsed	+20	0

Fig. 2. The points schedule for tiebreaks from [1]

These point values can be summarized as net gains or losses for the attacker in question: −1 for breaking the lance, +3 for knocking off the helm, +10 for injuring the opponent, and +20 for unhorsing them. Note in the matrix that injury "I" results only happen simultaneously with an unhorsing "U" result (for a total attacker net gain of + 30 points, possibly reduced by 1 if the lance is also broken).

Two somewhat puzzling rules stand out in the preceding. The first is that breaking the lance penalizes the attacker in points; in most historical treatments, and modern Renaissance Fair jousting, breaking the lance earns the attacker positive points, being seen as evidence of a successful and solid strike [3]. The second is that a knight who suffers from a "B" or "H" result is then, on the next ride, restricted to position 4, the "Steady Seat" defense (per the asterisked footnote at the bottom of the matrix). The reason for this rule is unclear, but an obvious implication is that the unfortunate party will definitely be unhorsed on the next ride by a rational opponent who picks the FP attack point, thereby ending the joust.

THE SHIELD:

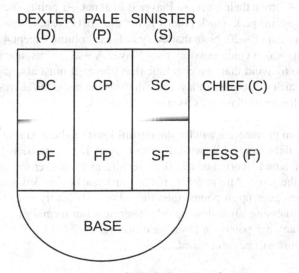

Fig. 3. Definition of the aiming points from [1]

While it is not of essential concern to the play of the game, to give some context, the aiming points such as "DC" and "CP" indicate classical heraldic names for different locations on an opposing knight's shield, as shown in Fig. 3.

3 Solving the Game

Solving the Chainmail Jousting game involves a number of separate analytic steps, as given below. We identify the two opponents as Player A and Player B.

3.1 Preliminary Analysis

The first detail to be careful about is to *not* make the mistake of using the points schedule given in Fig. 2 to construct the formal payoff matrix for the Chainmail Jousting game. Again, the contest is concluded and won by whoever scores the first unhorsing event, and the points given are only used to break ties by that criterion. By careful consideration, we can eliminate the given point values entirely from our analysis; our payoff matrices will only involve values of +1 for a result in which a player wins the joust (whether by unhorsing the opponent or on points), −1 for the reverse, and 0 if neither player does so (including the case where the joust ends in a tie as both players are unhorsed).

The possibility of a player being required to take the "Steady Seat" defense (position 4) is of critical importance; we will henceforth call this situation a "restricted ride". As noted, a rational opponent can automatically unhorse a player taking a restricted ride and end the joust by picking the FP attack. As a result, any points-scoring event will guarantee that the joust concludes on that ride or the next – the "B" or "H" results trigger a restricted ride (ending the joust on the next ride), the "U" result ends the joust by definition, and the "I" result only happens in tandem with "U".

Consider the case where Player A has a restricted ride, while Player B does not. Based on the preceding, Player B must be ahead in points to have reached this situation; e.g., say Player A broke their lance, so Player B is at net +1 point. The best that Player B can do is to (again) pick attack point FP, for the "B/U" result, resulting in a net + 19 points, and a total of +20. Note that every defense column except 4 has at least one clean "U" result, which could possibly earn Player A +20 points, and thereby end the joust in a tie; so to avoid that, we conclude that Player B must also pick defense 4 in this situation – such that the best Player A can do is the same "B/U" result for net +19 points, thereby losing to Player B's total of +20 points.

To summarize the prior paragraph – as soon as one player scores and takes a lead in points, they can guarantee a win for the overall joust on the next ride (if they haven't already won by unhorsing). Likewise, if both players have a restricted ride, then both must pick the FP attack, scoring equal "B/U" results, and whoever was previously ahead in points wins the joust. Alternatively, if the joust reaches its 3rd and final ride, and either player then goes up in points, then that player obviously wins on points at that time, without witnessing any follow-up ride. Therefore our formal game devolves to just trying to score any net points on any single non-restricted ride; once that occurs, the winner of the joust will be determined.

3.2 Iterated Elimination of Dominated Strategies

As provided by the game's PDP/AP column, there are a total of 33 different combined possible moves for each player; so we can form a 33×33 payoff matrix for Player A, representing the result of each of Player A's 33 move options versus each of Player B's 33 move options. In this symmetric game, the transpose of that matrix is the payoff matrix for Player B. The entries of these matrices are, as noted earlier, $+1$ if the result wins the joust for the given player, -1 for a win by the opponent, and 0 if the result is a tie. Note that our formalization makes this a zero-sum game.

The resulting formal game is a degenerate one; meaning that for some moves by one player, the other player has many best-response moves with which to win (i.e., maximize our payoff to $+1$ as above), not any unique one. For example, say Player A chooses the CP/1 move; then Player B actually has 12 different response moves that can win the game for them – including unhorsing results by attacks DC, CP, or FP, in combination with either of defenses 3 or 4, as well as other options. Therefore, we should not expect a unique solution to this game (per Avis [4]).

Fortunately, for brevity and computational simplicity, we can strike out a number of move combinations as being at least weakly dominated by some other one. For example, the DC and DF attack options have a worse result than CP in almost every defense column – with only a tie in columns 3 and 4 – so they can be discarded. Likewise, defense 5 has a worse result than 4 in most rows – only tying against DC, SC, and SF – so we can remove that option as well. Note that each of these removals actually represent a number of attack/defense combination moves (per the PDP/AP allowance), in fact 13 in total; so now we are reduced to a 20×20 sized payoff matrix.

We can continue this IEDS process further (eliminating at least weakly dominated strategies), although at this point it's convenient to use software to trim down the 20×20 sized matrix. Custom software written by the author was used for this purpose. At the end of this process, we arrive at a 13×13 sized payoff matrix. Table 1 shows this for

Table 1. The reduced 13×13 payoff matrix after IEDS.

Move	Helm/4	Helm/6	CP/3	CP/4	CP/6	SC/2	SC/4	SC/6	FP/2	FP/3	FP/4	SF/4	Base/4
Helm/4	0	−1	1	1	1	0	1	0	−1	−1	−1	1	1
Helm/6	1	0	−1	−1	−1	−1	−1	−1	1	1	1	1	1
CP/3	−1	1	0	−1	1	1	0	1	1	1	0	−1	−1
CP/4	−1	1	1	0	1	1	−1	1	1	1	1	1	0
CP/6	−1	1	−1	−1	0	0	−1	1	1	1	0	−1	0
SC/2	0	1	−1	−1	0	0	0	1	0	−1	0	0	0
SC/4	−1	1	0	1	1	0	0	1	−1	−1	−1	0	1
SC/6	0	1	−1	−1	−1	−1	−1	0	1	0	1	0	1
FP/2	1	−1	−1	−1	−1	0	1	−1	0	−1	1	1	1
FP/3	1	−1	−1	1	−1	1	1	0	1	0	1	0	−1
FP/4	1	−1	0	1	0	0	1	−1	−1	−1	0	1	1
SF/4	−1	−1	1	1	1	0	0	0	−1	0	−1	0	1
Base/4	−1	−1	1	0	0	0	−1	−1	−1	1	−1	−1	0

Player A, with Player A's move in the rows, and Player B's move in the columns (again, with the transpose being the payoff matrix for Player B).

The reader can find spreadsheets used to generate the full and reduced payoff matrices, the code which performed the IEDS step, and other supporting documents, at https:// danielrcollins.commons.gc.cuny.edu/solving-chainmail-jousting.

3.3 Finding Nash Equilbria

At this point we'd like to find Nash equilibria for the Chainmail Jousting game. For this purpose we turned to the *lrs* solving program outlined by Avis et. al. [4], and the online version of that program maintained by Rahul Savani [5]. We briefly considered the alternative *EEE* algorithm given in [4], but the authors write, "*EEE* performs poorly on degenerate games", and since Chainmail Jousting falls into that category, we abandoned the idea.

Entering our reduced 13×13 payoff matrix into Savani's online solver, the solution is produced in about 2 s, and reports 9 different extreme equilibria. Conveniently, there is just a single connected component of the solution space, including 3 distinct and interchangeable mixed strategies, with the 9 extreme equilibria being all possible arrangements of the 3 mixed strategies between the 2 players. These 3 critical mixed strategies are given in Table 2.

Table 2. The three critical mixed strategies in the Nash equilibria.

Strategy	Moves and Probabilities
Mix 1	CP/3, FP/4 (1/2 each)
Mix 2	Helm/4, Helm/6, CP/3, CP/4, FP/3 (1/5 each)
Mix 3	Helm/6 (1/6), CP/3 (1/4), CP/4 (1/6), FP/3 (1/12), FP/4 (1/4), SF/4 (1/12)

This being a symmetric and zero-sum game, the expected payoff for any pairing of these strategies is 0. Also, in a case like this with a single connected component to the solution space, any linear combination of the 3 critical mixed strategies will also be a best response to any of the others. Therefore this degenerate game has an infinite number of Nash equilibria, involving an infinite number of mixed strategies (see [4] for elaboration).

In summary, for the player interested in a minimalist protocol, there's no better strategy in the Chainmail Jousting game than flipping a coin to pick between either the CP/3 or FP/4 moves on any non-restricted ride (i.e., Mix 1). If for aesthetic reasons one wished to use one of the more sophisticated strategies (Mix 2 or Mix 3), then a 10-sided or 12-sided die, commonly available to players of D&D, could be used to randomly select moves from those mixed strategies.

3.4 Timing and Other Tests

Savani's web version of the *lrs* solver [5] lists a maximum matrix size of 15×15, so even our reduced 13×13 matrix is barely within the scope of that tool to handle. For further testing, we installed a local application of that solver program, which permits handling of larger matrix sizes. For the 13×13 matrix, with the solver running on a personal computer (using a single 3.4 GHz core, with 8 GB of RAM available), the solution seen in Table 2 is found in 1.7 s.

As a double-check on our custom IEDS program, we also input the manually-reduced 20×20 matrix. In this case the solver took 79.2 s (a bit less than 1 min and 20 s) to find the exact same solution. That is: one connected component of the solution space, with the same 3 critical mixed strategies, in all arrangements for the same 9 extreme equilibria.

We also attempted to run the solver on the full, un-reduced 33×33 matrix. This has an indefinite run time, and the run was canceled after one day. In that time the same connected component was found (3 mixed strategies forming 9 extreme equilibria), with no other solutions.

These timing results are similar to those found in the Avis paper [4]. Moreover, it highlights the necessity of our performing IEDS and eliminating weakly dominated strategies in our formal game; if we had not done that, our existing solving tool would not halt in a reasonable amount of time. On the other hand, it leaves open the question of whether the weakly-dominated moves might form part of mixed strategies in some other Nash equilibria; in this author's opinion, that seems highly unlikely.

3.5 Comparing the Mixed Strategies

Given the 3 critical mixed strategies that we find in the extreme-equilibria solution space, we know that any pairing of them give the same expected payoff value for our formal game; namely zero (0). That is to say: it's always equally likely for either player to emerge as the winner of the joust. However, the strategies may differ in other interesting ways, such as exactly what the mutual chance for a win is, and what the chance is for a tie, in any particular pairing of the strategies.

By complete enumeration of all the supported moves and their respective probability distributions, we compute the respective win and tie probabilities, as shown in Table 3 (Mix 1, Mix 2, and Mix 3 refer to the three mixed strategies given in Table 2).

Table 3. Win and tie rates for each pairing of critical mixed strategies.

Player A	Player B	A Wins	B Wins	Ties
Mix 1	Mix 1	0.000	0.000	1.000
Mix 1	Mix 2	0.444	0.444	0.112
Mix 1	Mix 3	0.285	0.285	0.430
Mix 2	Mix 2	0.435	0.435	0.131
Mix 2	Mix 3	0.436	0.436	0.128
Mix 3	Mix 3	0.369	0.369	0.262

Note, for example, that a match-up between mutual Mix1 strategies (the coin-flip between CP/3 and FP/4 moves), is guaranteed to result in a tie joust. Looking back to the original game's Jousting Matrix, if both players in this case choose CP/3, then both get a "G" glancing-off result for no points. If both choose FP/4, then a mutual "B/U" unhorsing occurs, ending the joust with equal points. Finally, if one side chooses CP/3 and the other FP/4, then both get "B" broken-lance results, forcing a restricted ride on each side, at which point the joust ends as both choose FP/4.

Other mixed-strategy pairings, obviously, have different possible outcomes. This brings to mind that the Chainmail Jousting game might be embedded in a larger context, such that the two players could have different overarching goals within a given joust. Say, for example, that a large tournament is held, including multiple jousts between two teams, and an overall count of jousts won is recorded. Depending on which team is ahead near the end, Player A might wish to maximize their chance of scoring a win (if they are behind in overall jousts), while Player B might wish to maximize their chance of not losing (in the case they are ahead).

This situation then spawns its own asymmetric meta-game. Each player has a 3 × 3 payoff matrix, where Player A's is the arrangements of win probabilities seen above, while Player B's is composed of the sum of win and tie probabilities for each cell. This game is easily solved by the *lrs* program, and is found to have a unique Nash equilibrium – Player A should play Mix1 2/161, and Mix2 159/161 of the time; while Player B should play Mix2 151/160, and Mix3 9/160 of the time. Most plays of this meta-game will see mutual Mix 2 strategies played by either side, for a 43.5% chance that either side wins, and a 13.1% chance of a tie.

4 Variants

A few variants to the Chainmail Jousting rules as written have been suggested or seen in active use. Of course, fairly small modifications to the rules of the game can greatly impact the optimal strategies.

4.1 Maximizing Points

One might consider bringing the Chainmail Jousting points schedule front and center (from Fig. 2), and determining the result of jousts directly from that. For example, it's been suggested that in a large tournament structure with teams of many knights competing, the overall tournament could be determined by summed points. In this case, we construct a new zero-sum matrix by taking the difference of the points scored by Player A and Player B for each combination of permissible moves.

Attempting to reduce this new 33 × 33 matrix by IEDS, we find that the only entries that are removable are those that were previously eliminated by manual inspection (the DC, DF, and defense 5 options), leaving a 20 × 20 matrix as the terminal reduction. Applying the *lrs* solver, we find one connected component to the solution space, with 2 distinct mixed strategies, in arrangements forming 4 extreme equilibria. These strategies are shown in Table 4.

Table 4. Critical mixed strategies for the maximizing-points game.

Strategy	Moves and Probabilities
Points 1	CP/3 (18/59), FP/2 (19/59), FP/3 (2/59), SF/4 (19/59), Base/4 (1/59)
Points 2	CP/2 (18/59), FP/2 (1/59), FP/3 (20/59), SF/4 (19/59), Base/4 (1/59)

Note that this partial analysis only considers the points from a single ride, not the effect of any follow-up rides.

4.2 GaryCon Variant

The author entered the Jousting Tournament at GaryCon in 2018 using a combination strategy of the equilibria shown in Table 2. However, he was surprised to learn that the rules in use were significantly altered from the book as written. In particular: (1) Three rides are performed in every joust, even if one of the players was previously unhorsed; (2) joust winners are determined by overall points; (3) on restricted rides, either defense 4 or 6 is permitted; (4) "T" injury results are removed from the table; and (5) the points schedule is completely rewritten. The revised point values are: 0 for a miss, 1 for a glancing blow, 2 for a broken lance, 4 for knocking off the helm, and 5 for unhorsing the opponent. In particular, note that the "B" broken lance result switched from a negative to a positive for the attacker (as we might have initially guessed); and the "G" glancing blow result went from zero to a positive value.

Of course, this is a totally different game. Arguably, it's a better one, with added strategic texture. (Reportedly, the later editor of D&D suggested the particular change in the restricted ride rule to Gary Gygax, who agreed that it would be an improvement [6].) The current paper has greatly benefited from the simplifications that any point-scoring event either ends the joust or triggers a restricted ride, that any such restricted ride has a single best move for each side, and that the game always ends with a predetermined winner at that time. Since all of these assumptions are cast side at GaryCon (and several of our IEDS reductions no longer apply, as well), our results are not applicable to that format. Considering how the results of one ride can effect multiple later rides in an inter-dependent fashion would seem to be a far more complicated problem to solve.

5 Conclusion

Chainmail Jousting is a sufficiently complex game that, to the author's knowledge, no complete analysis of the strategy space has been accomplished in the 50 years of study and exploration since its introduction. It seems to be the case that finding apparently-complete solutions for the game is just barely within the capacity of the mathematical and software tools currently available. Having accomplished this, we do find that there are optimal strategies that are close to trivial. That said, variants of the game – such as that played at GaryCon – can again increase the strategy space to something significantly more difficult to solve.

At the 2018 GaryCon tournament, the author did win his joust in the first round, but was eliminated in the second. The author hopes to make a full analysis of the altered GaryCon rules and re-enter the tournament at some point in the future.

Acknowledgments. The author wishes to thank Nataniel Greene and Stephen Wendell for encouragement in writing this paper.

References

1. Gygax, G., Perren, J.: Chainmail: Rules for Medieval Miniatures. 2nd edn. Guidon Games, Belfast Maine (1972)
2. Gygax, G., Arneson, D.: Dungeons & Dragons. Tactical Studies Rules, USA (1974)
3. The Order of the Boar: Rules of Jousting. https://www.jousting.co.nz/jousting/rules-of-jou sting. Accessed 30 Aug 2022
4. Avis, D., Rosenberg, G., Savani, R., von Stengel, B.: Enumeration of nash equilibria for two-player games. Econ. Theory **42**, 9–37 (2010). https://doi.org/10.1007/s00199-009-0449-x
5. Solve a Bimatrix Game. https://cgi.csc.liv.ac.uk/~rahul/bimatrix_solver. Accessed 30 Aug 2022
6. OD&D Discussion. https://odd74.proboards.com/post/206676/thread. Accessed 30 Aug 2022

An Algorithm for Multiplayer Games Exploiting Opponents' Interactions with the Player

Kyle Sacks[1](✉) and Brayden Hollis[2](✉)

[1] Northeastern University, Boston, MA 02115, USA
sacks.k@northeastern.edu
[2] Air Force Research Laboratory, Rome, NY 13440, USA
brayden.hollis.1@us.af.mil

Abstract. In multiplayer games, it is often the case that some actions of one player will not influence the decisions of another, either until much later in the game or not at all. Existing algorithms make use of this idea and arbitrarily limit their models of the opponents, or partially ignore them, in order to explore more of the player's options. These limitations can go too far in the opposite direction, however, and miss crucial pieces of interaction between player and opponent. This paper attempts to solve both these problems, by introducing an algorithm which guides its search based on the player's interaction with the opponents. Specifically, it conducts a breadth-first, MaxN style search that builds its search trees by grouping together states that have the same interaction with the player.

Keywords: Interaction · Tree Search · MaxN

1 Introduction

The difficulty with multiplayer spaces is at once obvious and daunting - the sheer number of possible moves between a player's individual turns makes a massive search space in which the player only has limited control due to opponents' influences. Attempts to address this challenge usually try to limit the search space, by restricting which moves they consider from the opponent [10] [2] or ignoring the opponents' moves to focus on their own actions [1] These methods see significant improvement from traditional agents, but can make important oversights in doing so. Their failure to accurately predict opponent actions can in some crucial moments lead to wrong decisions, which might influence the whole of the game.

In multiplayer games, not all of an opponent's actions immediately or significantly affect the decision of the next player. Often, players will make moves

---

This material is based upon work supported by the Air Force Office of Scientific Research (AFOSR) under award number 21RICOR039.

which affect only themselves, setting themselves up for later positions. Sometimes, they will act against a third party, in such a way that the agent does not care about the result of this interaction. Consider the game of Chinese Checkers - in it, two to six players compete to move their pieces from a starting area into a goal area, which is unique for each player and directly across from them on the board. In between all the players sits a no-man's land for them to traverse while attempting to achieve their objectives. In this game, it stands to reason that one must only consider their opponent's actions when those actions affect how far one can move, i.e., there are times where the player is far enough from opponent pieces they do not matter [3].

Our algorithm attempts to exploit this pattern to restrict which paths the agent explores while avoiding to miss significant interactions between players. It does this by grouping together states where the agent's opponents' moves have interacted with the player in a similar matter, treating them as the same state. These groupings are treated as single nodes in a MaxN [7]-style algorithm, and an action taken from one member of the group counts for all of them. These groupings allow the agent to reduce the number of opponent moves which it must consider. The algorithm also accounts for moves which may not immediately seem relevant to the player but in fact are important for moves deeper into the game, and must be considered separately. To this end, it constructs search trees from the perspective of each player as it explores, and checks for discrepancies between these trees which would indicate an important over-simplification or something missed.

The contributions of this paper are 1) providing a definition of interaction that is specific and usable by algorithms; 2) proposing a new structure for searching game trees using this definition; and finally, 3) outlining and evaluating an algorithm using the definition and structures for playing multiplayer games.

2   Background

This section describes the MaxN breadth-first search algorithm we build upon. We then describe the state of the art algorithms BRS+ and OMA.

BFS and MaxN - Breadth-First Search(BFS) explores a game tree by simply exploring all possible moves from each state in turn, finishing every state at one turn before moving on to the next [6]. It explores the root, than each action taken from the root, than each action taken from the resulting states, than each action from *those* resulting states, and so on. MaxN [7] is a method of assigning and backpropagating values in a game tree - in it, each node contains a set of values, one for each player. If that node has children, this value corresponds to the set of values amongst it's children which maximizes the score for the player currently moving at that node. While an optimistic approach that often performs worse in practice when paired with BFS, MaxN is capable of finding a Nash equilibrium and can outperform in non-BFS search patterns, such as MCTS [8].

BRS+ - A common approach to multiplayer games is the paranoid assumption, which assumes all other players act against the root player, simplifying the game into essentially a two player game [11]. Best-Reply Search+ (BRS+) [10] relaxes the paranoid assumption by only selecting the one action between all opponents that is determined to be most harmful to the player. It then assigns all other opponents a move from a given move-ordering function. A generalization of this algorithm has been proposed in [2].

BRS+ is effective for a few reasons: first, it limits the problem of complexity by reducing the sets of opponents's it explores. Alpha-beta pruning can also be applied to the search trees created by BRS+, further increasing its efficiency. One can view BRS+ through the lens of interaction: it assumes that a player's actions are most important, and finds the move it thinks has the most important interaction with the player, which it defines as the most harmful move, and assumes only this one interacts with the player. Thus, it is a useful comparison for our algorithm, as one which is both effective and which abstracts almost all interaction away from the game.

OMA - Opponent Move Abstraction(OMA) is a recent state of the art algorithm by [1]. It is a variant algorithm of Monte-Carlo Tree Search [4], which explores without the use of rollouts. The main difference is that OMA uses both the regular UCT evaluation function as well as making use of a value it calls the OMA value estimate - this is an estimate calculated for actions at abstract states which only consider the player's move history, regardless of the actual board state. It maximizes the following modified equation: $\beta \bar{X}_a^{OMA} + (1-\beta)\bar{x}_a + k\sqrt{\frac{\ln n}{n_a}}$, where $\bar{X}_a^{OMA}$ is the OMA value estimate for move a, and β is a weighing coefficient which regulates the OMA value's influence. [1] The OMA algorithm makes use of both the UCT and OMA estimates scaled at a proportional rate to the number of times a particular action has been explored from a state - favoring the less accurate, more quickly calculated OMA estimate at first and later utilizing the more accurate standard estimate. The OMA algorithm also makes use of progressive widening [5], a technique which initially limits the number of available actions explored from a particular state to the ones with the highest heuristic estimate, gradually relaxing this restriction as time passes.

The OMA concept served as an inspiration for the structure of interaction trees - the idea of abstracting over the different histories of opponent moves and treating multiple states as the same for the purpose of a value estimation, was something we explored further. The OMA value is essentially the assumption that there is no interaction, and the algorithm which uses it finds the middle ground between no and all interaction(standard UCT) by assigning an arbitrary weight to each one and combining them. In our work, we try to explicitly track interaction, only grouping states with similar interactions with the player.

3   Interaction Tree Search

Interaction - Up to this point we have used the term interaction, but have not given it direct attention. Commonly, interaction deals with how two things impact each other. We are interested in how one player's actions impact another player's decision making; and, since we are interested in grouping similar interactions together, we evaluate interaction similarity by examining the impact on a player from that player's perspective. For this work, we focus on the resulting state's heuristic value and what actions the player can take from that state, grouping together interactions for a particular player if they match by these metrics. We use these characteristics as they are the primary features an AI uses for decision making and we claim interactions that cause differences in these characteristics are necessarily distinct. While necessary, we do not consider these similarities to be sufficient; our interaction groupings are only candidate sets that we do separate if some addition criterion (which we refer to as higher order interactions) is violated - this is discussed further in the subsection on splitting.

Interaction Trees - As our method for comparing interactions only relies on characteristics of the resulting states, we can use it to group states and build what we call *interaction trees*. Interaction trees are constructed of special nodes called *interaction nodes*. These nodes hold within them a set of states; states that resulted from similar interaction from the player's perspective (i.e., the player's available moves are the same, and the player's heuristic value of all the states are the same). The children of an interaction node contain states resulting from actions taken from the states in the parent. We do not allow the same action to map to different children nodes (this is one of the higher order interaction criteria we use); however, different actions can (and often will) map to the same child node, as seen in Fig. 1. For this work, we also assume that each distinct action of a player is a distinct interaction from their perspective, i.e. the each of the player's actions from one of their interaction nodes will map to a unique child interaction node. Note that we evaluate interactions from the perspective of individual players, so each player will have a unique interaction tree. Figure 1 shows an example of players' interaction trees, and the corresponding full tree.

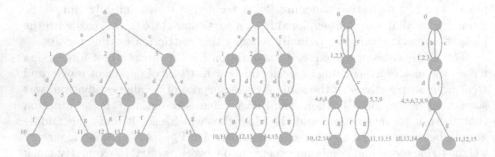

Fig. 1. The tree on the left is what a normal search tree would look like for the states and actions shown in the example. The other three trees represent the interaction trees from the perspectives of the three different players in the hypothetical game, who take the first, second, and third action of the game respectively. Curved edges are one edge with multiple actions, depicted separately for clarity.

The underlying hypothesis of these interaction sets is the player will make the same decision after the interactions in the same set. Our approach exploits this hypothesis by assuming exploring each action from a interaction set once is sufficient, i.e. it is not necessary to explore that action from each state in the interaction node, which results in a reduced branching factor and allows for greater search depths. The rest of the section details the our approach built on these concepts of interaction.

Exploration - Our agent explores its search space in a manner reminiscent of breadth-first search - when an action from a state is queued up for exploration, it is queued with a priority equal to the turn of the state(with lower turns being explored first). At first, every action from the root state is added to the queue. The algorithm does the following when exploring a new state-action pair.

1. Take the action from the given state.
2. For each player's interaction tree:
   (a) Determine the interaction estimate(the heuristic value and feasible actions) of the state for that player.
   (b) If the interaction node which contains the given state already has a child for the action:
       i. If there is no interaction between the existing child and resulting state, group them together.
       ii. Else, room must be made by splitting the parent node(or it's parents, if the parent cannot be split) until there is room.
   (c) If the action taken was not previously explored by the tree's player, determine if the parent interaction node has any children with the same interaction estimate. If one is found, group the resulting state into that interaction node, and that node will be the child of the action taken in the parent interaction node.
   (d) If no matching states were found, or if the action was taken by the tree's player, create a new interaction node as a child of the explored action, containing the resulting state.

After adding the state to each player's interaction tree, a random action is queued from the resulting state and then the agent moves on to the next node.

Every time the agent finishes exploring a level(turn), it additionally does two things. First, it ensures that all created interaction nodes have at least one child for every possible move, by queuing up moves from states within each of those interaction nodes to fill the gaps. Then, it compares the MaxN value for the agent in the agent's interaction tree to the value for that agent in every other interaction tree. If any are not equal, a node is split in one of the trees and exploration resumes, repeating the process until all values match. Once they do, the agent can move on to the next level and continue exploration.

In order to find which node to split, checks are run in the following order, in a BFS search that follows each tree simultaneously (alternating between each tree as long as there still remain nodes from both on each level of the search). In all cases, for a node to be split it must contain multiple states, with at least two different actions taken to reach those states.

1. A node which has a direct child with the score for the other player among their values, but does not have that score as it's own.
2. A node which has a descendant matching the same conditions as 1.
3. A node which has a sibling the score at the top of the other player's tree, while it does not.
4. A node which has a sibling with a descendant matching the same conditions as 3.
5. A node which can be split.

Splitting - Sometimes, it is the case that an interaction tree is determined by the agent to have missed some higher-level interaction, and as such two states which were previously considered together must be considered separately. In order for a node to be split, it must contain multiple states abstracted within it, and there must be at least two states such that they were explored from different actions. To split a node, the algorithm selects a particular action, gathers all states within the interaction node reached by that action or sequence, and takes the following steps, which are shown being carried out in Fig. 2:

1. Create a new child of the parent interaction node, for the action(or actions) which were taken to reach the states being split out.
2. Distribute the children of the old interaction node as follows: children from states exclusively in the old node remain, children from states exclusively in the new node are moved, and children from both states are recursively split, with a new interaction node containing the states from those split out as a child of the previously created node.
3. The MaxN values of the tree are updated to reflect the change, and state-action pairs are queued up for exploration to fill in any gaps created (In Fig. 2, this step would involve exploring g from state eight and f from state nine).

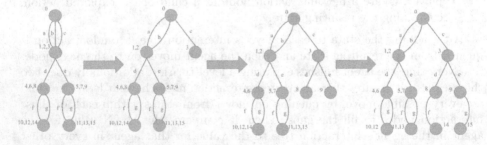

Fig. 2. This shows the steps in splitting out a node, and proliferating the split down the rest of an interaction tree. On the far left is the original interaction tree, which corresponds to the interaction tree of player 2 in Fig. 1. State 3 is split from it's interaction node in the next image, and the trees follow the splitting out of children explored from state 3, with the far right showing the resulting interaction tree after the split is completed.

Backpropagation - The MaxN values of nodes are updated whenever a new node is added, starting from that node, and additionally whenever a new node is split out, starting from both the previously existing and newly added node, to ensure the MaxN value of each tree is always up to date. While the algorithm is running, it needs to keep track of the current MaxN [7] scores for each node in its interaction trees. Each node in a tree is assigned with a value for each player, initially a heuristic value from each player's perspective. These heuristic values are calculated from the state within the interaction node which maximizes the heuristic for the player which made the action to reach it. After a node is created and assigned this value, the value is propagated upwards until no more changes are necessary - the parent node reconsiders all of its children, and if the score of the new child is considered better than it's current score(or if the new child is it's first), it takes the scores of the new child for each player as its own. Scores are compared as follows, from the perspective of a particular interaction node:

1. The player who is making the next action in the node's scores are compared, with the higher being taken.
2. If the previous is a tie, the value with the lowest sum of scores across all other players will be taken.
3. If there is still a tie, then the scores of each player from first to last will be compared, and whenever a difference appears the set of scores with the lower value will be taken.

Final Selection - After the algorithm runs out of time, it selects which action to take by comparing all children of the root of the interaction tree corresponding to the agent's player, and selecting the action among them which leads to the child with the greatest MaxN score.

4   Experiments

We tested our algorithm in the game Chinese Checkers, with both four and six player games, because the game has phases with low numbers of distinct interactions. The game is for two to six players, on a star-shaped board, with each player's pieces starting in a point of the star. The goal of each player is to move all of their pieces into the opposite point - a piece may move one tile in any direction, or jump over any number of adjacent pieces in a chain. We use a smaller board where each player starts with 6 pieces, in order to speed up testing.

Our algorithm, as well as our baselines, require an evaluation function from each player's perspective. We used a simple function: the summed distance of each of a player's pieces to their end goal, over the total distance that player had to move, such that the value remains between zero and one. Our Monte-Carlo(UCT) [4] baseline, uses a modified version of the evaluation function which normalizes each player's value over the total of all player's evaluations of the state instead of rollouts. Some baselines also required a move-ordering function, such as OMA, and for this we kept its move-ordering function the same, which orders moves by how much closer they bring a piece to the goal area [1].

We ran our experiments in Ludii [9], a Java-based system designed for running games using AI agents. Ludii takes a set of agents and covers all possible permutations of positions as many times as possible within the given number of games. It outputs results using a system which collects an average of placements in each game, via a score scaled to the number of players. In the case of ties, the tying players will split between them the score of the place they tied for. Ludii also provides a confidence interval for these average scores. Our experiments ran sets of 240 games each. Note that Ludii implements Chinese Checkers with each jump in a turn as a separate action, and we have simplified this to consider each sequence of jumps as one action.

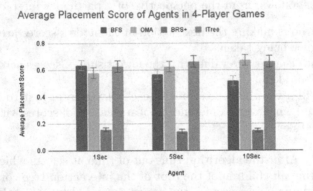

Fig. 3. Average placement scores in 4-player games, in experiments where agents had 1, 5, and 10 s to consider their moves. This placement score was awarded as follows at the close of each game: 1st - 1.0, 2nd - 0.66, 3rd - 0.33, 4th - 0.0.

In our four player experiments, there was no clear algorithm which was superior to the other three. Outside of BRS+, which consistently performed poorly and scored highest at 0.156 with 1 s moves, BFS, OMA, and our algorithm were within each others confidence intervals for $1\,s(0.63 \pm 0.042, 0.579 \pm 0.037,$ and 0.62 ± 0.043 respectively) and $5\,s(0.56 \pm 0.037, 0.625 \pm 0.039, 0.66 \pm 0.042)$, and OMA and Interaction Tree Search continued this pattern at $10\,s(0.67 \pm 0.041, 0.66 \pm 0.041)$.

For our six player experiments, We introduced a Monte-Carlo MaxN agent, as well as an attempt at an Interaction Tree Monte Carlo Search(which performed poorly and thus is not the focus of this paper). Our six player experiments saw a similar pattern of parity for the most part, with the notable exception of 5 s decisions, where Interaction Tree Search clearly outperformed the other algorithms(0.71 ± 0.039), with the next highest scoring 0.59 ± 0.038. OMA performed worse than with 4 players, with scores of 0.55, 0.52, and 0.56, and Monte Carlo took it's place in the three-way ties of $1\,s(0.59 \pm 0.04(MCTS), 0.629 \pm$

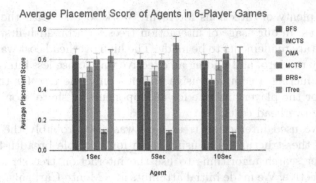

Fig. 4. Average placement scores in 6-player games, in experiments where agents had 1, 5, and 10 s to consider their moves. This placement score was awarded as follows at the close of each game: 1st - 1.0, 2nd - 0.8, 3rd - 0.6, 4th - 0.4, 5th - 0.2, 6th - 0.0

0.04(BFS), 0.62 ± 0.042(ITree)) and $10 \text{ s}(0.638 \pm 0.043, 0.592 \pm 0.043, 0.6385 \pm 0.045)$ alongside MaxN BFS and Interaction Tree Search.

BRS+ probably performed poorly due to the longer game times and issues with the paranoid assumption in Chinese Checkers, where players often act greedily instead of trying to stop opponents, while the time helped BFS reach the minimum depths to stay relevant. Our algorithm tended to do better with more time and more players - with more time, grouping together states allows more and more actions to be ignored, and with more players each tree had less nodes where it could not group together multiple different actions.

5   Discussion

In this paper, we use a focus on interaction within games to introduce a new algorithm, modeled on MaxN-style search. This algorithm attempted to only account for opponent's moves which interacted with the player and ignore the rest in such a way as to focus more on the player's own actions. The results we got from testing this algorithm were mixed. On the one hand, with enough players and enough time, we saw the algorithm be competitive with and even perform better than its baseline and other state-of-the-art algorithms, however, with fewer players and less time it often failed to stand out.

As we were testing the algorithm, we noticed that although it is effective in cutting down the number of nodes a tree needed to use to represent the game at each level, there was a significant overhead cost in the creation and maintenance of interaction trees, not to mention the requirements of creating simultaneous trees for each player. OMA and BFS respectively explored approximately three and ten times as many nodes as our approach, with the most significant time of our approach being spent upkeeping the MaxN values of all the interaction trees and splitting taking between 10 and 20% of the time. With enough time, however, this overhead cost hurdle was able to be overcome and the benefits of the algorithm shone through.

There are plenty of directions for future work to take with the concept of interaction trees. In our usage of interaction trees for a breadth-first search, for instance, there are refinements to be made. The high overhead cost was a problem we consistently ran into, and finding an effective way to use less interaction trees while still conducting a comprehensive search - only one tree for the game, or perhaps one for the player and one for all opponents to share, would go a long way to cutting overhead costs.

The way we used interaction trees here was also probably the most basic - constructing the structures and using them for a simple breadth-first search. Adapting other search algorithms to use the interaction tree structure might prove more effective. We made initial attempts at a Monte-Carlo algorithm using interaction trees, and while ours was not very effective there are probably better ways to integrate our concepts of interaction. Determining which algorithms would benefit the most from interaction trees, and determining how they would use them, is probably the most fruitful direction for future research.

References

1. Baier, H., Kaisers, M.: Guiding multiplayer MCTS by focusing on yourself. In: 2020 IEEE Conference on Games (CoG), pp. 550–557 (2020)
2. Baier, H., Kaisers, M.: Opponent-pruning paranoid search. In: International Conference on the Foundations of Digital Games (2020)
3. Bell, G.: The shortest game of Chinese checkers and related problems. Integers 9 (2008). https://doi.org/10.1515/INTEG.2009.003
4. Browne, C.B., et al.: A survey of monte Carlo tree search methods. IEEE Trans. Comput. Intell. AI Games **4**, 1–43 (2012)
5. Chaslot, G., Winands, M., Herik, H., Uiterwijk, J., Bouzy, B.: Progressive strategies for monte-carlo tree search. New Math. Natural Comput. **04**, 343–357 (2008). https://doi.org/10.1142/S1793005708001094
6. Holdsworth, J.: The nature of breadth-first search (1999)
7. Luckhardt, C.A., Irani, K.B.: An algorithmic solution of n-person games. In: Proceedings of the Fifth AAAI National Conference on Artificial Intelligence, pp. 158–162. AAAI Press (1986)
8. Nijssen, J.A.M.: Monte-Carlo Tree Search for Multi-Player Games. Ph.D. thesis, Maastricht University (2013)
9. Piette, É., Soemers, D.J.N.J., Stephenson, M., Sironi, C.F., Winands, M.H.M., Browne, C.: Ludii - the ludemic general game system. In: ECAI (2020)
10. Schadd, M.P.D., Winands, M.H.M.: Best reply search for multiplayer games. In: IEEE Transactions on Computational Intelligence and AI in Games, pp. 57–66 (2011). https://doi.org/10.1109/TCIAIG.2011.2107323
11. Sturtevant, N.R., Korf, R.E.: On pruning techniques for multi-player games. In: AAAI/IAAI (2000)

Incentivizing Information Gain in Hidden Information Multi-Action Games

Nathan Lervold, Gilbert L. Peterson[(✉)] [iD], and David W. King [iD]

Air Force Institute of Technology, 2950 Hobson Way, WPAFB, Dayton, OH, USA
{nathan.lervold,gilbert.peterson,david.king}@afit.edu

Abstract. Wargames often include fog of war, i.e. hidden information, and multi-action turns, where each turn requires making multiple, sequential action choices. These properties provide unique challenges
for Artificial Intelligence agents. Extensions to Monte-Carlo Tree Search
(MCTS) allow it to perform well in games with hidden information as
well as multi-action games. However, these extensions do not specifically
consider both properties simultaneously nor how information-gaining
actions could improve agent performance. Information-gaining actions
are important in multi-action turns where initial actions can reveal state
information, thus improving later action decisions. This paper presents
enhancements to MCTS that add an information gain incentive and a risk
determinization to balance locating opponent pieces while minimizing
exposure to enemy fire. The information gain incentive and risk functions
are implemented in Perfect Information-MCTS (PIMCTS) and Information Set-MCTS (ISMCTS) and evaluated on the multi-action hidden
information game TUBSTAP. Results show that these additions improve
performance over the baseline algorithms and against a Cheating MCTS
implementation.

Keywords: Multi-action turn-based games · Hidden Information ·
Monte-Carlo Tree Search

1 Introduction

Wargames employ many game elements that greatly increase the complexity
beyond a game of checkers or chess. These may include fog of war (hidden information), taking multiple actions each turn (multi-action turns), having different
capabilities for each unit (such as unit mobility), or having a large board size
[9]. Additionally, war games utilize a variety of maps and starting pieces to
accommodate different scenarios. The complex interactions between units and
environment make developing artificial intelligence (AI) agents difficult.

The views expressed in this article are those of the author and do not necessarily
reflect the official policy or position of the Air Force, the United States Department of
Defense, or the United States Government.

Monte Carlo Tree Search (MCTS) has proven to be very successful in games with multi-action turns [8] and games with hidden information such as Bridge [2], Kriegspiel [11], and Magic the Gathering [6]. One shortcoming of MCTS applied to multi-action hidden information games, is that it does not consider taking actions for the benefit of gaining information, such as moving a unit to uncover fog of war to give future moves more certainty.

Two MCTS hidden information extensions are Perfect Information MCTS (PIMCTS) and Information Set MCTS (ISMCTS). Both utilize determinizations at the root of the game tree, but differ in tree structure. Each determinization is a possible sample of the opponent's hidden information.

Evaluation of the information gain and risk extensions to PIMCTS and ISM-CTS uses TUBSTAP extended to include fog of war. TUBSTAP, the TUrn Based Strategy Academic Package [8], is a multi-action turn-based strategy game loosely based on Advance Wars that encompasses many complexities of wargaming. TUBSTAP includes map customization, various unit types and compositions, and terrain that imposes restrictions and bonuses. In a TUBSTAP game, two teams compete to eliminate all units of the opposing team.

Our main contributions focus on adding probability maps (pmap), information gain incentive and risk determinizations to MCTS agents playing the game of TUBSTAP. These concepts exist in current literature; however, this is the first work to explore their impact on an MCTS agent playing a game that contains both hidden information and multi-action turns.

Results indicate that the probability map consistently improves both PIMCTS and ISMCTS. The addition of information gain and risk offset is greater in PIMCTS where sampling determinizations is more limited, and there is little benefit over the probability map in ISMCTS.

2   Related Work

Monte Carlo Tree Search (MCTS) is an anytime stochastic algorithm that searches the game space asymmetrically, focusing on the most promising nodes [3]. Each iteration of MCTS completes four phases: Selection, Expansion, Simulation, and Backpropagation. MCTS has had broad applicability in games with large branching factors, and has been extended to address hidden information and multi-action turns.

2.1   Imperfect Information MCTS Extensions

There are several MCTS extensions for imperfect information games. The simplest is Perfect Information MCTS (PIMCTS). PIMCTS creates x determinizations from the game state, then performs a separate MCTS search on each determinization [10]. Once complete, the action with the highest cumulative UCT score is chosen. PIMCTS has the shortcomings of strategy fusion and nonlocality [7]. Strategy fusion is due to each determinization being evaluated on separate trees: an action may look favorable when considering partial information independently when in reality, dependencies between determinizations affect the value of information. Non-locality occurs when PIMCTS samples determinations with uniform probability. In reality, some states are more likely than others since the opponent is rational.

ISMCTS addresses strategy fusion by including all determinizations in a singular tree [5]. Each node is part of an information set, a set of possible states that can be reached from an action. Each action can connect one node to an information set of nodes. In each iteration, ISMCTS samples a new determinization at the root. During selection, ISMCTS only selects nodes compatible with the root determinization. Additionally, expansion may occur at a non-leaf node if selection finds no compatible nodes in the information set. After backpropagation, each parent node of an information set consolidates all the information of nodes in the set, overcoming strategy fusion. ISMCTS still suffers from non-locality since all determinizations are considered with the same probability.

2.2 Multi-Action Turn MCTS Extensions

While MCTS is a powerful search algorithm, large search trees can inhibit how deep the algorithm can search each turn. If given enough time, MCTS should return the optimal move from the current game state. However, guiding the search through the use of heuristics or pruning the game tree can yield deeper and more effective searches. Multi-action games generate more complex trees as nodes in a multi-action game tree can either represent a complete action sequence (full turn) or single actions (partial turn) applied sequentially. This means MCTS has to be modified to account for these full and partial turn nodes in combination with a pruning methodology to ensure a deeper search.

Most partial turn enhancements address the additional space complexity of multi-action games by limiting/pruning the tree space. Sato and Ikeda [12] present three forward pruning techniques applied to TUBSTAP: fixing the movement order of units, applying selective unit action generation, and applying limited unit actions. Selective unit action generation groups attack and movement actions by certain criteria, such as target unit, and only selects one action per group. Lastly, limited unit action performs a smaller tree search on only the most influential units (ignoring units with low HP or far out of combat range). These forward pruning techniques improved TUBSTAP agents by allowing deeper searches on the tree focusing on more promising nodes.

Baier and Cowling created Evolutionary MCTS [1] for a multi-action hidden information game Hero Academy. Each node in the tree is a genome that encompasses a full turn (each action is a gene). However, Evolutionary MCTS ignores the hidden information aspects of the game.

Progressive widening or progressive unpruning [4] limits the number of child nodes added to any node until a certain threshold is reached. The threshold can increase with the number of iterations, slowly unpruning or adding more children to each node. This has been applied to TUBSTAP [8] with an emphasis on attack actions. Progressive unpruning can be paired with progressive bias which uses heuristic knowledge to influence node selection. As the number of iterations increases, the heuristic influence decreases. Progressive bias could be an effective solution to TUBSTAP given the development of effective heuristic state evaluators such as phase division [13]. The phase division heuristic evaluator is based on unit positioning and matchups rather than simply HP and unit type as in [8].

3   Information Gain and Risk for MCTS

To account for information gain in multi-action hidden information games, we make two modifications to MCTS in the form of an information gain incentive function during selection and a risk function used during determinization. These additions leverage a visibility matrix and a probability map. The visibility matrix is what the player sees at a specific turn and includes visible units. The probability map maintains a distribution of where enemies are most likely to be based on their last known position.

3.1   Probability Map

The probability map (pmap) is represented by a set of tiles $t_{(x,y)} \in T \wedge t = \{plains, mountain, forest, road, ocean\}$. Each tile type affects movement and may grant a defensive bonus. From the perspective of the active player, F is the set of all friendly units, F_A is the set of friendly units that still have an action left to take this turn, and E is the set of all enemy units. Each unit has a location, health, and type. Unit type dictates movement, vision, and attack power against other unit types.

A visibility matrix $\{V_{(x,y)}\}$ tracks which tiles are visible. Visibility determines whether an enemy unit can be seen on that tile. If $V_{(x,y)} = 1$, then $t_{(x,y)}$ is visible. If $V_{(x,y)} = 0$, then $t_{(x,y)}$ is not visible. The matrix $v(f)$ contains all tiles visible for unit $f \in F$.

The pmap $\{P_{(x,y,e)}\}(e \in E)$ tracks the probability of an enemy unit being on each tile. The probability that enemy e is on tile $t_{(x,y)}$ is $p_{x,y,e}$. The pmap update maintains a distribution of the possible positions of enemy units based on the visibility matrix, the range of each enemy unit, and the pmap from the prior turn. The player begins with an initial assumption that enemy units are in a mirrored configuration to their own.

Figure 1 shows an example of how the pmap tracks the legal moves of enemies. Each unit has a movement and vision of 2. Figure 1a depicts the possible locations each enemy could be this turn with an assumed starting location (red squares for enemy 1, blue squares for enemy 2, and purple squares for both). Figure 1b shows the visibility of the player at the start of the turn. In Fig. 1c, a unit is moved from a4 to a2 revealing more tiles; although c4 is now out of visible range, it is still included since it was visible at start of the turn. Before the next move, the player updates the pmap with the added information in Fig. 1d. Tile c2 cannot contain an enemy since it is now visible. Without any added belief, the probabilities of each enemy are uniformly distributed among the tiles. For

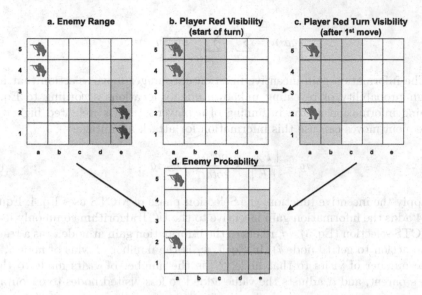

Fig. 1. Tracking possible enemy moves.

determining the enemy range next turn, the pmap checks the range at each edge tile (tiles c1, d2, and e3 for enemy 2).

3.2 Information Gain Incentive

The information gain incentive function combines information from the visibility matrix and pmap to create a heuristic for guiding MCTS selection. In TUBSTAP with hidden information, the damage calculation favors the attacker over the defender. Additionally, a unit cannot attack a unit that is not visible. Finding enemy units becomes critical for maintaining attack advantage as well as organizing defense.

The total number of unknowns in the probability map is calculated according to Eq. 1. Figure 1a contains 14 unknowns (6 possible tiles for the enemy on e1 and 8 possible tiles for the enemy on e2).

$$total = \sum_{p_{x,y,e} \in P} k(x, y, e) \tag{1}$$

$$k(x, y, e) = \begin{cases} 1 & \text{if } 0 < p_{x,y,e} < 1 \\ 0 & \text{else} \end{cases}$$

Set G contains all the new visible tiles gained from the last action. In Fig. 1c, $G = \{a1, b1, b2, c2\}$. The number of unknowns uncovered is calculated for each enemy according to Eq. 2. The move in Fig. 1c results in uncovering 1 unknown on tile c2.

$$gain = \sum_{e \in E} \sum_{g_{x,y} \in G} k(x, y, e) \tag{2}$$

The information gain incentive function encourages move selection that has a high probability of revealing unknown enemy locations according to Eq. 3. Gaining information at the beginning of a player's turn is weighted higher as subsequent moves can use this information for attack advantage.

$$ig = \frac{|F_A|}{|F|} \times \frac{gain}{total}; \ 0 \leq ig \leq 1 \tag{3}$$

To apply the incentive function, the Selection phase of MCTS uses Eq. 4. Equation 4 adds the information gain incentive to the UCT algorithm commonly used in MCTS selection (Eq. 5). ig_i refers to the information gain at node i (as a result of the action to get to node i). In Eq. 5, w_i is the number of wins of node i, n_i is the number of visits to that node, N_i is the number of visits made to that node's parent, and α adjusts the value added to less visited nodes to encourage exploration.

$$u(i) = (1 - \beta) \ UCT_i + \beta \ ig_i \tag{4}$$

$$UCT_i = \frac{w_i}{n_i} + \alpha \sqrt{\frac{\ln(N_i)}{n_i}} \tag{5}$$

This work only uses Eq. 4 when selecting the first layer of nodes in the game tree due to complications of maintaining the pmap throughout the gametree. Subsequent layers use normal UCT.

3.3   Risk Determinization

Taking an information-gaining action often comes with risk. When a player unit moves into a position that reveals an opponent unit, the opponent unit gains a potential attack advantage the next turn (given it has a similar sight range).

The risk determinization accounts for this risk by sampling from a worst case enemy unit distribution called fringe weighting. Fringe weighting takes pmap with a uniform distribution and multiplies each pmap probability $p_{x,y,e}$ by a value r. The value of r is different for each tile and increases as the associated tile gets closer to the edge of the player's vision. Figure 2 shows how r values increase for each tile. Looking at tile b1 in Fig. 2, $p_{b,2,e}$ in the pmap is multiplied by an r value of 16 (r values are squared). Values are then normalized between 0 and 1 and sum to 1 for each enemy.

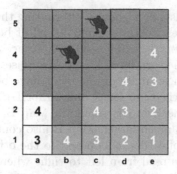

Fig. 2. Applying uneven fringe weighting to the pmap. Grey tiles represent turn vision. Red squares represent possible locations of an enemy unit. (Color figure online)

4 Results

TUBSTAP with hidden information is used as the testing environment to evaluate the information gain incentive function and risk determinization additions (IGR) to MCTS. The addition of hidden information extends the base TUBSTAP implementation [8] and adds the fog-of-war and unit visibility range mechanic from Advance Wars. Table 1 shows the added Unit Vision values.

Table 1. Unit Vision and Movement.

	Attack Jet	Fighter Jet	Anti-Air	Infantry	Tank	Artillery	Scout
Vision	3	3	2	2	2	1	4
Movement	7	6	5	4	5	2	6

ISMCTS variants complete 10,000 iterations, while PIMCTS variants split this budget between 20 determinizations (or trees) of 500 iterations. They use an exploration constant for UCT of 0.20 and an information incentive β of 0.05. This paper compares the following four MCTS variants:

1. PIMCTS-Pmap/ ISMCTS-Pmap: PIMCTS and ISMCTS using the probability map with a uniform distribution to guide determinizations. The information gain and risk functions are not used.
2. PIMCTS-IGR/ ISMCTS-IGR: PIMCTS and ISMCTS using the information gain incentive during selection and risk function applied to the pmap.
3. PIMCTS-S/ ISMCTS-S: PIMCTS and ISMCTS without the use of a probability map. They instead use the simplified determinization method of distributing enemy units uniformly among unseen tiles.
4. Cheating MCTS: Acts with complete knowledge of opponent hidden information and does not need to make determinizations.

Each comparison consists of 30 games, alternating the starting player so that each player starts 15 games. Scores above 0.50 reflect better performance. Each score is calculated by $(wins - losses + 30)/60$, to account for ties which may occur if a game exceeds the turn limit. Comparison uses the two maps shown in Fig. 3. A game ends when all units of one color have been eliminated or when a turn limit has been reached (15 for A and 25 for B). In Map A, information is gained quickly since the board is small. In Map B, information gain stays relevant for longer as it is much larger. Map B also contains a Scout which has an increased sight range of 4 tiles as opposed to the other units' sight range of at most 2 tiles. Tables are read from left to right where each row contains the scores of the player against each opponent.

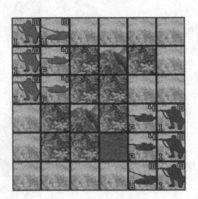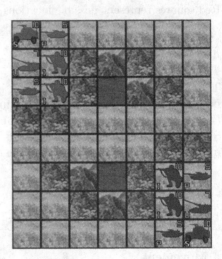

Fig. 3. Map A (left) and Map B (right).

Table 2 shows the win rates on Map A. Overall, the additions of the pmap and the IGR result in both PIMCTS and ISMCTS outperforming the base variants. The pmap addition has a much larger positive influence on ISMCTS then PIMCTS. Since information is gained quickly, the pmap is largely only used in the first couple of turns or when an opponent unit is occasionally lost. However, since ISMCTS makes a determinization at each iteration, the pmap helps prune these determinizations to sample a much more accurate board. The other item to note is that on both maps adding in pmap and IGR results in additional wins/ties against the Cheating agent.

Table 3 shows results on Map B. As with Map A, the additions of the pmap and IGR result in improved performance over the baseline implementations. Map B contains more unknowns than Map A. This may make information gain more relevant but riskier as a player's units can become more separated. The pmap appears to perform better on map B. The primary reason is that the pmap restricts the sampling space to reachable states, and limits exploring highly

Table 2. MCTS variants Map A

Player	Opponent					
	PIMCTS			ISMCTS		
	S	Pmap	IGR	S	Pmap	IGR
PIMCTS-S	–					
PIMCTS-Pmap	0.58	–				
PIMCTS-IGR	0.82	0.55	–			
ISMCTS-S	0.45	0.33	0.28	–		
ISMCTS-Pmap	0.82	0.60	0.62	0.82	–	
ISMCTS-IGR	0.82	0.78	0.68	0.70	0.42	–
Cheating MCTS	0.92	0.83	0.73	0.95	0.78	0.77

Table 3. MCTS variants Map B

Player	Opponent					
	PIMCTS			ISMCTS		
	S	Pmap	IGR	S	Pmap	IGR
PIMCTS-S	–					
PIMCTS-Pmap	0.68	–				
PIMCTS-IGR	0.65	0.68	–			
ISMCTS-S	0.68	0.62	0.58	–		
ISMCTS-Pmap	0.87	0.75	0.63	0.70	–	
ISMCTS-IGR	0.82	0.63	0.63	0.63	0.42	–
Cheating MCTS	0.93	0.75	0.82	0.8	0.72	0.78

unlikely areas. Because PIMCTS has a fewer number of determinizations, the improvement is even more marked. The information gain incentive with risk offset (IGR) also increases the performance of PIMCTS reflecting that information gain is important for PIMCTS to guide the limited number of determinizations. However, ISMCTS-IGR does not outperform the ISMCTS-pmap as the UCT selection with a large number of determinizations is still effective. As on Map A, on Map B, the additions increase the score of MCTS variants against Cheating MCTS.

5   Conclusions and Future Work

This paper introduced an information gain incentive that is applied during the selection phase of MCTS, a risk offset applied to MCTS determinizations, and the introduction of a probability map to prune unrealizable determinizations in the game of TUBSTAP. These additions are implemented in PIMCTS and ISMCTS. In both cases, the additions lead to improved performance over the baseline algorithms and improves their performance against a Cheating MCTS player. However, the incentive with risk did not improve ISMCTS over just including the pmap as ISMCTS completes sufficient sampling such that guiding the sampling is less critical. However, this does not mean that it would not impact ISMCTS on larger, more complex maps.

Currently, the information gain incentive is only applied at the first node layer during selection. Future work should determine if applying it at every node, with the addition of incentive decay as the selection reaches deeper in the tree, could improve performance. Additionally, as mentioned in Sato, et al. [13], there is a strong opening and mid-game transition that impacts move ordering. The addition of hidden information magnifies this impact and determining when the transition occurs, and what the move ordering should be, in these two phases should be explored.

Acknowledgment. This document is the result of a research project funded by the Air Force Research Laboratory's STRATAGEM Program, under program manager Brayden Hollis.

References

1. Baier, H., Cowling, P.I.: Evolutionary MCTS for multi-action adversarial games. In: 2018 IEEE Conference on Computational Intelligence and Games (CIG), pp. 1–8. IEEE (2018)
2. Bethe, P.M.: The state of automated bridge play (2009). Unpublished
3. Browne, C.B., et al.: A survey of monte Carlo tree search methods. IEEE Trans. Comput. Intell. AI Games 4(1), 1–43 (2012)
4. Chaslot, G.M.J., Winands, M.H., Herik, H.J.V.D., Uiterwijk, J.W., Bouzy, B.: Progressive strategies for monte-carlo tree search. New Math. Nat. Comput. 4(03), 343–357 (2008)
5. Cowling, P.I., Powley, E.J., Whitehouse, D.: Information set monte Carlo tree search. IEEE Trans. Comput. Intell. AI Games 4(2), 120–143 (2012)
6. Cowling, P.I., Ward, C.D., Powley, E.J.: Ensemble determinization in monte Carlo tree search for the imperfect information card game magic: the gathering. IEEE Trans. Comput. Intell. AI Games 4(4), 241–257 (2012)
7. Frank, I., Basin, D.: Search in games with incomplete information: a case study using bridge card play. Artif. Intell. 100(1–2), 87–123 (1998)
8. Fujiki, T., Ikeda, K., Viennot, S.: A platform for turn-based strategy games, with a comparison of monte-carlo algorithms. In: 2015 IEEE Conference on Computational Intelligence and Games (CIG), pp. 407–414. IEEE (2015)
9. Keller, C.J., Averna, R., Matcheck, D.: How to master wargaming: commander and staff guide to improving course of action analysis 20–06. Mission Command Center of Excellence (2020)
10. Long, J.R., Sturtevant, N.R., Buro, M., Furtak, T.: Understanding the success of perfect information monte Carlo sampling in game tree search. In: Twenty-Fourth AAAI Conference on Artificial Intelligence (2010)
11. Russell, S., Wolfe, J.: Efficient belief-state and-or search, with application to kriegspiel. In: IJCAI, vol. 19, p. 278 (2005)

12. Sato, N., Fujiki, T., Ikeda, K.: Three types of forward pruning techniques to apply the alpha beta algorithm to turn-based strategy games. In: 2016 IEEE Conference on Computational Intelligence and Games (CIG), pp. 1–8. IEEE (2016)
13. Sato, N., Ikeda, K.: Phase division and simplification game offline tree search for phase evaluation value composition in turn-based strategy games. In: Game Programming Workshop, pp. 61–68 (2015)

Solving Games

QBF Solving Using Best First Search

Yifan He$^{(\boxtimes)}$ and Abdallah Saffidine$^{(\boxtimes)}$

The University of New South Wales, Sydney, Australia
harryheyifan99@gmail.com, abdallah.saffidine@gmail.com

Abstract. Quantified Boolean Formula or QBF is similar to a two-player strategy game on a theoretical level. While most search-based QBF solvers are based on a depth-first search based QDPLL procedure, many game solvers use best-first search algorithms such as proof number search. In this paper, we examine how to design a best-first search based QBF solver that combines some well-known QBF solving techniques such as backjumping and clause learning. We evaluate the performance of the resulting algorithm on a set of standard QBF benchmarks.

1 Introduction

Quantified Boolean Formulas (QBFs) was proposed in the 1970s as a natural generalization of propositional logic. Since then, many problems have been addressed by expressing them as a QBF and evaluating the formula with a *QBF Solver* [24]. Solving a QBF is a computationally difficult task, and the fastest known algorithms for this problem have a worst-case complexity exponential in the number of variables. Yet, in practice, QBF solvers routinely solve formulas with a few hundred or thousands of variables. This success can be attributed to several key algorithmic improvements. Of particular note are unit propagation, pure literal elimination [1], backjumping [5], QCDCL [6,26], and CEGAR [10].

Game solving has also witnessed significant heuristic algorithmic improvements over the last 30 years. Best-First Search (BFS) algorithms maintain information about the search space in memory and use it to decide where to explore next. In particular, Proof Number Search (PNS) and Monte Carlo Tree Search (MCTS) have proven quite effective [3,12]. This contrasts with the traditional Depth-First Search (DFS) algorithm which risks being trapped on the wrong side of the search space. For example, traditional DFS algorithms can rarely solve Shogi positions more than 17-move deep whereas a PNS variant identified up to 100-move deep strategies [23]. Although there are DFS algorithms such as MTD(f) [19] and DF-PN [12] that can reduce the chances of being trapped on the wrong side of the searching space, it is not the main focus of this paper.

QBFs are typically written as a quantifier *prefix* followed by a quantifier-free propositional formula called *matrix*. Any QBF can be interpreted as a strategy game where two players, *Existential* and *Universal* take turn assigning truth value to the variables in the quantifier prefix. If the resulting assignment satisfies the matrix, then Existential wins, otherwise Universal wins. Thus, typical QBF

C. Browne et al. (Eds.): CG 2022, LNCS 13865, pp. 73–86, 2023.
https://doi.org/10.1007/978-3-031-34017-8_7

can be seen as games with branching factor 2 and a depth exceeding 100. This parallel between formulas and games carries to the algorithm level: E.g., QPDLL explores the space of variable assignments for a QBF in the same order as would the DFS approach to solve the corresponding strategy game [6]. Similarly, MCTS was adapted to SAT, the special case of QBF with only existential variables, as early as 2011 [20], and then to the MaxSAT variant [7]. Eventually, the most important heuristic in SAT solving, Clause Learning (CDCL), was combined with MCTS into a single SAT-solving algorithm [22].

Previous work on combining CDCL with MCTS crucially assumed the absence of any universal variables in the prefix. How to extend this work to handle the full range of QBF is an algorithm design challenge. On the other hand, combining game tree search algorithms with quantified logical formula solving is not a completely new idea. Alpha-beta pruning algorithm and learning techniques have already been combined in the field of Quantified Integer Programming (QIP) [2]. However, alpha-beta pruning is still a depth-first search algorithm, [2] did not fully address the interesting research question of how to design a best-first search based QBF solver. Seeing the appeal and success of BFS for solving games with deep strategies and traps in the search space and the importance of specific algorithmic techniques for QBF such as backjumping and CDCL, this paper investigates the following research questions.

- How to integrate BFS and CDCL in an elegant algorithm for QBF solving?
- What of the other main heuristics: cube learning and pure literal elimination?
- Is the new BFS any better than traditional DFS for any class of QBF?

To answer the last question, we focused on PNS, but any method in this paper can be easily generalized to other BFS algorithms including MCTS.

The paper is structured as follows: first, we review the foundations of game tree search algorithms, QBF solving as well as Schloeter's combination of MCTS and CDCL. In Sect. 3, we describe how to design a PNS-based QBF solver that integrates Backjumping and CDCL. Experimental results for this new algorithm is presented in Sect. 4.

2   Background

2.1   Game Solving with Best First Search Algorithms

Best-first search (BFS) algorithm is a class of search algorithms that prioritize the search in the direction of the most promising node. The "most promising direction" is usually determined by some heuristic functions. BFS has achieved massive success in both game-playing and game-solving. For example, the application of Proof number search (PNS) in solving Connect 6, Othello, and Checkers [12]. Also the application of Monte Carlo tree search (MCTS) in many general game-playing programs [8]. Many classic BFS algorithms are implemented iteratively. Each iteration consists of 3 phases: selection, expansion, and backpropagation. We would briefly review 2 BFS algorithms in this section, PNS and MCTS.

PNS is suitable for 2-player strategy game solving. In its default setting, each search tree node stores the proof number (pn) and the disproof number (dn). The proof number (resp. disproof number) gives a lower bound estimate of the minimum number of nodes in the subtree that needs to be proved (resp. disproved) to conclude the maximizer (resp. minimizer) would win in the current subtree. The most promising direction at a node N is a child with the minimum pn (resp. dn) if N is controlled by the maximizer (resp. minimizer). The selection continues until we reach a leaf called the most proving node (MPN), we expand and initialize its children with domain knowledge and propagate backward to update the proof and disproof number all the way to the root [12].

MCTS is very similar to the process of PNS. When the algorithm is applied to game solving, each node needs to explicitly store whether the node has been solved. The most promising direction for an internal node N is determined by [21]:

$$\begin{cases} \operatorname{argmax}_c\left(\frac{R(c)}{S(c)} + \sqrt{\frac{\ln S(N)}{S(c)}}\right) & N \text{ is controlled by the maximizer} \\ \operatorname{argmax}_c\left(-\frac{R(c)}{S(c)} + \sqrt{\frac{\ln S(N)}{S(c)}}\right) & N \text{ is controlled by the minimizer} \end{cases} \quad (1)$$

Here $S(n)$ means the total number of simulations for a node n, and $R(n)$ means the current reward of the node. When a leaf is reached, we expand its children, and the initial reward of a child is normally determined by random playouts. Similar to proof number search, this information is propagated back to the root in the final phase of an iteration.

2.2   Search Based QBF Solving

In this paper, we assume the readers are familiar with the basic terminologies of SAT and QBF such as their semantics, unit propagation, pure literal elimination, and Q-resolution; otherwise, please refer to [1,6]. The task of QBF solving is to decide the truth value of the QBF expression. There are two types of QBF solvers, expansion-based and search-based. In this paper, we focus on the latter technique. Search-based QBF solvers only consider assignments consistent with the order of variables in the quantifier prefix.

Definition 1 (Assignment [6]). *An assignment μ for a QBF ϕ is a sequence of literals $\mu = l_1; \ldots l_n$ with $n \geq 0$ where each literal l_i is a unit literal or is bound in the outermost quantifier block in $\phi_{l_1;\ldots l_{i-1}}$ where ϕ_μ is the formula obtained from ϕ by assigning literals in μ. A variable that is not unit in an assignment is a branching variable.*[1]

For any assignment μ, we define $S(\mu)$ as the set of literals in μ, $A(\mu)$ as the set of universal literals in μ. For any formula ϕ, if unit propagation on ϕ does not derive a contradiction, then it always results in the same set of

---

[1] If pure literal elimination is enabled, assignments may also contain pure literals [5], and branching variables in an assignment are those that are neither unit nor pure.

literals assigned, regardless of the order of propagation.[2] We denote by $U(\phi)$ the resulting assignment of unit literals, in an arbitrary order.

Search-based QBF solving is usually based on a depth-first search procedure called QDPLL that combines the semantics of QBF, unit propagation, and pure literal elimination [1,6]. Unlike SAT where the importance of pure literal elimination is debatable, it is widely believed that for QBF solving, pure literal elimination is beneficial [14]. Notable improvement on the QDPLL algorithm includes conflict-solution driven backjumping (CBJ + SBJ) [5,6] and QCDCL (CDCL + SDCL) [6,26]. In both backjumping and QCDCL, we associate each solved search state with a resolvent (either a clause or a cube). We associate each false search state with a μ-contradicted clause, and each true search state with a μ-satisfied cube. The resolvents are maintained and calculated during the backtracking phase of QDPLL based on a sequence of Q-resolution [6,26]. The definition of the resolvent is as follows.

Definition 2 (Resolvent [6]). *Let μ be an assignment. A clause C is μ-contradicted if for each literal $l \in C$, we have $l \notin \mu$, and for each existential literal $l \in C$, we have $\neg l \in \mu$. A cube T is μ-satisfied if for each literal $l \in T$, we have $\neg l \notin \mu$, and for each universal literal $l \in T$, we have $l \in \mu$. A resolvent is either a μ-contradicted clause or a μ-satisfied cube derived by Q-resolution depending on whether ϕ_μ is falsified or not.*

In backjumping, the main benefit of calculating the resolvent is we can prune the right branch of the searching space if the resolvent associated with the left child does not contain the branching variable [5,6]. The QCDCL algorithm extends the idea of backjumping by allowing any resolvent to be learned (i.e. added to the formula conjunctively or disjunctively) without affecting the correctness of the algorithm. This has the advantage over backjumping that the learned clauses/cubes may allow stronger unit propagation when searching on a different path. In the QCDCL algorithm, if we replace cube learning (SDCL) with solution-driven backjumping (SBJ), we can associate each node with not just a μ-satisfied cube but a μ-entailed cube [6].

Definition 3 (μ-entailed cube). *Let μ be an assignment. A cube T is said to be μ-entailed if and only if each literal $l \in T$, we have $l \in \mu$.*

Any μ-entailed cube is also a μ-satisfied cube. However, when SDCL is activated, cubes are added to the formula. And because of the existence of universal unit propagation, associating every satisfied node with a μ-entailed cube is no longer possible.

2.3 Schloeter's CDCL Based SAT Solver

Combining a best-first search based algorithm with clause learning (CDCL) is non-trivial. The main difficulty for such a combination is best-first search a node might be visited more than once. If new clauses are added to the formula, more

---

[2] This property is folklore in the context of SAT and it is easy to establish it for QBF.

unit propagation might occur and some root to leaf assignments may no longer be valid. For example, consider the root to x_3 path in Fig. 1.

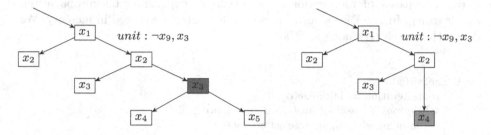

Fig. 1. Schloeter's method

Assume in the first visit of the red node, the assignment is $x_1; \neg x_9; x_2$, and the branching variable stored in the red node is x_3. It is possible that in a later iteration, the branching variable x_3 becomes unit when some new clauses are added to the formula. In this case, we can no longer branch on x_3 when we reach the red node.

One approach to solve this issue is to postpone some unit propagation (i.e. the unit propagation x_3), however, in most cases, this would significantly decrease the efficiency of the solver. In 2017, Schloeter proposed an algorithm to combine CDCL with MCTS in the field of SAT to overcome this issue [22]. Whenever a branching variable v stored in a node is propagated as a unit literal because of the learned clauses, we check if it has been assigned positively or negatively. If v has been assigned positively (resp. negatively), we just remove the current node and link up its parent with the left-child (resp. right-child). For the given example, we check that the unit literal is $+|x_3|$, we would simply link up the parent of x_3 (i.e. x_2) with the left child of x_3 (i.e. x_4) and continue the search from the green node. This approach allows us to lazily maintain the search tree such that each root to leaf path we traverse during the selection phase still corresponds to a valid assignment and no additional unit propagation caused by learned clauses needs to be postponed.

3 Best-First Search and QBF Solving

3.1 Best-First Search Based QBF Solver with CDCL and SBJ

Schloeter's method does not automatically fit to QBF. Firstly, in the context of SAT, no tree node corresponds to a "solution", because whenever a solution is reached, the solver terminates. In QBF, however, we need to deal with both conflicts and solutions. In addition, Schloeter's paper does not address a critical aspect of backjumping and QCDCL: how to associate each solved search state with a resolvent. In this section, we explain how to design a BFS-based QBF solver. In this solver, we support unit propagation, traditional conflict-driven clause learning (CDCL) [6,26], and solution-driven backjumping (SBJ) [5].

As we can see from Algorithm 1 that the BFS based QBF solving algorithm works in iterations. The iteration would not terminate until the root is solved (i.e. we can associate the root with an empty clause or empty cube). Every iteration consists of four major steps: selection, expansion, backpropagation, and learning. In the BFS algorithm, all search states are stored in memory. We define the search tree node as follows:

```
BFSsolve(φ)
    root, iteration := initialize(φ), 0
    while root is unsolved and ++iteration do
        most_proving_node := selection(root, φ)
        expansion(most_proving_node, φ)
        current := most_proving_node
        while current ≠ NULL do
            current := backpropagation(current, φ)
            current := parent(current)
        learn(φ)
    return root is satisfied
```

Algorithm 1: BFS based QBF solving procedure: take a QBF expression ϕ and return its truth value

Definition 4 (Best-first search tree node). *A best-first search tree node N at an instant (iteration) t is a tuple (i, h, v, μ, R) where i is a unique identifier, h is the heuristic information, μ is a partial assignment made on the path from root to N, v is the branching variable associated to N, and if N is solved by iteration t then R is the resolvent (i.e. μ-contradicted clause or μ-entailed cube[3]).*

During the selection phase in iteration t, we select the child of node (i, h, v, μ, R) which subtree contains the most proving node using the heuristic information stored in the children. There are two cases. Firstly, suppose $v \in \mu$ or $\neg v \in \mu$, this means the branching variable v has been assigned unit in μ because of additional unit propagation caused by clause learning. In this case, we just link up the parent of node i with the correct children of i according to the method discussed in Sect. 2.3. Secondly, if the branching variable has not been assigned, we continue the regular BFS selection. The selection formula depends on the type of BFS we apply. For example, the PNS selection formula described in [12], the DeepPN selection formula described in [9], and the MCTS selection formula described in [22] are all applicable in our case. If the most proving node is on the left (resp. right) subtree of N, we assign v (resp. $\neg v$) to the formula and perform unit propagation until there exists no unit literal in $\phi_{\mu;v}$ (resp. $\phi_{\mu;\neg v}$), and continue the search procedure from the left (resp. right) child. The

---

[3] The resolvent corresponds to each satisfied node is a μ-entailed cube in this case because we are not doing any cube learning.

selection phase would end when we reach a leaf that is the most proving node of the current search tree.

Once we have reached the most proving node (i, h, v, μ, R), we expand it and initialize its two children. We only explain the initialization of the left child, the right child being symmetric. The left-child is given by $(i^l, h^l, v^l, \mu^l, R^l)$, in which i^l is a fresh identifier, h^l is the heuristic information corresponds to a newly created node, some popular initialization heuristics can be found in [9,11,12]. $\mu^l = \mu; v; U(\phi_{\mu;v})$, and R^l is the μ^l-contradicted clause or μ^l-entailed cube if ϕ_{μ^l} contains a contradicted clause or has all clauses satisfied, or NULL otherwise. Note that R^l (i.e. conflict or model) can be computed in polynomial time with methods described in [6]. If ϕ_{μ^l} does not contain a conflict or solution, we pick the next branching variable v^l from ϕ_{μ^l} based on some branching heuristics [16]. Based on our implementation, the following property holds for the selection algorithm. For convenience, we introduce the notation $\phi[t]$ to represent the QBF expression with empty assignment before iteration t

Proposition 1 (Property of the Selection Algorithm). *Suppose node i is visited in iteration t_1 and t_2 ($t_1 < t_2$). Let its state be (i, h_1, v, μ_1, R_1) and (i, h_2, v, μ_2, R_2) respectively. If $\phi[t_2]_{\mu_2}$ has no contradicted clauses, we have that $A(\mu_1) = A(\mu_2)$ and $S(\mu_1) \subseteq S(\mu_2)$.*

The interpretation of the proposition is as follows: if the same node is visited in a later iteration, and the formula corresponds to the node is not contradictory, the set of universal assignments we made is always the same as the one in the earlier iterations, and the set of assignment we made in a later iteration is always a superset of the assignment we made in earlier iterations. The superset is because of additional unit propagation caused by learned clauses. Note that such property is critical for the correctness of our solver.

During the backpropagation phase of the algorithm, we need to update the information of (i, h, v, μ, R) based on the information stored in the left child $(i^l, h^l, v^l, \mu^l, R^l)$ and right child $(i^r, h^r, v^r, \mu^r, R^r)$. In many BFS algorithms, h can be calculated with h^l and h^r [9,12,22]. Besides, we need to calculate R based on R^l and R^r. There are two steps: firstly, we need to calculate the resolvent R'_l (resp. R'_r) corresponds to the assignment $\mu; v$ (resp. $\mu; \neg v$) based on the resolvent R^l corresponds to the assignment $\mu^l = \mu; v; U(\phi_{\mu;v})$ (resp. $\mu^r = \mu; \neg v; U(\phi_{\mu;\neg v})$). Secondly, we calculate R based on R'_l and R'_r. Both of these steps can be done with a sequence of Q-resolution, and in our implementation, we used the algorithm of *RecResolve* described in [6]. There are three cases we need to consider: (1) One of R'_l and R'_r can be calculated, and the branching variable v appears neither positively nor negatively in it. Let's say v does not appear in R'_l (R'_r is symmetric). This is the backjumping condition in which we can directly assign R to be R'_l and prune the right branch of node i. (2) Both R'_l and R'_r can be calculated, and the branching variable v appears in both of the resolvents. Then, we set $R = RecResolve(R'_l, R'_r)$. (3) Otherwise, R cannot be calculated yet, and we leave it as NULL. One critical remark about the backpropagation procedure is there are two cases we need to consider when we query the resolvent R^l (similar to R^r) when we want to calculate R. If $\phi_{\mu;v;U(\phi_{\mu;v})}$ contains a contradicted clause, we replace the resolvent R^l stored on i^l by the contradicted clause. Otherwise, we simply use the resolvent we stored in i^l (i.e. the original R^l) as R^l. The discussion on why this step is necessary is left to the appendix.

After the backpropagation phase terminates, we can add any clause calculated by Q-resolution to the formula ϕ conjunctively. In our implementation, we applied the 1-UIP learning schema [6,26], and in every iteration, we would learn at most 1 clause. One remark about this algorithm is that we only execute CDCL and SBJ so that if a node is solved, we store the resolvent (either a μ-contradicted clause or a μ-entailed cube) in the corresponding node, however, we only learn clauses when the method *learn*() is called. In addition, for simplicity, once a clause is learned, it is never deleted.

3.2 Complications with Cube Learning and Pure Literal Elimination

Unlike the depth first search situation where clause learning and cube learning are often dual, in BFS adding cube learning is complicated. This is because, with cube learning, the concept of universal unit propagation appears [6], and the additional universal unit propagation might break part 2) of proposition 1 and make our reusability discussion in the appendix no longer hold. In short, we may have stored a contradicted clause C in some internal node, but after the universal unit propagation take place, C might not be contradicted anymore. This breaks the invariant of the QCDCL algorithm that we must associate each false node with a contradicted clause. Besides, one should note that all of the discussions about BFS and clause learning we have made so far are based on the assumption that we have disabled pure literal elimination. If we only execute backjumping (CBJ + SBJ), such deactivation is unnecessary, because 1) the QBF formula does not change during the solving procedure, and 2) with careful implementation, we can guarantee that when we return to the same node twice, the partial assignment we make is always the same. However, with clause learning, some literals that are pure on a root to leaf path might no longer be pure after additional clauses are added to the formula. Note that such a case is hard to be dealt with in the context of BFS because it would make some original root to leaf assignment invalid after some pure literal elimination on this root to leaf path is blocked. The reusability discussion in the appendix holds only if we can guarantee proposition 1, and apparently, if some pure literal elimination is blocked, such property does not hold.

4 Experimental Results and Discussion

We are interested in elucidating the following questions: 1) is clause learning is beneficial to a BFS-based QBF solver? and 2) how does the performance of DFS- and BFS-based solvers compare on standard QBF benchmarks?

After more than 30 years of research into building highly optimized solvers for SAT and QBF, implementing a competitive QBF solver is a massive undertaking and our experiments are preliminary in nature. As such, we only have implemented semi-naive DFS- and BFS-based solvers. We call our solvers *semi-naive* because we have implemented the main algorithms used search-based QBF solving (unit propagation, backjumping, QCDCL) and corresponding appropriate data structures, including watched-literals to support efficient unit literal propagation and clause-watching to support efficient pure literal elimination [4]. However, we have not implemented additional heuristics that can help in practice and that are used in some state-of-the-art modern solvers, such as dynamic blocked clause elimination [13] which aims to enhance learning, and pseudo unit propagation [15] which aims to deal with the exponential blown-up problem of the *RecResolve* procedure in [6]. For this reason, we compare our BFS solvers with our own DFS solvers instead of state of art search-based solvers such as DepQBF.

We use a variation of the Proof Number Search algorithm called DeepPN as the underlying search method for the BFS approach. The aim of the DeepPN algorithm is to reduce the seesaw effect of standard proof number search. A more detailed description of the algorithm can be found in [9]. For both our DFS and BFS solvers, the baseline approach corresponds to the backjumping algorithm, to which we can add either pure literal elimination or clause learning. These 6 resulting combinations define a solver variant that we evaluate on a subset of 2004 QBFEVAL instances as well as on *gttt4x4* instances [17], each solving attempt has a time limit of 900 s. The number of instances solved from each benchmark family by each solver combination are shown in Table 1.

Table 1. The number of instances solved by different combinations of methods on a subset of the 2004 QBFEval and gttt4 × 4 instances. Each domain family has 8 instances, except logn (2 instances) and gttt4 × 4 (96 instances).

Search method	DFS			BFS		
Pure literal elim.	N	Y	N	N	Y	N
Clause learning	N	N	Y	N	N	Y
blocks	2	3	3	0	1	1
chain	8	8	8	7	7	6
counter	3	3	4	2	2	2
k_d4_p	8	8	8	1	1	8
k_ph_n	4	4	6	4	4	6
k_ph_p	2	2	2	2	2	2
k_lin_n	3	3	5	2	2	4
k_lin_p	2	3	8	1	1	3
k_dum_n	3	4	6	2	2	5
k_dum_p	3	3	7	1	1	7
k_path_n	3	3	5	3	3	3
k_path_p	3	3	3	3	2	3
k_poly_n	1	1	3	1	1	2
k_t4p_n	0	0	1	0	0	1
k_t4p_p	1	1	2	1	1	2
logn	2	1	2	0	0	2
toilet	6	6	6	7	7	7
tree	6	6	8	6	6	8
Total	60	62	87	43	43	72
gttt4x4	14	41	16	19	39	21

We propose three observations. First, in all benchmark families except for "chain", enabling clause learning does not worsen the performance of the

DeepPN-based solver, and in many families learning improves the performance. It has long been known that clause learning is useful in DFS-based solvers and we have established that this is also true for a Proof Number Search-based solver.

Second, Pure Literal Elimination is useful for the BFS-based solver. For the gttt4 × 4 group, the backjumping-based solver with PLE can even outperform the clause-learning solver. This matches the studies done in the QDPLL world [14].

Third, while some families are better tackled by BFS than by DFS, a larger number of families are solved by DFS better than by BFS.

The third observation is not what we were hoping for but we have some elements of explanations for this result. One reason is that in BFS, each tree node can be visited many times. For example, for the families listed in table 1, the average number of times each node is visited during the search ranges from 11 to 98. Since time is normally the evaluation metric for QBF solving, repeatedly visiting the same node is undesired. This phenomenon is not unknown to the game-solving community and approaches such as the ε-trick have been proposed to improve the situation [18].

Another reason, the ratio between the number of existential and of universal variables is very unbalanced for many QBF instances. In the family "blocks" for example, this ratio can be as high as 100:1, and usually the first universal branching variable assignment happens after more than 30 existential branching variable assignments. In the gttt4 × 4 family, however, the ratio is around 15:1, and the first universal branching variable assignment happens only after 10 existential branching variable assignment. This might also explain why BFS-based solvers perform comparatively better on gttt4 × 4 than on blocks. Our current implementation uses DeepPN with default selection, initialization, and backpropagation as described in [9]. Since many successful applications of PNS-based algorithms are for balanced games with alternating moves' (e.g., Shogi, Othello, and Checkers), we can expect that directly applying the algorithm to unbalanced games might not work well. Hence, designing better initialization heuristics for QBF or trying other types of BFS algorithms such as MCTS are natural avenues for future work.

5   Conclusion

Using best-first search algorithms to solve QBF is not a completely new idea. For example, researchers have attempted to use the neural MCTS algorithms to solve QBF [25]. However, this paper is one of the first attempts at solving QBF using a BFS algorithm that combines traditional reasoning techniques such as backjumping and clause learning. We have discussed that a technique proposed by Schloeter that combines MCTS and CDCL in the SAT world can be generalized to the context of QBF when the solver contains CDCL and SBJ. However, we have pointed out that the technique might not work when universal unit propagation or pure literal elimination is allowed. In our implementation, we have disabled both SDCL and pure literal elimination. Our experimental results showed that in the context of PNS, CDCL can significantly improve the solver's performance on the set of selected benchmarks. However, because of the nature of the PNS algorithm that each search state might be visited significantly more than once, and our current node initialization heuristic is not ideal for unbalanced games, in both the context of backjumping and CDCL, none of the PNS based solvers can outperform the traditional QDPLL based solvers which use the same proof system in most families of instances. Although all the experiments were completed in the context of PNS, the algorithm combination technique discussed in this paper can be easily transformed to other types of best-first search algorithms such as MCTS as long as the heuristic information for each node only relies on the heuristic information stored in the children. In the future, the following two tasks would be addressed: one is investigating how to activate SDCL and pure literal elimination in BFS not necessarily based on Schloeter's technique, and another is experimenting the solver with other best-first search strategies in order to improve its performance.

A   Correctness Discussion of the BFS Based CDCL Solver

There is a critical problem we have not explained in algorithm 1, which is the reusability of the resolvent. We have mentioned in the paper that during back-propagation when we want to query the resolvent corresponding to a node, we only need to consider two cases. In the appendix, we would explain 1) why this is necessary, and 2) why this is correct. Recall that, we let $\phi[t]$ represent the QBF expression at iteration t. According to the definition of a BFS node, at iteration t each node i has an assignment μ_t^i associated with it. If we only execute backjumping (i.e. CBJ + SBJ), the formula does not change during the solving procedure, hence for any t and t' when node i is visited we have $\mu_t^i = \mu_{t'}^i$. Note that with careful implementation, even if we activate pure literal elimination, this property would hold. However, when CDCL is enabled, this property might no longer hold. We have discussed that in the backpropagation phase, we would use the resolvent we store in the children to derive the resolvent of the current node. However, in BFS each node can be visited more than once, and more clauses might be added to the formula which could create more unit propagation. In other words, suppose node i is visited in iteration t and t', it is possible that $\mu_t^i \neq \mu_{t'}^i$. When we attempt to derive the resolvent associated with a node i with the resolvents we stored in its children, it is possible that the resolvent we stored in the children corresponds to a different assignment. For example, suppose the left child was solved in iteration $t' < t$ and the information associated with the node is $(i^l, h_{t'}^l, v^l, \mu_{t'}^l, R_{t'}^l)$. When we want to calculate the resolvent of node i with state (i, h, v, μ_t, R), we need to make a query of the resolvent of the left child i^l which corresponds to the assignment $\mu_t^l = \mu_t; v; U(\phi[t]_{\mu_t;v})$. However, because of the additional unit propagation caused by clause learning, it is possible that $\mu_{t'}^l \neq \mu_t; v; U(\phi[t]_{\mu_t;v})$, hence, we can no longer use $R_{t'}^l$ as a valid resolvent for the left child! We would update the resolvent we have previously stored in a node as follows:

- If $\phi[t]_{\mu_t^l}$ contains a contradicted clause, we can recalculate R_t^l based on the conflict in linear time [6].
- Otherwise, we can reuse $R_{t'}^l$ as a resolvent for node i^l.

The correctness of this update method does not always hold, however, in our implementation of the generalized Schloeter's method proposition 1 holds. With this proposition, we should realize the following two lemmas related to the μ-contradicted clause and μ-entailed cube trivially holds.

Lemma 1. *For a QBF expression ϕ, if C is a μ-contradicted clause, and μ' is an assignment such that $A[\mu'] = A[\mu]$ and $S(\mu) \subseteq S(\mu')$, then C is also a μ'-contradicted clause.*

Proof. By the definition of μ-contradicted clause, we must show that for any literal $l \in C$, $l \notin \mu'$, and for each existential literal $l \in C$, we have $\neg l \in \mu'$. We consider two cases: 1) $l \in C$ and l is existential. Then, since C is μ-contradicted, we have $\neg l \in \mu$. Because $S(\mu) \subseteq S(\mu')$, we have $\neg l \in \mu'$ as well. In addition, since μ' is an assignment, whenever $\neg l \in \mu'$, $l \notin \mu'$.

2) Suppose $l \in C$ and l is universal. Then, because $A[\mu'] = A[\mu]$, we can easily show that $l \notin \mu'$.

By definition 2, we conclude that C is also a μ'-contradicted clause.

Lemma 2. *For a QBF expression ϕ, if T is a μ-entailed cube, and μ' is an assignment such that $A[\mu'] = A[\mu]$ and $S(\mu) \subseteq S(\mu')$, then T is also a μ'-entailed cube.*

Proof. Analog to the proof of lemma 1, the lemma trivially holds by the definition of μ-entailed cubes.

Note that in iteration t, if $\phi[t]_{\mu_t^l}$ contains a contradicted clause, we can easily replace R_t^l with the contradicted clause. Otherwise, because of the consequence of proposition 1, we have

$$S(\mu_{t'}^l) \subseteq S(\mu_t^l) \tag{2}$$

and,

$$A(\mu_{t'}^l) = A(\mu_t^l) \tag{3}$$

Since we only execute conflict-driven clause learning and solution-driven back-jumping, the resolvent we initialized for a node is μ-contradicted or μ-entailed at the time it is calculated. According to lemma 1 and lemma 2, the $\mu_{t'}^l$-contradicted clause (resp. $\mu_{t'}^l$-entailed cube) we have calculated previously is still a μ_t^l-contradicted clause (resp. μ_t^l-entailed cube). Therefore, as long as $\phi[t]_{\mu_t^l}$ does not contain a contradicted clause, we can reuse the reason we have calculated in a previous iteration, and the method we have discussed just now is correct.

Note that this discussion also explains the exact difficulty of combining BFS with SDCL. When SDCL is activated, universal unit propagation comes in, proposition 1 does not hold anymore, because when a node is visited more than once, it is possible that $A(\mu_{t'}) \neq A(\mu_t)$ due to universal unit propagation. If this condition is falsified, lemma 1 does not hold, and the resolvent we previously stored in a node might not be reused.

References

1. Cadoli, M., Giovanardi, A., Schaerf, M.: An algorithm to evaluate quantified Boolean formulae. AAAI/IAAI **98**, 262–267 (1998)
2. Ederer, T., Hartisch, M., Lorenz, U., Opfer, T., Wolf, J.: Yasol: an open source solver for quantified mixed integer programs. In: Winands, M.H.M., van den Herik, H.J., Kosters, W.A. (eds.) ACG 2017. LNCS, vol. 10664, pp. 224–233. Springer, Cham (2017). https://doi.org/10.1007/978-3-319-71649-7_19
3. Ewalds, T.V.: Playing and solving Havannah. Master's thesis, University of Alberta, Canada (2012)
4. Gent, I., Giunchiglia, E., Narizzano, M., Rowley, A., Tacchella, A.: Watched data structures for QBF solvers. In: SAT, pp. 25–36 (2003)
5. Giunchiglia, E., Narizzano, M., Tacchella, A.: Backjumping for quantified boolean logic satisfiability. AI 145(1–2), 99–120 (2003)
6. Giunchiglia, E., Narizzano, M., Tacchella, A.: Clause/term resolution and learning in the evaluation of quantified Boolean formulas. JAIR **26**, 371–416 (2006)
7. Goffinet, J., Ramanujan, R.: Monte-Carlo tree search for the maximum satisfiability problem. In: CP, pp. 251–267 (2016)
8. Goldwaser, A., Thielscher, M.: Deep reinforcement learning for general game playing. In: Proceedings of the AAAI Conference on Artificial Intelligence, pp. 1701–1708. AAAI Press, New York (2020)
9. Ishitobi, T., Plaat, A., Iida, H., van den Herik, J.: Reducing the seesaw effect with deep proof-number search. In: ACG, pp. 185–197 (2015)
10. Janota, M., Klieber, W., Marques-Silva, J., Clarke, E.: Solving QBF with counterexample guided refinement. In: SAT, pp. 114–128 (2012)
11. Keszocze, O., Schmitz, K., Schloeter, J., Drechsler, R.: Improving sat solving using monte Carlo tree search-based clause learning. In: IWSBP, pp. 107–133 (2020)
12. Kishimoto, A., Winands, M.H., Müller, M., Saito, J.T.: Game-tree search using proof numbers: the first twenty years. ICGA J. **35**(3), 131–156 (2012)
13. Lonsing, F., Bacchus, F., Biere, A., Egly, U., Seidl, M.: Enhancing search-based QBF solving by dynamic blocked clause elimination. In: LPAR, pp. 418–433 (2015)
14. Lonsing, F., Biere, A.: Depqbf: a dependency-aware QBF solver. JSAT **7**(2–3), 71–76 (2010)
15. Lonsing, F., Egly, U., Van Gelder, A.: Efficient clause learning for quantified Boolean formulas via QBF pseudo unit propagation. In: SAT, pp. 100–115 (2013)
16. Marques-Silva, J.: The impact of branching heuristics in propositional satisfiability algorithms. In: EPIA, pp. 62–74 (1999)
17. Mayer-Eichberger, V., Saffidine, A.: Positional games and QBF: the corrective encoding. In: SAT, pp. 447–463 (2020)
18. Pawlewicz, J., Lew, L.: Improving depth-first PN-search: 1+ ε trick. In: CG, pp. 160–171 (2006)
19. Plaat, A.: Mtd (f), a minimax algorithm faster than negascout. arXiv preprint arXiv:1404.1511 (2014)
20. Previti, A., Ramanujan, R., Schaerf, M., Selman, B.: Monte-Carlo style UCT search for boolean satisfiability. In: AI*IA, pp. 177–188 (2011)
21. Saffidine, A.: Solving games and all that. Ph.D. thesis, Université Paris Dauphine-Paris IX (2013)
22. Schlöter, J.: A monte Carlo tree search based conflict-driven clause learning SAT solver. In: INFORMATIK 2017, pp. 2549–2560 (2017)

23. Seo, M., Iida, H., Uiterwijk, J.W.: The PN2217-search algorithm: application to tsume-shogi. AI 129(1–2), 253–277 (2001)
24. Shukla, A., Biere, A., Pulina, L., Seidl, M.: A survey on applications of quantified Boolean formulas. In: ICTAI, pp. 78–84 (2019)
25. Xu, R., Lieberherr, K.: Solving QSAT problems with neural MCTS. arXiv:2101.06619 (2021)
26. Zhang, L., Malik, S.: Towards a symmetric treatment of satisfaction and conflicts in quantified Boolean formula evaluation. In: CP, pp. 200–215 (2002)

Oware is Strongly Solved

Xavier A. P. Blanvillain[✉]

Amsterdam, The Netherlands
research@48stones.com

Abstract. On 23 January 2021, Xavier Blanvillain solved the Abapa variant of the classic strategic game Oware, with a single computer and with multi-threaded, brute-force algorithms. The results of all 827,240,309,058 possible positions were calculated. It has been determined that if each player makes only perfect moves, the games end in a draw. In other words, the starting player doesn't have a first-move advantage and should open the game with the right-most pit. In situations with 2, 3, 4, 7 or 9 seeds remaining on the board, the resolution required human intervention to force the results of repeating positions, known as loops. An 11-seed loop and a 13-seed loop, previously unknown to Oware players, were discovered during the research. Although these loops cannot be solved with Abapa rules, the research proved that it was possible to continue the resolution. The end result shows that Oware was solved strongly.

Keywords: Oware · Strong solution · Möbius loops · Parallel Backward Propagation

1 Solution

The starting position for the South player to play is strongly solved (see Fig. 1). The bottom row indicates the result of each move with the number of seeds that the South player would win at the end of a game, if each player makes perfect moves. 24 indicates therefore a draw (24–24), while 23 indicates a loss (23–25).

North player

4	4	4	4	4	4
4	4	4	4	4	4
23	23	23	23	23	24

South player

Fig. 1. Solution for the starting position.

Oware European Vice-Champion 2000, 3rd International Champion 2019, Elo 2048.
Co-founder of the International Association of Warri Players (IAWP), Switzerland
Member of the Oware Society (OWS), United Kingdom.

Solving an abstract strategy game means determining the end result of each legal position using logic alone. L. V. Allis [1] and T. R. Lincke [2] defined 3 degrees of solutions: ultra-weakly solved, weakly solved and strongly solved. Solving a game 'strongly' means that the best move can be found (within a reasonable timeframe) from every position in the game.

2 Introduction

2.1 Rules of Oware, Abapa Variant

These are the official rules played during international competitions organized by the OWS, in the Mind Sports Olympiads (MSO), recognized by the IAWP organization.

The board contains 2 rows of 6 pits. Each player owns a row. They alternate turns after each move. The game starts with 4 seeds in each pit (Fig. 1). A player takes all seeds from one of his pits, and sows them 1 by 1 in the adjacent pits, counter-clockwise, skipping the pit where the seeds came from if need be (Fig. 2 A). If the last seed ends in the opponent's pit and the pit contains 2 or 3 seeds after the sowing, the seeds in that pit are captured. Going clockwise, the seeds of the adjacent pits are captured if the same conditions apply (Fig. 2 B). After a move, a player is not allowed to capture all his opponent's seeds. In that case, all the seeds stay in place (Fig. 3). If the opponent is left without any seeds, the player must play a move that leaves at least 1 seed in the opponent's row. If this is not possible, the game stops and the player keeps the remaining seeds (Fig. 4). In case of repeating positions, the players agree to stop playing and share the remaining seeds. The player who captured the highest number of seeds wins.

4	4	4	4+1	4+1	4+1
4	4	4	4	-	4+1

-	-	-	1	2	1
-	-	-	-	3	1

A - Sowing: South just played a 4-seed pit   B - Capturing: South will capture 5 seeds

Fig. 2. Basic principles: sowing and capturing

-	-	-	-	2	1
-	-	-	-	-	2

-	-	-	-	3	2
-	-	-	-	-	-

South to play   >>>   Result of sowing = no capture

Fig. 3. 'Grand Slam' situation

2.2 History: 30 Years of Research

In 1990, a variant named 'Awari' was created and became the reference for use by computer scientists [3]. It was used not only in computer science research but also in computer programming competitions.

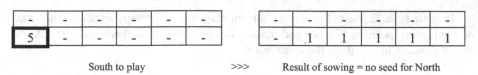

South to play   >>>   Result of sowing = no seed for North

Fig. 4. 'Starving' situation

In 2002, a team of computer scientists in The Netherlands found a solution to the Awari variant by applying a parallel retrograde analysis using a network of 144 computers [4, 5]. It was a major technical accomplishment, demonstrating the abilities of what a distributed system could do. The Awari solution was published in the form of an online database, named 'The Oracle', hosted and served by the University of Amsterdam. H.H.L.M. Donkers questioned this resolution [3] since the rule of splitting a seed, in case of repeating positions, is not known in human play and not used in MSO. Eventually, the infrastructure supporting The Oracle database was dismantled.

X.A.P. Blanvillain's project to strongly solve Oware began in 1999. And was supported by the OWS and the IAWP. The resolution of the 'Abapa' variant was more difficult since it dealt with the settlement of repeating positions without splitting a seed.

2.3 Key Milestones

Inventory of Possible Positions. On 24 September 2011, a 12-core machine with 128 GB of memory and 10 TB of storage, searched all Oware positions with mono-threaded brute-force algorithms, starting from the initial position (see Fig. 1). It took 12 days, 1 h and 22 min to report a state space of 827,240,309,058 legal positions.

Creation of an Endgame Book. On 15 February 2012, results lead to the conclusion that Oware could not be solved by a computer without human intervention: the solution for 'loops' with 2, 3, 4, 7 and 9 seeds had to be entered manually into the database. These loops are a series of repeating positions where these positions depend on each other's results. It is in the interest of each player to keep playing a loop. There is no rule that a computer can apply to solve these loops. Identifying unequivocally the 'key' position in a loop, with which to force the result manually, was a challenge. In the simplest example of a 2-seed loop (Fig. 5), there is a moment where the 2 seeds are on the same side of the board. The computer can't take that position and settle the end-result 2–0 for South. Players know that the end-result is 1–1 because 'most of the time', playing a loop, the seeds distribute evenly on the board.

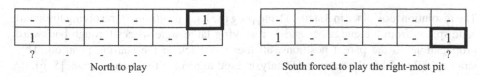

North to play   South forced to play the right-most pit

Fig. 5. 2-seed loop situation

In January 2022, the online game platform playok.com wrongly attributed the score of a repeating position (Fig. 6) and made a Grand Master lose his game. It took the wrong position to distribute the seeds from.

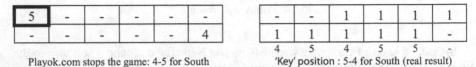

5	-	-	-	-	-
-	-	-	-	-	4

Playok.com stops the game: 4-5 for South

-	-	1	1	1	1
1	1	1	1	1	-
4	5	4	5	5	

'Key' position : 5-4 for South (real result)

Fig. 6. 9-seed loop settlement

Only loops with 10 seeds or less are commonly encountered by players, and these have been documented in an endgame book.

Discovery of New Loops: the Möbius Loops. As the research continued with an increasing number of seeds, 11-seed and 13-seed repeating positions were discovered and reported on 20 April 2012, during the Board Game Studies Colloquium XV in Munich, Germany. What makes these loops special is the way the positions repeat themselves. In these loops, a position initially played by South, is then played by North at the next repetition, and so on (details of the 11-seed loop in Fig. 7). It is like the Möbius strip (or loop), formed by attaching the ends of a strip of paper together with a half-twist.

These loops were not known to the players as they are difficult to recognize. During the execution of these loops, there is no particular player that has permanently more seeds than the other, hence there is no way to determine an end-result. This raised a question around the arbitration of such loops. One can't call a draw by evenly distributing the seeds among players because of the odd number of seeds (splitting a seed to settle the game is not allowed in the Abapa variant). To unblock the resolution of the game, a contingency perspective was taken and is described in this paper (see Sect. 3.3).

Resolution of Oware Completed. On 23 January 2021, a 24-core machine with 768 GB of memory made it possible to parallelize the brute-force algorithms over 46 threads while addressing all the game positions of very large size state spaces, in a reasonable amount of time.

3   Method

3.1 Strategy

The resolution took place in 3 steps: 1) mapping the legal positions; 2) resolving the small state spaces from the endgames and 3) resolving large state spaces through backward propagations to the parent positions, all the way back to the starting position. This strategy differs from the retrograde analysis used to resolve the Awari variant [5, 6].

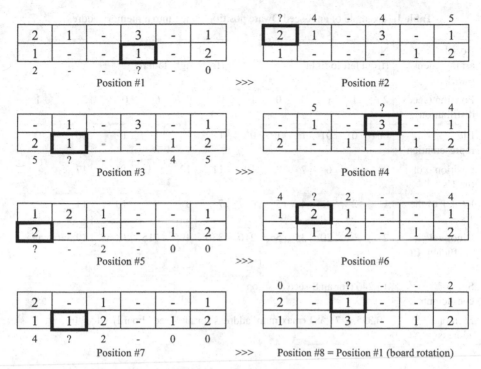

Fig. 7. 11-seed Möbius loop

3.2 Step 1: Mapping the Legal Positions

Objective. Having a map of legal positions speeds up the resolution by focusing on those positions that require a resolution. The key constraints for this step were time and storage. Operating on main memory only allowed the high performance of search and resolution algorithms: crawling through all positions, calculating all the possible moves and fetching the results the fastest.

Database Partitioning. The expected outcome of this step was a map with the results of all legal positions. Since the database had ca. 1 trillion entries, it was organized around 47 partitions based on the number of seeds on the board (state space).

Direct Addressing. Mapping one on one the index of a position with the address of the main memory was crucial to the resolution. The data access time was limited to the speed of the bus between the CPU cores and the main memory. Each Oware position was coded into a memory address using binomial coefficients (Table. 1). The binary representation of a position consists of replacing each seed by a 0 and separating each pit by a 1. Each pit separator has a position based on the number of seeds and combined with its rank on the board (1 for North left-most pit to 12 for South left-most pit, going clockwise), it gives a unique coefficient. The sum of these coefficients gives a unique address. When we know the number of seeds in play, the last pit (South left-most) doesn't need to be coded as it can be deduced.

Table 1. Example of an 8-seed Oware position coded into a memory address

Board arrangement (clockwise)	North (from left to right)						South (from right to left)					
Position (seeds distribution)	2	1	1	0	0	1	0	0	0	0	2	1
Bit representation	001	01	01	1	1	01	1	1	1	1	001	0
Position p of the 1's	2	4	6	7	8	10	11	12	13	14	17	-
Rank r of the 1's	1	2	3	4	5	6	7	8	9	10	11	-
Binomial coefficient $C(p, r)$	2	6	20	35	56	210	330	495	715	1,001	12,376	n/a
Sum of coefficients	15,246 (for an 8-seed position)											
Memory address	$60,335 = 75,581$ (maximum address for an 8-seed board) $- 15,246$											

1-bit and 8-bit Memory Maps. The database consisted of an 8-bit map built to store the result of a position on 7 bits plus 1 bit to mark the position as resolved. A 1-bit map was created to record whether a position at a specific address was legal or not.

Calculation of a Position Resulting from a Move. Since the distribution of the seeds contained in a pit is predictable, masks of the board were created with all ways to distribute the seeds for each of the 6 playable pits and for each possible number of seeds (from 1 to 48). Playing a move consisted of selecting the corresponding mask and applying it to the current board, thus limiting the CPU calculations to 11 sums. The potential captures were then assessed and applied by nulling the amount of seeds in the corresponding pits, except for Grand Slam situations that are not allowed.

Depth-First Search (DFS). From the opening position, every position resulting from a move was calculated and marked as legal in the 1-bit map. This was done 1 partition at a time using a DFS (mono-threaded) algorithm. The vertical fringe of positions from the same state space was stored in a LIFO stack in the main memory. The positions with fewer seeds than the size of the state space under resolution (positions resulting from a capture of seeds) were stored in their own LIFO stacks.

3.3 Step 2: Resolving Small State Spaces

Objective. The ambition was to create a playbook with easy-to-identify situations that occur with a limited number of seeds. The arbitrary definition of a small state space resides in the type of situations with a small number of seeds (1 to 15), which require specific resolution methods. Three situations that are not found in bigger state spaces can occur: 1) 'starving' positions, 2) traditional loops, and 3) the Möbius loops. The starving positions constituted the foundation of the game's resolution because the results are known and could be propagated backward. The resolution began with 1-seed state space and progressively propagated backwards the results. Then the bigger state spaces were resolved, one at a time, in ascending number of seeds, from 2 to 15.

Detection and Resolution of Starving Positions. The resolution started by setting each result with a default value, indicating an unknown result. The 1-bit map was crawled linearly from its 1st address, and each time a legal position was reported, a check was done to see if North was left without seeds and if South could not make a move to give North a seed. In this case, the result for South equaled the number of seeds of the state space. During this step, the partition began to be filled with first resolved results.

Backward Propagation Principle. Once the resolution of the starving positions was completed, the 1-bit map was again crawled. For each legal position that hadn't been resolved already in the 8-bit map, for a given move from South, the score of the resulting North position was looked up in the database and reported. If a move ends up with the maximum score that South can obtain (because it corresponds to the number of seeds in the state space), then there is no need to look up the other potential moves in that position because there is no better possible score. The position was therefore marked as resolved and its result set to the maximum score. The 8-bit map was crawled until no more resolved positions were found after a full crawling pass. At this stage, the resolution of all maximum scores is complete.

Settling the Resolution on Best Achievable Scores. All the positions that showed a score equaling to the number of seeds of the state space (S) were the best possible scores. More importantly, this also meant that the positions that showed a score S-1 seed were the best possible results, as no higher score was possible. The crawling could then restart. Each time the result of a position reached this new lower limit S-1, then the resolution of that position was considered settled. The process continued, lowering the best possible score limit by 1-seed increments each time, until the score limit reached S/2 for an even number of seeds on the board, or until the score limit reached (S + 1)/2 for odd number of seeds on the board. If no positions were updated after 2 full cycles, then a check was done to see whether all positions had been resolved, or whether a loop had been found.

Detection and Resolution of Traditional Loops. Once the series of crawling and backward propagations cycles was completed, the state spaces with 2, 3, 4, 7, 9, 11 and 13 seeds required special attention. Two types of positions were still unresolved: a) loops containing positions that depended on each other's results and b) the parent positions of a loop waiting for its resolution. In an actual game with loops containing 2, 3, 4, 7 or 9 seeds, 'key' positions are commonly recognized by the players. The results of these key positions were entered as described in Sect. 2.3.

Handling the Möbius Loops. The 11-seed and 13-seed loops were a challenge to handle. This research suggests that the 11-seed loop gives a result of at least 5 and at most 6 seeds to a given player. Similarly, for a 13-seed loop, the result is 6 or 7 seeds to a given player. In order to continue the resolution of Oware, this outcome had to be considered. For example, for a 14-seed position depending on the result of the 11-seed Möbius loop, after a 3-seed capture, its result is 8 or 9. So we need to mark this uncertainty on the 7-bit format, while keeping track of the captures along the way. The solution was to consider the relative scores between the 2 players instead of the absolute scores. This means that in a state space of an even number of seeds, the difference in scores between the 2 players is even. Similarly, for an odd number of seeds, the difference in scores is odd. For these Möbius loops, the relative score is set to zero as a marker, giving an even difference in scores, in state spaces with that have odd number of seeds: 11 and 13. In effect, any parent positions that inherit directly or indirectly from the score of a Möbius loop, have the parity of its relative result marked by not matching the parity of the number of seeds of their state space. This explains why the results were initially coded on 7 bits, to accommodate negative values.

3.4   Step 3: Resolving Large State Spaces

Objective. With the size of the state space increasing exponentially with the number of seeds, the parallelization of work was required. The positions with 16 to 25 seeds could be resolved with a mono-threaded (serial) backward propagation algorithm in a reasonable amount of time. For positions with more than 25 seeds, a scalable multi-threaded (parallel) backward propagation algorithm was required.

Technical Considerations. In the period up to 2020, off-the-shelf technologies for dealing with large databases were still not powerful enough. Instead, the solution was to optimize the whole technology stack of a single machine, combining hardware configurations, Linux-based operating system (OS) behaviors and low-level programming for an ultra-fast parallelization of work. The memory allocations were done to avoid any memory swap or compression from the OS. Any computation was initiated from a freshly booted OS, so no memory caching was done, which would have relied on the OS to guarantee the integrity of the cache. The code was produced in plain C and compiled with gcc. Both were optimized for fast computation. More than 200 trillion (15 digits) of computations took place in a couple of weeks.

Database Management. The main challenge with databases is the concurrent access to data with a risk of deadlock during write accesses. The use of semaphores to orchestrate the write accesses created an expensive overhead and slowed down the resolution. Instead, it was decided to fragment each partition of a state space into memory segments of equal size, and then designate a thread to own each segment. Each partition was divided into 46 segments corresponding to the threads available from the machine. A thread could only operate a write access on its own memory segment, while it could read access any other memory segments. The concurrent read accesses were queued and managed directly by the bus between the CPU and the main memory, thus ensuring a maximum overall performance.

Parallel Backward Propagations – Stage 1. The resolution of a state space began by loading its partition in memory and by attributing a thread (called 'crawler') to each segment. Each time seeds were captured, the results from the subsequent position needed to be searched in the corresponding partition (with a number of seeds lowered by the number of captured seeds). That meant that 14 partitions containing these positions needed to be searched (captures vary from 2 to 15 seeds). They couldn't be loaded all at once due to the memory space limitation, hence the need to use them one by one. Once a partition loaded (aka cached), each crawler started exploring their segment. For each legal position, they calculated the position resulting from any move. They retrieved the results only of captures corresponding to the number of seeds of the smaller partition that was cached. They reported it and compared it to the result of the current position. In case of a better outcome, the result of the position was updated. Once all crawlers finished their scan, the cached partition was unmounted, leaving the memory space to cache the next one. The process with the crawlers was repeated. After all the smaller partitions had been explored, the crawlers started a last scan for consolidation. Each time they detected that a position contained only moves that provoked a capture, then the position was marked as resolved. At this stage, the partition under resolution contained positions that were resolved by captures and these results were ready to be propagated backward further.

Parallel Backward Propagations – Stage 2. The final resolution of the partition continued by kick-starting all crawlers again, this time focusing on the moves that didn't capture seeds. They updated the result of a position only when the result of a move gave a better outcome (from a subsequent position that was resolved). Only when all moves of a position referred to resolved positions, was the result of the position marked as resolved. In effect, the crawlers kept running, calculating the moves over and over again until all the moves of a position were resolved. After 3 full cycles in which no positions were updated, a crawler would indicate to the monitoring system that it was going in 'idle' and would stop crawling. Once all the crawlers were idle, the monitoring system terminated them. It started a final mono-threaded crawl to resolve the rare positions that were waiting for the resolution of a position that had been resolved during the transient period of some crawlers going into idle mode. If no positions were updated after 2 full cycles, then a check was done to see whether all positions had been resolved, or whether a loop had been found. (No loops were found for state spaces with 14 seeds or more.) The partition would then be resolved. The resolution of the next partition with a higher number of seeds could start and the process be re-iterated with caching, parallel crawling and finally serial crawling.

Strong Resolution. The end result of Oware's resolution showed -2 or 0 relative scores for South (corresponding to the respective absolute scores of 23 or 24). In a 48-seed state space, this means that perfect games do not inherit (or depend on) the resolution of these Möbius loops because of the parity match. In light of this, the resolution of Oware is therefore claimed to be strong.

4 Validation and Conclusion

The basic verifications included the Error Correction Code (ECC) from the hardware and the memory usage monitoring from the OS (neither swap nor compression allowed). On the rare occasions when an ECC memory bank reported a correction, the computation was restarted and accepted until no ECC correction occurred. The serial and parallel backward propagations algorithms delivered the same results for the resolution of 16 to 25 seeds positions. And because of the use of the crawlers, the database segments were calculated not once, but 50 times on average.

The most important phase is the validation of the database. As expected, the database playing against itself resulted in a draw. Some of the world's best Oware players and computer scientists were invited to play against the database, under the supervision of the Oware society [9]. To date, the database is still undefeated.

On 24 December 2021, T. Simon, International Grand Master from Antigua & Barbuda, became the first to play against the database and attain a score of 23–25. On 17 April 2021, computer scientist J. Sala Soler from Spain played with his AI engine Aalina 1.2.0, also scoring 23–25. And on 3 May 2022, M. Smits from The Netherlands played with his AI engine, in addition to using a database with fewer than 36 seeds, scoring 23–25 as well. The invitation to play against the database is still open since the possible tie result hasn't yet been reached [9].

The database has been named '48 Stones' and there is a website dedicated to it [7]. The documentation of the findings referred to in this paper, such as loops, games transcripts and related articles are all available on the website [8]. The database is not (yet) available to anyone in order to avoid misuse by online players, especially during competitions. How the results of this research can be used is still being discussed with the Oware Society and is open for discussion with computer scientists.

References

1. Allis, L.V.: Searching for solutions in games and artificial intelligence. In: Ph.D. Thesis, University of Limburg, The Netherlands (1994)
2. Lincke, T.R.: Exploring the computational limits of large exhaustive search problems. In: Ph.D. Thesis, ETH Zurich, Switzerland (2002)
3. Donkers, H.H.L.M.: Comments on the awari solution. In: ICGA J. 25(3), 166–167 (2002)
4. Romein, J.W., Bal, H.E.: Awari is Solved. In: ICGA Journal 25(3), 162–165 (2002)
5. Romein, J.W., Bal, H.E.: Solving the game of Awari using parallel retrograde analysis. Computer 38(10), 26–33 (2003)
6. Goot, R.: Awari retrograde analysis. In: Marsland, T., Frank, I. (eds.) CG 2000. LNCS, vol. 2063, pp. 87–95. Springer, Heidelberg (2001). https://doi.org/10.1007/3-540-45579-5_6
7. 48 Stones. https://48stones.com. Accessed 06 Nov 2022
8. 48 Stones, research. https://48stones.com/research/. Accessed 06 Nov 2022
9. 48 Stones, open invitation to the Master Challenge. https://48stones.com/challenge/. Accessed 06 Nov 2022

Solving Impartial SET Using Knowledge and Combinatorial Game Theory

Jos W. H. M. Uiterwijk[✉] and Lianne V. Hufkens

Department of Advanced Computing Sciences, Maastricht University,
Maastricht, The Netherlands
uiterwijk@maastrichtuniversity.nl, uiterwijkjwhm@gmail.com,
l.hufkens@alumni.maastrichtuniversity.nl, lianne.hufkens@ou.nl

Abstract. Standard SET is a card game played between any number of
players moving simultaneously, where a move means taking a number of
cards obeying some predetermined conditions (a Set). It is mainly a game
of pattern recognition and speed. The winner is the player obtaining the
most Sets.

To enable analyzing SET in a more mathematical and game-theoretic
sense we transformed the game into an impartial combinatorial game. SET
versions may differ depending on the number of characteristics c on the
cards and the number of values v of each characteristic. We indicate a particular version of SET for some v and c as SET-v-c.

We analyze different versions of Impartial SET using $\alpha\beta$ search with
several enhancements from mathematical SET theory and from Combinatorial Game Theory. We first show using SET theory that all SET-2-c versions for $c > 1$ are second-player wins and that SET-v-2 versions are first-
player wins for odd v and second-player wins for even v. We next show how
to compute solutions using search. We give some results and discuss how
solving efficiencies were dependent on the enhancements used. Especially,
the use of a pruning method based on symmetry of positions was pivotal
for a large efficiency enhancement. Also the use of two methods based on
endgame databases filled with Combinatorial Game Theory values proved
very useful in further enhancing the solving efficiency.

Using all enhancements together the complex SET-4-3 game was solved,
needing the investigation of some 2 billion nodes. This game is (maybe
counterintuitive) a first-player win.

1 Introduction

Standard SET is a real-time card game played with a deck of 81 cards. The
symbols on the cards have four characteristics: color, shape, filling, and number
of shapes. Each of these characteristics has three possible values and the deck
contains every possible combination exactly once.

In SET any number of players can participate. At the start of the game
twelve cards are open on the table. The players move simultaneously, searching

---

This paper is based on the M.Sc. thesis [7] of the second author.

for a Set among the cards. A valid Set is a combination of three cards where for each characteristic the values either are all the same or all different. After a Set is found and taken the remaining cards are supplemented with three new cards from the deck. Play continues until the deck is empty or no more Set can be found. The player with the most Sets in their possession wins.

To avoid ambiguity in the remainder of this paper we reserve the notion 'SET' (with all capitals) for the game, the notion 'Set' (only first letter capital) for a tuple of cards obeing the conditions in the rules as given above, and the notion 'set' for the mathematical concept of a set as a collection.

2   Impartial SET

Standard SET is based on pattern recognition and notoriously on speed. To be able to analyze SET in a game-theoretic way, we transformed the game into a 2-player perfect-information version. This version is denoted as Impartial SET, further in this paper just called SET.

Definition 1. *Impartial SET is a two-player variant of SET where the two players move alternately. All cards are open on the table. A move consists of taking a single Set out of all Sets present. There is no time constraint on taking a Set. The win condition is changed into: the player who makes the last move (taking the last Set) wins the game, so as soon as a player is unable to move he loses.*

With these constraints the game is converted into a *combinatorial game*, for which a whole theory, the Combinatorial Game Theory (further CGT in short), is developed [1, 2, 4]. Since in a position both players have the same moves (called *options* in CGT) when to move, the game belongs to the class of *impartial* combinatorial games.

We investigate different versions, defined by the number of *characteristics* c and the number of *values* v for every characteristic (with each characteristic having the same number of values). We denote such SET version as SET-v-c. It is easy to see that the Set size necessarily is v.

We present a few general definitions and formulas.

- Since there is exactly 1 card for every combination of values for all characteristics, the number of cards N for SET-v-c is given by v^c.
- The number of Sets at the start of the game is denoted by S_0.
- The number of Sets from which a card is part is indicated by s. Note that this number depends on the card in question. However, at the start of the game this is the same for every card, and this number is indicated by s_0.

So SET-2-3 is the game with three characteristics (e.g., color, shape, and filling), for which each characteristic can have two values (e.g., {purple, red} for color, {squiggle, oval} for shape, and {empty, full} for filling). The Set size is 2 and there are $2^3 = 8$ different cards. At the start of the game there are 28 different Sets (S_0) and every card is part of 7 Sets (s_0). For SET-versions with three possible values per characteristic we add 'green', 'rectangle', and 'shaded' to the respective value sets. So SET 3-3 with Set size 3 has $3^3 = 27$ different cards being all combinations of color $\in$ {purple, red, green}, shape $\in$ {squiggle, oval, rectangle}, and filling $\in$ {empty, full, shaded}. Standard SET is SET-3-4 with $3^4 = 81$ different cards with as fourth characteristic number $\in$ {one, two, three}.

To illustrate a SET game, we take as example SET-3-3. In Fig. 1 we show all 27 cards at the beginning of the game. All cards are open on the table. (The order of the cards is of no importance.) The IDs in the Figure are just added to identify the cards.

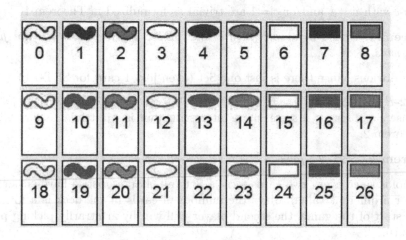

Fig. 1. A complete deck of SET-3-3 cards.

An easy to spot Set is for instance (0 1 2) where for two characteristics (color and shape) the values of the cards in the Set are all equal, whereas the third characteristic (filling) has three different values in the Set (therefore we denote this Set as of type *eed*). Note that a Set of type *eee* is impossible, since all three cards would have equal values for all three characteristics, and hence the Set should contain three identical cards, whereas exactly one copy of each card is present. A second example Set is (0 4 8), where only one characteristic (color) has equal values in the Set, and two characteristics shape and filling have different values. This type of Set is clearly *edd*. The most difficult (for humans that is) type of Set to spot is *ddd*, with all three characteristics having different values for all cards, exemplified by the Set (0 13 26).

This complete deck of SET-3-3 contains 117 different Sets. The first move by the starting player (in CGT often indicated as player Left) then makes a first move, say taking Set (0 1 2). Note that not only Set (0 1 2) is now removed, but also all other Sets having at least one card in common with Set (0 1 2), like Sets (0 9 18), (0 10 20), etc, with 80 Sets remaining. Then the second player (Right) makes a move (taking a Set), and play continues alternately, until there is no more card on the table or there is no Set among the cards on the table. The last player having taken a Set is the winner.

3   SET Theory

In this section we focus on knowledge of several SET-v-c versions. Where possible (without investigation by search) we give some mathematical details [5] of the versions introduced. We formulate this knowledge in the form of theorems. Formal proofs are omitted for reasons of space, but can be found in [7].

SET-1-c and SET-v-1
SET-v-c with $v = 1$ and/or $c = 1$ are trivial as formulized in Theorem 1.

Theorem 1. *SET-1-c for arbitrary c and SET-v-1 for arbitrary v are first-player wins.*

This is obvious, since there is just one Set (even just 1 card for SET-1-c).

SET-2-c with $c > 1$
The case $v = 2$ for $c > 1$ seems more interesting, but is still trivial as formalized in Theorem 2.

Theorem 2. *SET-2-c for $c > 1$ is a second-player win.*

This holds since every two cards form a Set (all characteristics have either the same or a different value). Since the number of cards in the deck is a fourfold at the start of the game, the second player will win by arbitrarily picking pairs each turn.

SET-v-2 with $v > 1$
Theorem 3 shows that SET with just 2 characteristics is also easy.

Theorem 3. *SET-v-2 for arbitrary v is a first-player win if v is odd, and a second-player win if v is even.*

As simple examples, the first player can win SET-3-2, SET-5-2 etc. by starting with taking a Set with 1 characteristic equal (the other necessarily different), such as all purple cards. After that the deck consists of disjoint Sets. The last Set (color) is taken by the first player, who thus wins the game. On the other hand SET-4-2 is won by the second player. If the first player again starts by taking a Set with 1 characteristic equal, the second player wins necessarily (since there are 3 disjoint Sets left). Alternatively, if the first player starts with a Set with both characteristics different, the second player can use some copy-strategy. For example, the Set {(purple squiggle), (red oval), (green rectangle), (yellow diamond)} is countered by the Set {(purple diamond), (red rectangle), (green oval), (yellow squiggle)}. This is possible, since the number of values is even. In this way the second player necessarily wins. For other even values of v a similar strategy for the second player will work.

SET-v-c with $v > 2$ and $c > 2$

No general Theorems have been found for these SET versions, so they have to be determined for specific SET versions by search. This will be done in the remainder of this paper. One interesting result for arbitrary SET versions was the following. As defined in Sect. 2, S_0 denotes the number of Sets at the start of a game. In [7] we derived a formula for S_0, as a function of v and c.

$$S_0 = \begin{cases} 1 & \text{if } v = 1 \\ \frac{v^c}{v!} \times \sum_{k=1}^{c} \binom{c}{k}((v-1)!)^k & \text{otherwise} \end{cases} \tag{1}$$

In this formula the factor v^c is the total number of cards N, from which the first card can be chosen, the second factor sums the number of ways the remaining cards can be chosen, and the divisor accounts for the permutations of the Set.

Another useful characteristic is the number of Sets an arbitrary card can be a member of. We denoted this by s, and at the start of the game by s_0. This is also the maximum s, since s can never increase during a game. From S_0 we now can easily derive s_0 as follows. Since the first card is settled we have to divide S_0 by $N = v^c$. Moreover, since the specific card is always taken as the first one, in order to account for the different order of picking cards in a Set we have to divide by the number of permutations for the 2nd up to the last card, so by $(v-1)!$ instead of $v!$, so multiplying S_0 by v. This gives for s_0:

$$s_0 = \frac{S_0}{v^{(c-1)}} \tag{2}$$

Finally, a useful theorem is the following.

Theorem 4. *If for an arbitrary SET-v-c version during game play with legal moves the situation is reached where there are exactly v cards left, these cards form a Set.*

Although this was already proven for SET-3-c (see e.g. [10]), it was not proven for arbitrary v. We have given an alternative proof valid for arbitrary v in [7].

4   Forward Pruning Using Knowledge and CGT

In [7] several SET versions were analyzed and solved using basic search techniques. Some enhancements based on SET theory were implemented, but were only useful in solving small SET versions. In the present contribution we report on four new pruning methods. The first one is based on equivalent move sequences, the second one on position equivalence using symmetry. Moreover, we introduce the use of CGT by incorporating two types of database support in our solver.

4.1 Forward Pruning Using Sequence-Based Equivalence

One method for filtering moves is based on the observation that any permutation of some move sequence leads to the same position. This follows from two facts: 1) the game is impartial, so in any position both players can make the same moves; and 2) moves in a sequence are independent, since interfering moves obviously can never be played in the same sequence. This leads us to the following technique, which we dubbed *Sequence-based Equivalence Pruning*. We only have implemented a simple version of this techniques, namely for sequences of length 2.

Suppose in some position P we investigate move a by the current player (say Left) and after investigating the position P_a after move a it turns out that a loses, say by response b by the second player (Right). Then obviously it is not useful for Left to investigate move b instead, since Right's response a then will win. Of course this technique is only useful when the move a investigated is losing, since if a wins (from every possible response) no further alternative for a need be investigated, due to the nature of $\alpha\beta$, and this branch is solved.

As an example (refering to Fig. 1), consider SET-3-3. In the position after the opening move (0 1 2) by the first player, there are 80 Sets remaining. The first move by the second player investigated is (3 4 5). This move turns out to be losing to (6 7 8). As a consequence, the move (6 7 8) need not be inspected at depth 1. Note that this process is cumulative. For instance, in our solver the second node investigated at depth 1 is (3 9 24) which loses to (4 10 25); then move (4 10 25) can also be dismissed. It turned out that in total 4 moves were dismissed. This is not a large amount, which stems from the fact that the move order is always similar, and as a consequence the best response is often already investigated before.

4.2 Forward Pruning Using Symmetry-Based Equivalence

Looking at the game of SET it is obvious that many equivalent positions exist. One way to use this is to look at all symmetries of a position. This includes for a given characteristic shuffling the values, which gives $v!$ equivalent permutations per characteristic, leading to in total $(v!)^c$ permutations. Moreover, characteristics may also be shuffled, giving another factor of $c!$ permutations. To give a striking example for the largest SET version in our test set, SET-4-3, the number of symmetries is $24^3 \times 6 = 82,944$.

As a trivial example: take SET-2-2. For any position on the board we can generate 8 equivalent positions. These can be divided into two classes: the first class contains those symmetries where always characteristic 1 concerns the color and characteristic 2 the shape (the default). Within this set of 4 equivalent symmetries we can transform the position to an equivalent position according to a permutation of the values of the color and a permutation of the values of the shape. The permutations are applied for each characteristic in order; (01) means that the first value (0) of each card stays 0, and the second value (1) stays 1, whereas (10) means that value 0 becomes 1, and 1 becomes 0. So the permutation

(01)(01) is the identity operation, the permutation (10)(01) transforms all purple (red) cards of the position into red (purple) without changing their shapes, the permutation (01)(10) transforms all squiggles (ovals) cards of the position into ovals (squiggles) without changing their colors, and the permutation (10)(10) combines the above two transformations. The second class consists of the same symmetry operations after exchanging the two characteristics.

Symmetrical children of some position are pruned. For this we store every child investigated so far. For a prospective new child we check if it is symmetry-equivalent with one of the already stored children, in which case we skip this new child. Of course, we then do not need to calculate all remaining symmetries. Moreover, as soon as a card of the prospective Set is not present in the comparison with a previously inspected child we can go at once to the next symmetry. A final enhancement is that we also store for each child investigated the number of differing characteristics $\#d$ in the Set. Since children with different values for $\#d$ can never be symmetry-equivalent, we only have to inspect stored children with the same $\#d$ as the prospective new child. We dubbed this technique as *Symmetry-based Equivalence Pruning*. By this procedure using symmetries is quite efficient, especially in the upper layers of the search tree. Lower in the tree the number of equivalent children becomes small, and the gain in diminishing number of nodes does not outweigh the decrease in solving speed. By some preliminary experiments we found that a maximum depth of 4 is best to use for Symmetry-based Equivalence Pruning.

Continuing our example of SET-3-3 (see Fig. 1) after the opening move (0 1 2), where the first child (3 4 5) loses to the response (6 7 8): it turns out that of the 75 moves to be investigated after applying the Sequence-based Equivalence Pruning technique 70 moves are further dismissed based on symmetry, like Set (6 7 8) being equivalent to Set (3 4 5). Consequently, only 6 responses to (0 1 2) had to be investigated (all shown to be losses, proving that SET-3-3 is a first-player win).

4.3 Forward Pruning Using CGT Subgame Databases

In this section we describe how we represent and construct endgame databases for sets of Sets. So we start with the representation of a set of Sets. The underlying notion is how the Sets are connected (i.e. which overlaps in cards there are). The most simple case is when the number of Sets $N_{Sets} = 1$, which is represented by the constant DB1 = 1 (meaning its value is nimber[1] $*1$).

For $N_{Sets} = 2$ we have two possibilities, Set1 being connected to Set2 or being not connected. This is represented by a single bit (with value 0 for no connection, 1 for connection), so we need a 1-bit array DB2. Its values are nimbers $*n$, represented by the associated integers n, in this case DB2[0] = 0 and DB2[1] = 1.

---

[1] A nimber $*n$ in CGT is defined as $*n = \{*0, *1, ..., *(n-1)\}$, meaning that the player to move can in one move reach any position with lower value than $*n$.

For $N_{Sets} = 3$ we need 3 bits, from left to right indicating a possible connection between Set1 and Set2, between Set1 and Set3, and between Set2 and Set3. So for DB3 we have 8 entries, from 000 to 111, with values 1, 0, 0, 2, 0, 2, 2, 1. For example, DB3[3] with index 011 stores the value of three Sets, with Set1 not connected to Set2, Set1 connected to Set 3, and Set2 connected to Set3 (a linear graph with Set3 in the middle). Regarding the values of the children: since taking Set1 removes also Set3 but not Set2, this child has value *1; since taking Set2 removes also Set3 but not Set1, this child has also value *1; since taking Set3 removes all three Sets, this child has value *0; therefore the value of this entry is the Mex() function (minimal excludant) applied to the values of the children, being *2 (represented by the value 2).

Continuing, for DB4 we will need 6 bits, for DB5 10 bits, etc. These are the well-known Triangular numbers 1,3,6,10,... and so on. So for the endgame database DBn for $n > 1$ we need $T(n-1) = (n-1) \times n/2$ bit entries. Storing in each entry a byte, the size of DBn therefore is $2^{T(n-1)}$ bytes, giving for DBn with n from 2 to 9 as sizes 1 B, 8 B, 64 B, 1 KB, 32 KB, 2 MB, 256 MB, and 64 GB. Clearly the last one, DB9 with 36-bits entries, exceeds our storage capacities. Therefore, the maximum DB-size used is 8 Sets.

Regarding the construction of the endgame databases, we have followed the same method as used for Cram [11]. Databases are constructed from small (2 Sets) to large (8 Sets). For each entry in a database we determine all children (which means deleting one of the Sets plus all directly connected Sets). The nimber value of each child can be directly looked up in the concerned smaller databases (constructed before), after which the value of the current position is determined as the Mex() function of the values of all children.

When during a game the position decomposes in subgames (fragments) of size(s) at most 8, we can lookup the value of each subgame in an endgame database and combine them using the Nim-addition rule.[2] We denote this technique as *Database SubGames Pruning*. It is evident that high in the tree it is not useful to check for a useful decomposition. We experimented with different settings of the minimum depth to apply the subgames pruning. The result was that it is best to only apply subgames pruning when the total number of Sets is at most 8 (the maximum database size), i.e., when it is sure that database pruning is guaranteed to be successful.

4.4 Forward Pruning Using CGT SubSET Databases

The main disadvantage of the subgame databases is that their size grows extremely fast with the number of Sets, leading to a largest feasible database of just 8 Sets. In practise, for larger (and more interesting) SET versions the set of Sets decomposes only quite deep and even then most subsets are too large to be useful (often with 12 Sets for SET-3-3). Based on these disadvantages we implemented another idea, namely to represent just cards in a database, which

---

[2] The Nim addition rule states that the sum of $*m$ and $*n$ is given by $*m \oplus *n$, where $\oplus$ is the exclusive-or operator applied to the binary representations of m and n.

is much more efficient than storing connections. This is obvious: in a deck of n cards every position can be represented by n bits (0 and 1 meaning that a card is present or not). Since we lose the information on connections between cards this is only possible if the databases represent pre-determined decks of cards.

One way of using pre-determined card decks is to build databases for complete SET-v-c decks. We have built the complete databases for the following SET versions: SET-2-2 (4 cards, $2^4 = 16$ entries), SET-2-3 (8 cards, $2^8 = 256$ entries), SET-2-4 (16 cards, $2^{16} = 64K$ entries), SET-3-2 (9 cards, $2^9 = 512$ entries), SET-3-3 (27 cards, $2^{27} = 128M$ entries), SET-4-2 (16 cards, $2^{16} = 64K$ entries), and SET-5-2 (25 cards, $2^{25} = 32M$ entries). It is evident that databases for much larger disjoint subsets can be built in this way and thus can be encountered much earlier in the search tree.

The construction of the databases is straighforward by performing a v-fold loop over all possible v-tuples in the database, and if such entry forms a Set (according to the convention of the concerning SET-v-c version), then the CGT value of the child is obtained from the entry after removal of the Set. As usual the value of the parent is the Mex() of the values of all children.

In the solver this database support is used by keeping track of the so-called *population vector* (PV in short). This vector stores for all characteristics and per characteristic for all values in predetermined order the number of cards with that characteristic/value pair. As an example, for SET-3-3 with 27 cards there are 9 cards for each characteristic/value pair, so the initial PV is the vector 9,9,9,9,9,9,9,9,9 (or easier to read 999 999 999 with each group of three denoting a characteristic). In general, at the start of a SET-v-c game, the PV is a $c \times v$ vector with each entry filled with the value $v^{(c-1)}$. When the first move in SET-3-3 is taking 3 cards with the same first value for the first characteristic and all different values for the second and third characteristic, the resulting position has PV 699 888 888. We use subSET pruning in a SET-v-c game as soon as an entry in the PV becomes 0, since this signals that 1 specific value for some characteristic is not present anymore, meaning that the deck consists of disjoint sets of Sets for the remaining values of that characteristic. Consequently, each disjoint set belongs to an appropriate SET-v-$(c-1)$ game, for which we have complete information. We denote this database support in the solving process as *Database SubSET Pruning*.

As a small but useful enhancement, note that from the start of a game an entry in the PV can decrease at most by v, meaning that we have to make at least $v^{(c-2)}$ steps before an entry can become zero. So testing the PV need not be done before we reach depth $v^{(c-2)}$.

5   Solving Impartial SET Versions

In this section we give an overview of our experimental analyses of different SET-versions.

5.1 Solving Using Basic Search Methods

In this subsection we give our first series of experiments. Our solver was written in C# using Microsoft Visual Studio. All experiments were performed on a MSI Prestige laptop with Intel® Core™ i7-10710U processor. Note that for the experiments we still include SET versions with known results according to Theorems 2 and 3, for testing and comparison purposes.

In Table 1 we give the experimental results for solving different SET versions. In these experiments no domain knowledge (except the rules of the game) is used. They are obtained using our basic MiniMax and $\alpha\beta$ [8] solver, and as enhancement the use of a standard transposition table [6] based on Zobrist hashing [13] (+TT). A simple *Deep* replacement scheme [3] is used. This table contains 2^{26} entries of 8 bytes each, so with a total size of 0.5 GB. Further the Early Transposition Cutoffs (+ETC) method [9] has been implemented and investigated. A column with a '+' heading means that the enhancement is cumulative wrt the previous column.

Table 1. Experimental results for different SET versions. No domain knowledge is used.

v	c	winner	MiniMax	$\alpha\beta$	+TT	+ETC
2	2	2	13	13	13	13
2	3	2	5,489	393	162	149
2	4	2	-	3,120,721	23,337	22,088
3	2	1	61	6	6	6
3	3	1	-	74,816	20,013	16,313
4	2	2	1,521	221	146	140
4	3		-	-	-	-
5	2	1	394,851	26	19	18

The table gives for each SET-v-c version solved the winner (a '1' denoting a first-player win, a '2' a second-player win) and the number of nodes investigated to solve the game. A '-' in an entry denotes that the SET version could not be solved with the solver configuration as indicated within a maximum of 1,000,000,000 nodes investigated.

We first observe that $\alpha\beta$ is obviously much better than MiniMax (with hardly any loss in speed). The use of transposition tables gives a mediocre improvement, but grows with larger SET versions. ETC clearly yields only minor improvements.

5.2 Solving Using Knowledge-Based Methods

A second series of experiments was performed with our program, where our new enhancements described in Sects. 4.1–4.4 were incorporated. An overview of the results is provided in Table 2.

Table 2. Experimental results for different SET versions. The enhancements are based on domain knowledge.

v	c	winner	Table 1	+SEQ	+SYM	+DBG	+DBS
2	2	2	13	7	5	1	1
2	3	2	149	141	17	6	6
2	4	2	22,088	22,076	1,246	933	892
3	2	1	6	4	4	2	2
3	3	1	16,313	15,256	1,107	477	261
4	2	2	140	123	9	4	4
4	3	1	-	-	-	-	1,870,533,469
5	2	1	18	15	6	2	2

The first data column denotes the best line of Table 1. The next columns show the improvement by incorporating respectively Sequence-based Equivalence Pruning (+SEQ), Symmetry-based Equivalence Pruning (+SYM), Database SubGames Pruning (+DBG), and Database SubSET Pruning (+DBS).

It is clear that Sequence-based Equivalence Pruning gives only a small increase in efficiency (but very simple to implement). Using Symmetry-based Equivalence Pruning has a very large positive impact on the solving efficiency of our solver. Database Subgames support and Database SubSET support lead to mediocre enhancements.

Using all four knowledge-based enhancements and with the nodes-limit disabled SET-4-3 was solved, proving that the game is a first-player win.[3]

6   Conclusions and Future Research

In this paper we have described the methods used to solve impartial SET-v-c, with $v = 2$ and $c = 2$-4, $v = 3$ and $c = 2$-3, $v = 4$ and $c = 2$-3, and $v = 5$ and $c = 2$. Of these only the games SET-3-3 and SET-4-3 are non-trivial.

Impartial SET-3-3 is (unsurprisingly for a game with an odd threefold number of cards) a first-player win. The win is however not straightforward, since there are still quite some lines leading to second-player wins and it is difficult to judge correctness of moves without deep calculations.

Impartial SET 4-3 is also a first-player win (which is more surprising for a game with an even fourfold number of cards). This means that the first-player is always able to play in such a way that not all cards can be taken. Closer inspection shows that the win for the first player is far from easy, with many non-optimal lines leading to second-player wins. However, it is hard to understand which moves will win and which will lose (typical for impartial games).

---

[3] This experiment took around 1 month of computation time. Due to some system failures the experiment needed a few restarts. Some useful information is lost between runs, such as the contents of the transposition table. As a consequence, the outcome is correct, but the number of investigated nodes is more than needed.

For future research we envision several further enhancements that proved worthwhile in another impartial combinatorial game, namely Cram [12]. These mainly concerned improvements or move-ordering heuristics based on CGT. Seeing the current time needed to solve SET-4-3 and knowing that SET-3-4 is inherently much more complex than SET-4-3 (with a deck size of 81 vs 64 and a maximum depth of 27 vs 16), it will be clear that we will need one or a few large increases in solving efficiency, so solving impartial SET-3-4 will probably be a tough challenge for future research.

References

1. Albert, M.H., Nowakowski, R.J., Wolfe, D.: Lessons in Play: An Introduction to Combinatorial Game Theory. A K Peters, Wellesley, MA (2007)
2. Berlekamp, E.R., Conway, J.H., Guy, R.K.: Winning ways for your mathematical plays. Academic Press, London (1982); 2nd edition, in four volumes: vol. 1 (2001), vols. 2, 3 (2003), vol. 4 (2004). A K Peters, Wellesley, MA
3. Breuker, D.M., Uiterwijk, J.W.H.M., van den Herik, H.J.: Replacement schemes for transposition tables. ICCA J. **17**(4), 183–193 (1994)
4. Conway, J.H.: On Numbers and Games. Academic Press, London (1976)
5. Davis, B.L., Maclagan, D.: The card game SET. Math. Intell. **25**(3), 33–40 (2003)
6. Greenblatt, R.D., Eastlake, D.E., Crocker, S.D.: The Greenblatt chess program. Proc. AFIPS Fall Joint Comput. Conf. **31**, 801–810 (1967)
7. Hufkens, L.V.: Investigating impartial SET, M.Sc. thesis, Dept. of Data Science and Knowledge Engineering, Maastricht University (2020)
8. Knuth, D.E., Moore, R.W.: An analysis of alpha-beta pruning. Artif. Intell. **6**, 293–326 (1975)
9. Plaat, A., Schaefer, J, Pijls, W., Bruin, A. de: Exploiting Graph Properties of Game Trees. AAAI-96 Proceedings, pp. 234–239 (1996)
10. Tucker, C.: Geometric models of the card Game SET. Rose–Hulman Undergraduate Math. J. **8**(1), 10 (2007). https://scholar.rose-hulman.edu/rhumj/vol8/iss1/10
11. Uiterwijk, J.W.H.M.: Construction and investigation of cram endgame databases. ICGA J. **40**(4), 425–437 (2018)
12. Uiterwijk, J.W.H.M.: Solving cram using combinatorial game theory. In: Cazenave, T., van den Herik, J., Saffidine, A., Wu, I.C. (eds.) Advances in Computer Games. ACG 2019. Lecture Notes in Computer Science, Vol. 12516, pp. 91–105. Springer, Cham (2020). https://doi.org/10.1007/978-3-030-65883-0_8
13. Zobrist, A.L.: A new hashing method with application for game playing. Technical Report #88, Computer Science Department, The University of Wisconsin, Madison (1970). Reprinted in ICCA J. **13**(2), 69–73 (1990)

Measuring Games

Which Rules for Mu Torere?

Cameron Browne[⊠]

Department of Advanced Computing Sciences, Maastricht University, Paul-Henri Spaaklaan 1, 6229 EN Maastricht, The Netherlands
cameron.browne@maastrichtuniversity.nl

Abstract. Mu Torere is a traditional board game played by the Maori people of New Zealand. It has simple rules, low complexity and has been fully analysed, but surprisingly is often described with incorrect rules in the literature. This paper compares the various known rulesets for Mu Torere to investigate which provides the most interesting game, as the first step in a more thorough analysis of this game.

Keywords: Mu Torere · Board Game · Game AI · Game Analysis

1 Introduction

Mu Torere is a traditional board game played by the Maori people of New Zealand [3]. The game is played by two players on the 9-point board shown in Fig. 1 (left). Both players start with four pieces of their colour initially set as shown (Fig. 1, centre).

 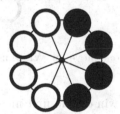 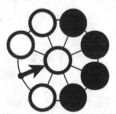

Fig. 1. The Mu Torere board (left), starting position (centre) and winning move (right).

Starting with White, players alternate moving a piece of their colour, according to the following basic rules:

1. The mover must move a piece of their colour to the adjacent empty point.
2. A player wins if the opponent cannot move on their turn.

However, a moment's analysis reveals a crippling problem with these basic rules. White immediately has a winning move from the starting position (Fig. 1, right), so the game is typically played with additional restrictions on movement.

The following five restrictions are found in the literature, giving five variant rulesets:

- **Ruleset A:** No restriction.
- **Ruleset B:** White cannot win on the first move.
- **Ruleset C:** The piece being moved must be adjacent to an opponent's piece.
- **Ruleset D:** The mover cannot win during the first two rounds.
- **Ruleset E:** The piece being moved must be adjacent to an opponent's piece if it is being moved to the centre point.

Unfortunately, it is not clear from the written accounts which of these rulesets is typically used in practice. This paper presents an analysis of the five rulesets to investigate which produces the most interesting game.

2   Ruleset A: No Restriction

Ruleset A represents the basic unrestricted form of the game. It is typically not found in historical descriptions of the game, but can be found in modern sources that oversimplify the description of the game.[1]

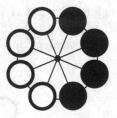

Fig. 2. Trivial win in one move for White using Ruleset A.

This ruleset allows White to win on the first move, as shown in Fig. 2. This ruleset should not be used.

3   Ruleset B: No Win on First Move

Ruleset B circumvents this win-in-1 problem by explicitly forbidding White to win on the first move. This ruleset is found in historical accounts including [6].

However, this ruleset does not solve the trivial win problem but rather just delays it slightly. Black can force a win every game as shown in Fig. 3. This ruleset should not be used.

---

[1] See for example: http://gamescrafters.berkeley.edu/games.php?game=mutorere.

Fig. 3. Trivial win in four moves for Black using Ruleset B.

4 Ruleset C: Move If Adjacent to Enemy

Ruleset C circumvents the trivial win problem of Rulesets A and B indirectly by forbidding moves that would allow the win-in-1 and win-in-4 cases. This ruleset is found in modern descriptions of the game.[2]

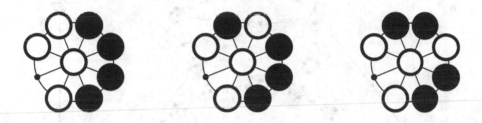

Fig. 4. The three basic winning patterns for White.

Unfortunately, this restriction is too successful in its aim and prevents *any* winning position from occurring. Figure 4 shows the three basic winning patterns from White's perspective; the restriction that pieces can only move if they are adjacent to an enemy piece does not allow any of theses positions to occur (for either player) so every game is guaranteed to become a perpetual cycle. This ruleset should not be used.

5 Ruleset D: No Win on First Two Rounds

Ruleset D is the most prevalent ruleset throughout the literature, both from historical sources [1–4] and from mathematical analyses of the game [10,11]. This ruleset simply forbids either player winning on their first two moves.

This rule is often described in more complicated terms, e.g. "For each player's first two moves, a stone can be moved from an outer node to the center only if it is adjacent to an opponent's stone" [10, p.384], but this is functionally equivalent to: "The mover cannot win during the first two rounds."

---

[2] See for example: https://cpb-ap-se2.wpmucdn.com/blogs.auckland.ac.nz/dist/7/67/files/2018/04/mu_torere_board-1b2pdv1.pdf.

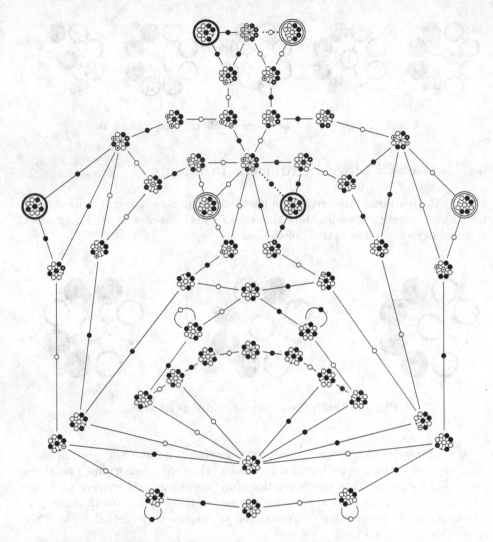

Fig. 5. Complete game graph for Ruleset D.

Figure 5 shows a full game graph expansion of Mu Torere played with Rule-set D. The format is based on Straffin's beautiful analysis of the game ([10] and [11]), except that the actual board positions are shown at each node for convenience and the game-theoretic value of each possible move is shown, from the perspective of each piece's owner, as follows:

- **Win** ⊙: The mover can force a win with this move.
- **Loss** ⊖: The opponent can force a win if the mover makes this move.
- **Draw (no marking)**: Move that leads to an infinite loop with optimal play.

The graph shows the 46 distinct positions that can occur during play, with each node representing all rotations and reflections of that position, and each edge between nodes representing all moves by the player indicated that produce a transition from one state to the other. The graph has six terminal positions representing winning or losing positions, each indicated by a surrounding circle in the winner's colour. The graph essentially provides a set of instructions for which moves to play – and not to play – from each position.

The initial state is shown at the centre top; note that this position and the position immediately below are effectively superpositions of these positions during the first two rounds (when winning moves – dotted – are forbidden) and subsequent later (when the dotted moves are allowed). Note that three of the symbols indicating moves as game-theoretic wins ⊙ and losses ⊖ in these positions are greyed; this indicates that these values only apply after the first two rounds.

6   Ruleset E: Move to Centre If Adjacent to Enemy

This variant is described by Bell [4, 5] – who hedges his bets by listing both variants D and E in [4] – and used by Jelliss in his excellent mathematical analysis of the game [7]. Reed's visual description of the game's rules through example [9] is compatible with both Rulesets D and E.

Figure 6 shows a full game graph expansion of Mu Torere played with Ruleset E. Jelliss [7] uses a more compact representation in his analysis that yields 26 distinct positions (each with a colour inversion flag) so that positions can conveniently be labelled by letters of the alphabet. However, Straffin's graph layout is used here for readability.

The game produced by Ruleset E is similar to that produced by Ruleset D except that more moves are forbidden. This can be seen in the game graph for Ruleset E, which is similar to the game graph for Ruleset D except that six winning moves shown in graph D are absent in graph E, and fewer moves are labelled as winning ⊙ or losing ⊖, hence more moves are drawish.

7   Which Ruleset: D or E?

It is clear that Rulesets A, B and C can be discarded due to producing: (A) a trivial win, (B) a trivial loss, and (C) the impossibility of a result. Rulesets D and E both produce relatively well-behaved and interesting games for the low complexity involved. Can we identify either of these superior rulesets as more potentially interesting than the other?

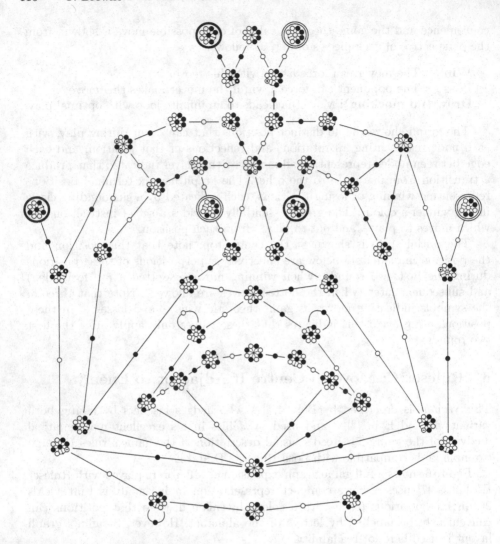

Fig. 6. Complete game graph for Ruleset E.

7.1 Drawishness

Mu Torere is a game of low complexity and is drawish in nature – no experienced player should ever lose a game – but it is still of interest to human players. It allows distinct skill levels and a skilled player will generally beat a beginner, and there is anecdotal evidence that (skilled) local Maori players have consistently beaten (unskilled) foreign opponents [2].

In order to make the game as interesting as possible, its rules should discourage draws and encourage a result as often as possible (assuming that both players are not experts). Table 1 gives some insight into the nature of Rulesets D and E by comparing the ratio of win, draw and loss game-theoretic values across positions and transitions that may occur during play.

Table 1. Distribution of Game-Theoretic Values Across Game Graphs D and E.

		Win	Draw	Loss
Ruleset D	Positions	6	25	15
	Transitions	24	74	32
Ruleset E	Positions	5	31	10
	Transitions	14	94	16

Ruleset D appears to be less drawish in nature. It only has fewer drawish positions than Ruleset E (25 compared to 31), more winning positions (6 compared to 5) and more losing positions (15 compared to 10). Similarly, Ruleset E has fewer drawish transitions (74 compared to 94), more winning transitions (24 compared to 14) and more losing transitions (32 compared to 16).

7.2 Playout Behaviour

Given that Ruleset D has fewer drawish positions than Ruleset E, what are the chances that a non-expert player will stumble into a losing move and produce a non-draw result? Table 2 shows the results of 1,000,000 random playouts for each ruleset A to E. Two playout types were implemented with a move limit of $L = 50$ moves per game, to reflect the approximate state space size:

1. **Random:** Strictly random move choice each turn until the game ends or the move limit L is reached.
2. **Greedy:** Strictly random move choice each turn (except that a winning move is made if one exists) until the game ends or the move limit L is reached.

Table 2. Results Over 1,000,000 Playouts.

		White Wins	Black Wins	Draws	Length
Ruleset A	Random	65.35%	26.30%	8.34%	10.80
	Greedy	100.00%	0.00%	0.00%	1.00
Ruleset B	Random	30.54%	52.71%	16.75%	20.58
	Greedy	0.00%	100.00%	0.00%	4.00
Ruleset C	Random	0.00%	0.00%	100.00%	50.00
	Greedy	0.00%	0.00%	100.00%	50.00
Ruleset D	Random	40.82%	36.79%	22.39%	26.13
	Greedy	**54.38%**	**37.89%**	**7.72%**	17.63
Ruleset E	Random	31.93%	33.32%	34.75%	31.78
	Greedy	**41.56%**	**44.39%**	**14.09%**	22.62

Strictly random playouts do not accurately reflect how games between intelligent human players are actually played and do not provide much insight. The greedy playouts, however, effectively mimic how a beginner might approach the game, playing experimentally and making winning moves if any present themselves. The results from the greedy playouts provide much more insight into the game.

Grredy playouts indicate a 100% win rate for White with Ruleset A, and 100% win rate for Black with Ruleset B, and a 100% draw rate for Ruleset C, all as expected. The results for rulesets D and E suggest much more interesting games. Rulset D has a low draw rate of 7.72% – about half that of Ruleset E – but Ruleset D also suggests a strong first move advantage with a White win rate of 54.38% versus a Black win rate of 37.89%. The win rates for Rulset E are much more balanced at 41.56% and 44.39%.

7.3   Mistake Potential

Chess Grandmaster Savielly Tartakower famously said:

The blunders are all there on the board, waiting to be made [8].

While mistakes are an embarrassment to the perpetrator that can ruin an otherwise beautiful game from their perspective, they can also inject excitement into the match for the opponent and spectators. Mistakes are in fact crucial to the success of such a simple and drawish game as Mu Torere, as without mistakes every game will end in a draw.

Mistakes can occur in any position that has moves with different game-theoretic values. However, since we want to achieve as many non-draw results as possible, we are most interested in mistakes in which the mover chooses a losing move when a winning or drawish move is available.

Table 3. Mistake Potential for Losing Moves by Position.

	P_m/P	Average Tension
Ruleset D	13/46	19.57 ($\pm$0.09)
Ruleset E	6/46	10.51 ($\pm$0.07)

Given the set of 46 known positions P, we define a position to have "mistake potential" if it is not a proven losing position but does contain one or more moves whose game-theoretic value is a loss. Table 3 shows the total number of positions with mistake potential P_m for rulesets D and E. Ruleset D has many more positions with mistake potential (13) than Ruleset E (6).

Observing the ratio of losing moves to available moves in each position gives an indication of the *tension* at each position. The second column of Table 3 shows the average tension for both players over all positions, with 95% confidence intervals. Both of these measurements suggest that Ruleset D provides greater potential for non-expert players to make mistakes that produce a non-draw result than Ruleset E.

8 Conclusion

It is incredible that such confusion should exist in the literature over the rules of such a simple game as Mu Torere, especially since the briefest analysis reveals the majority of those rulesets described (A, B and C) to be trivially flawed. This highlights the ease with which errors can be introduced into official accounts of games, and the care with which *any* description of a game must be approached, even those from noted authorities.

Ruleset D – stipulating that the mover cannot win on the first two rounds – is the most prevalent ruleset found in the literature and the most promising ruleset according to the simple analysis performed above. It is conceptually simple, maximises the number of potential wining moves, and gives non-expert players ample opportunity to make mistakes (but it does show indications of strong first move advantage).

Ruleset E – stipulating that the piece being moved must be adjacent to an opponent's piece if it is being moved to the centre point – is a plausible alternative. However, it is conceptually less simple, imposes greater restriction on movement (allowing fewer potential winning moves) and provides less opportunity for non-expert players to make mistakes than Ruleset D.

Future work will involve a full strategic decomposition of Mu Torere and comparison of strategies induced by the two plausible rulesets D and E. It would also be useful to determine if the game is still played, and if so what rules are typically used.

Acknowledgements. This work was funded by the European Research Council as part of the Digital Ludeme Project (ERC CoG #771292).

References

1. Armstrong, A.: Maori Games and Hakas. A. H. and A. W. Reed, Wellington, New Zealand (1964)
2. Ascher, M.: Mu Torere: an analysis of a Maori game. Math. Mag. **60**(2), 90–100 (1987)
3. Ascher, M.: Ethnomathematics: A Multicultural View of Mathematical Ideas. Chapman & Hall, London (1991)
4. Bell, R.C.: Board and Table Games From Many Civilizations. Dover Publications Inc, New York, revised edn (1979)
5. Bell, R.C.: Discovering Old Board Games. Shire Publications, London, second edn (1980)
6. Best, E.: Notes on a peculiar game resembling draughts played by the Maori folk of New Zealand. Man **17**, 14–15 (1917)
7. Jelliss, G.: Mu Torere. Games Puzzles J. **2**(17), 302–303 (1999)
8. Pandolfini, B.: Treasure Chess: Trivia, Quotes, Puzzles, and Lore from the World's Oldest Game. Random House, New York (2007)
9. Reed, A.W.: An Illustrated Encyclopedia of Maori Life. A. H. and A. W. Reed, Wellington, New Zealand (1963)
10. Straffin, P.D.: Position Graphs for Pong Hau Kí and Mu Torere. Math. Mag. **68**(5), 382–386 (1995)
11. Straffin, P.D.: Corrected figure for position graphs for Pong Hau Kí and Mu Torere. Math. Mag. **69**(1), 65 (1996)

Measuring Board Game Distance

Matthew Stephenson[✉], Dennis J. N. J. Soemers, Éric Piette,
and Cameron Browne

Department of Advanced Computing Sciences, Maastricht University, Paul-Henri
Spaaklaan 1, 6229 Maastricht, EN, The Netherlands
{matthew.stephenson,dennis.soemers,eric.piette,
cameron.browne}@maastrichtuniversity.nl

Abstract. This paper presents a general approach for measuring distances between board games within the Ludii general game system. These distances are calculated using a previously published set of general board game concepts, each of which represents a common game idea or shared property. Our results compare and contrast two different measures of distance, highlighting the subjective nature of such metrics and discussing the different ways that they can be interpreted.

Keywords: Ludii · Concepts · Board games · Distance

1 Introduction

Ludii is a relatively recent general game system that contains a large variety of different board games [1]. This includes games with stochasticity and hidden information, alternating and simultaneous move formats, between one and sixteen players, piece stacking, team-based scoring, among many other features. Games in Ludii are described using ludemes, which are specific keywords that are defined within the Ludii Game Description Language (L-GDL). While individually simple, these ludemes can be combined to express complex game rules and mechanics. A previous study demonstrated that it is possible to use a game's ludemes to accurately predict the performance of various game-playing heuristics [2]. However, representing a game solely as the set of ludemes within its description can lead to issues.

Because these ludemes are often combined to express more complex rules and mechanics, their specific order and arrangement can dramatically alter a game's behaviour. Just looking at the ludemes that are present within a game's description is often not enough to understand their wider context and intended effect. For example, knowing that a game contains the move ludeme "hop" does not tell us whether this type of move can be done over friendly or enemy pieces. We are also not able to detect how frequently "hop" moves occur in typical play, compared to other types of moves. To address these and other similar limitations, a set of general board game concepts was proposed [3]. These concepts were created as a way to identify and extract higher-level features within each game, thus providing a more complete representation.

C. Browne et al. (Eds.): CG 2022, LNCS 13865, pp. 121–130, 2023.
https://doi.org/10.1007/978-3-031-34017-8_11

In this paper, we explore how these concepts can be used to calculate a measure of distance between any two games in Ludii. In addition to providing insight into the types of games currently available within Ludii, being able to measure the distance between two games has a variety of practical applications. One example is the ability to improve the performance of general game playing agents on unknown games, by identifying similar known games with pre-existing knowledge and results. This application has already motivated prior investigations into measuring game distance within other general game systems, including both the Stanford GGP framework [4,5] and the General Video Game AI framework [6–8]. Along with this, measures of game distance can be used by recommender systems to suggest new games to users based on their prior preferences and ratings [9,10], for transfer learning between similar games [11], to examine the variety of games within a specific subset [12], or for game reconstruction purposes [13].

The remainder of this paper is structured as follows. Section 2 describes the games and concepts that will be used. Section 3 provides visualisations of the overall distribution of concept values across all games within Ludii. Section 4 presents several different approaches for calculating distances between two games using their concept values, and provides two specific examples based on Cosine Similarity and Euclidean distance. Section 5 summarises and discusses the results of these two distance measures when applied to all pairs of games. Section 6 summarises our findings and suggests possibilities for future work.

2   Datasets

This section describes the two datasets that were used for this study, that of the games within Ludii and their associated concept values. These datasets were obtained from v1.3.2 of the Ludii database, which is publicly available online.[1]

2.1   Games

As of the time of writing, Ludii version 1.3.2 includes 1059 fully playable games. While some of these games also contain multiple options and rulesets for providing different variations of the same base rules, for the sake of simplicity we will only be considering the default version for each game as provided by Ludii.

Due to the fact that Ludii was developed as part of the Digital Ludeme Project [13], the majority of the board games it contains are traditional games that date back many hundreds of years. Even though a large assortment of modern abstract games have also been implemented within Ludii, this set of games is unlikely to be fully representative of the complete population of different games that exist within the modern board game industry. For example, Ludii does not currently include any card games, even though many modern board games often use cards in some capacity. Nevertheless, Ludii still contains a substantial variety of different abstract games, and an analysis of its full game library is worth performing.

---

[1] www.ludii.games/downloads/database-1.3.2.zip.

2.2   Concepts

Each concept represents a specific property of a game as a single numerical value. These concepts can be binary (e.g. if the game contains hidden information), discrete (e.g. the number of players), or continuous (e.g. the likelihood of a game ending in a draw). The Ludii database currently lists 499 distinct concepts with computed values for every game. Each of these concepts is associated with one of six categories based on what aspect of the game they represent, see Table 1.

Table 1. Concept Categories

Category	Examples	Count
Properties	Num Players, Stochastic, Asymmetric	21
Equipment	Mancala Board, Hex Tiling, Dice, Hand	74
Rules	Hop Capture, Turn Ko, Draw Frequency	302
Math	Multiplication, Intersection, Union	33
Visual	Go Style, Chess Component, Stack Type	42
Implementation	Playouts Per Second, Moves Per Second	27

Concepts also differ in the way they are computed. Compilation concepts can be calculated from just the game's description, and will be the same every time they are computed. Playout concepts instead require one or more game traces in order to compute them, and will often vary for the same game if different traces are used (although using a large number of traces can reduce this variance). For this study, 87 of the concepts used were playout concepts. These were computed for each game using 100 game traces generated from random play, with a maximum limit of 2500 moves per game trace (after which the result is a draw).

Due to the different value ranges that each concept can take, we decided to normalise each concept to the same scale. However, one issue with these concepts is that they are susceptible to having outlier values. For example, games played on implied "boards" of potentially unbounded size (e.g. Dominoes) are modelled in Ludii using extremely large static boards. Another example would be the game *Hermit* which, due to the unique way in which each player's score is represented, produces an average score variance of over 100 million points. Due to cases like these, directly applying Min-Max scaling to our concept values would overemphasise these outliers and make all other values irrelevant. To mitigate this problem, we first applied a bi-symmetric log transformation on all concept values [14], see Equation (1).

$$f(x) = \begin{cases} log_2(x+1) & x \geq 0 \\ -log_2(1-x) & x < 0 \end{cases} \qquad (1)$$

This transformation reduces the impact of the more extreme positive and negative values, while ensuring that binary concepts are unaffected. These new transformed values are then normalised using Min-Max scaling, to give the final concept values for each game. Thus our full dataset consists of 1059×499 matrix, detailing the concept values for each game.

3   Data Visualisation

Before calculating any game distances, we decided to first visualise the overall distribution of concept values across all games within Ludii. To do this, we applied t-distributed stochastic neighbor embedding (t-SNE) [15] to reduce our concept dataset to two dimensions, see Fig. 1. From this visualisation, we identified four distinct clusters of games. The orange cluster contains 207 games, the green cluster contains 147 games, the red cluster contains 105 games, and the blue cluster contains 600 games.

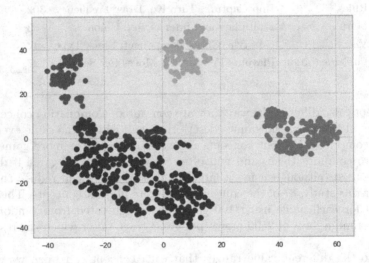

Fig. 1. Game concept dataset reduced to two dimensions using t-SNE. Points are coloured based on identified game clusters.

Analysing these clusters closer reveals some general trends within each group.

- The orange cluster contains all games with a Mancala Board, such as *Oware* or *Kalah*. These games are highly separated with a very distinct way of playing, leading to a lot of concepts that are unique to them such as the mechanic of sowing stones. It therefore makes sense that these games would form their own distinct cluster.
- The green cluster contains all games with both dice and a track for pieces to move along (e.g. *Backgammon* or *Snakes and Ladders*), as well as a few other games such as *EinStein Würfelt Nicht* and *So Long Sucker*. Despite the clear separation of the games in this cluster from the rest, this distinction is not the sole result of any one game element. Instead, it seems that such games would

be better characterised as those with a high degree of uncertainty, either because stochastic elements have a large impact on the game or because of other player's decisions.

- The red cluster contains all games with a "Threat" mechanism, predominantly used in Chess-like games when seeing if the king is in Check, as well as some other similar games such as *Ploy* and *Chaturaji*. Like the green cluster, this group of games is not characterised by a single concept. The key aspects that group these games together, seem to be the combination of a large number of pieces for each side, as well as complex movement rules for each individual piece.
- The blue cluster contains all other games which do not fall into the previous clusters.

From this, we can first see that the blue cluster is considerably larger than the others, making up more than half the total number of games. While this cluster could probably be split up further into sub-clusters, the separation is not as clear as for the clusters identified. Admittedly, the separation between the blue and red clusters is also not as distinct as the others, but is clear enough that we felt it worth mentioning. With the exception of the orange cluster, which is uniquely defined by the existence of the "Mancala Board" concept, there is no single concept that is responsible for any one cluster. Each cluster is instead defined by a combination of multiple concept values, making previous attempts to categorise games based on singular properties incapable of creating such a distinction. Based on these findings, it is clear that the recorded concept values provide significant information about a game's mechanics and properties, and are likely to be an effective basis for measuring the distance between two games.

4   Game Distance

When it comes to calculating the distances between games, each game is represented as a vector of 499 normalised concept values. Comparing two games can therefore be done using a variety of different vector distance/similarity measures. This includes Euclidean distance, Manhattan distance, Cosine similarity, Jaccard index, Jenson-Shannon divergence, among many other options.

Additional pre-processing can also be applied to adjust the importance of each concept. For example, Inverse Document Frequency (IDF) could be applied to all binary concepts, increasing the weights for concepts that occur in fewer games while decreasing the weights for those that occur in many. Each concept category could also be adjusted as a whole. For example, each concept could be scaled relative to the size of its category, resulting in each category carrying equal collective weighting. Some categories could even be excluded completely, as the importance of each category will likely vary based on the intended application. For example the "Visual" category of concepts has no bearing on actual gameplay, and would provide no benefit for the application of training a general game-playing agent.

Unfortunately, due the lack of any concrete benchmarks for measuring game distance, the effectiveness of these different measures and weight adjustments cannot be objectively evaluated without a specific application in mind. Due to the open-ended nature of this exploratory study, we decided to only compare the Cosine similarity and Euclidean distance measures, two of the most popular vector distance measures, without any additional pre-processing or weight adjustments. We encourage other researchers who wish to use this dataset for their own work, to experiment with these different distance measure approaches and identify what works best for their desired application.

The normalised Cosine distance between two games G_1 and G_2, with concept vectors denoted by $\vec{c}_1$ and $\vec{c}_2$ respectively, is given by Equation (2).

$$CosineDistance(G_1, G_2) = \frac{1}{2}\left(1 - \frac{\vec{c}_1 \cdot \vec{c}_2}{\|\vec{c}_1\|\|\vec{c}_2\|}\right) \tag{2}$$

The normalised Euclidean distance between two games, using the same terms in the previous equation and n denoting the total number of concepts, is given by Equation (3).

$$EuclideanDistance(G_1, G_2) = \frac{\|\vec{c}_1 - \vec{c}_2\|}{\sqrt{n}} \tag{3}$$

Both of these distance measures are normalised within the zero to one range, with one representing maximal difference and zero representing maximal similarity.

5   Results

Both Euclidean and Cosine distances were calculated between each possible pair of our 1059 games, giving a total of 560,211 unique game pairs for each distance measure.

Figure 2 presents a box plot visualisation of each distance measure across all game pairs. From this, we can see that the Euclidean distance is typically larger than the Cosine distance. The inter-quartile range for Cosine distance is situated almost exactly equally between its minimum and maximum values, while the inter-quartile range for Euclidean distance is skewed much closer to the maximum value. The difference between the median values of each distance measure (0.1358) is also much larger than the difference between their maximum values (0.0572).

Figure 3 provides further details on this observation, showing the general trend for each distance measure across all game pairs when ordered from smallest to largest along the x-axis. Looking at the 10% - 90% interpercentile range, represented by the area between the two green dashed lines, shows that the gradient of each distance measure is approximately equal. The most significant difference between the trends of these two distance measures is instead located at the extremities. While both distance measures begin at zero, the Euclidean

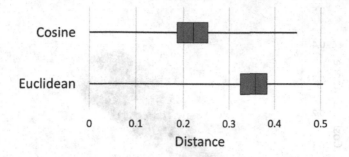

Fig. 2. Box plot for Cosine and Euclidean distances across all game pairs.

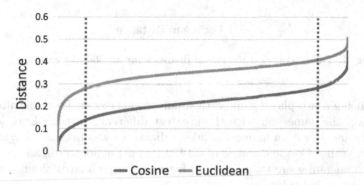

Fig. 3. Cosine and Euclidean distance trends, ordered by size along the x-axis.

distance initially increases far more rapidly than the Cosine distance. The opposite is true at the upper percentile end, with the Cosine distance taking a sharp increase to raise itself closer to the Euclidean distance.

Figure 4 visualises the differences between the Cosine and Euclidean distances for each individual game pair. From this we can see that there is a strong positive relationship between both distance measures, with a Pearson correlation coefficient of 0.7574. The overall upward curve of the points also reiterates our prior observation, that the rate at which the Euclidean distance increases is initially much higher, but then gradually falls to be more in line with that of the Cosine distance.

5.1   Discussion

While these statistical results provide a broad overview of how these distance measures compare across all games, we also explore how they differ with regard to specific game pairs. The game pair with the greatest difference in their Cosine and Euclidean distances (with a higher Cosine distance) was between *Magic Square* and *Rock-Paper-Scissors*, with a Cosine distance of 0.4438 and a Euclidean distance of 0.3036. Both of these games are relatively simple and share very little in common, with *Magic Square* being a logic puzzle and *Rock-Paper-*

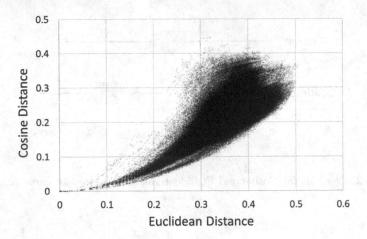

Fig. 4. The Cosine and Euclidean distance for all 560,211 game pairs.

Scissors being a two-player game with simultaneous moves. From the alternative perspective, the game pair with the greatest difference in their Euclidean and Cosine distances (with a higher Euclidean distance) was between *Tenjiku Shogi* and *Chex*, with a Cosine distance of 0.1429 and a Euclidean distance of 0.3792. Both of these games are very complex, featuring large boards along with many different pieces and rules.

Based on these two contrasting game pair examples, it initially seems that Cosine distance is greatest between simpler games with relatively few high-value concepts, while Euclidean distance is greatest between more complex games with a larger number of high-value concepts.

To dive deeper into how each distance measure compares across multiple game pairs, we looked at which game pairs received the largest values from each measure. One immediate observation was that the majority of the largest Cosine and Euclidean distances were between a logic puzzle, such as *Sudoku*, *Kakuro* or *Hoshi*, and non-puzzle game. This significant logic puzzle presence makes intuitive sense, as they are a unique type of game that would likely produce very distinct concept values.

For the Cosine distance measure, all of the 20 largest game pair distances involved either *Rock-Paper-Scissors*, *Morra* or *Aksadyuta*. All three of these games are very simple in terms of their rules, and are essentially purely random in terms of their outcome. These games contain no boards or pieces (at least in the traditional sense), and typically last for only a few moves. It would therefore make sense for these games to be highly distant from most other games, and further backs up our theory that the Cosine distance measure gives the greatest distance values to game pairs that include a simpler game with less common concepts.

For the Euclidean distance measure, all of the 20 largest game pair distances involved either *Beirut Chess*, *Ultimate Chess* or *Chex*. These games are all Chess variants with some unique twist on their rules. All three of these games would probably be considered more complex than the majority of other games in our dataset. This likely results in a substantial number of large value concepts for each game, again supporting the idea that the greatest Euclidean distances are typically given to game pairs that involve at least one high complexity game.

Based on these further comparisons, it appears that neither distance measure is inherently better than the other. It instead seems likely that each approach, as well as the other suggested measures that we did not explore deeper, has its own strengths, weaknesses and biases. The choice of which distance measure is most suitable is a highly subjective decision, and would depend on the intended application. We therefore reiterate our previous statement that multiple approaches should be tested and evaluated for each specific use-case, rather than attempting to develop a single correct measure of game distance.

6   Conclusion

In this paper, we have investigated the use of general board game concepts to measure the distance between pairs of games. Based on the same original concept dataset, two different measurements were proposed based on Cosine and Euclidean distance. Our results highlight the differences between these approaches. Cosine distance tended to give its highest values to pairs of relatively simple games with very few shared concepts. Euclidean distance on the other hand, appeared to include larger and more complex games in its highest value pairs, where any similarities between the games were outweighed by their differences. While we are unable to conclude which distance measure might be better or worse for any specific application, the contrasting outputs between these two distance measures illustrates the importance of experimenting with multiple distance measurement approaches.

Possible future work could involve a more complete analysis and summary of a larger range of distance measurements, as well as the effect that different pre-processing and weight adjustment techniques has on their outputs. Additional concepts could also be added to fill knowledge gaps within the existing dataset. One addition could be the inclusion of playout concepts based on alternative game traces, such as those produced from different game-playing agents or human players. Rather than adding more concepts, a more nuanced and critical look at the existing corpus may instead lead to the removal or weight reduction of certain items. It may not make sense to treat meaningful concepts, such as whether a game involves hidden or stochastic information, with as much importance as overly niche concepts, such as whether the game includes pieces that move backwards to the left. However, such alterations to the concept dataset are likely to be application specific, as adding or removing concepts for one purpose may inadvertently affect another.

Acknowledgements. This research is funded by the European Research Council as part of the Digital Ludeme Project (ERC Consolidator Grant #771292) led by Cameron Browne at Maastricht University's Department of Advanced Computing Sciences.

References

1. Piette, É., Soemers, D.J.N.J., Stephenson, M., Sironi, C.F., Winands, M.H.M., Browne, C.: Ludii - the ludemic general game system, In: Proceedings of the 24th European Conference on Artificial Intelligence (ECAI 2020) 325, pp. 411–418 (2020)
2. Stephenson, M., Soemers, D.J.N.J., Piette, É., Browne, C.: General game heuristic prediction based on ludeme descriptions In: Proceedings of the 2021 IEEE Conference on Games. IEEE, pp. 878–881 (2021)
3. Piette, É., Stephenson, M., Soemers, D.J.N.J., Browne, C.: General board game concepts. In: Proceedings of the 2021 IEEE Conference on Games (COG), pp. 932–939 (2021)
4. Jung, J.D.A., Hoey, J.: Distance-based mapping for general game playing. In: IEEE Conference on Games (COG), pp. 445–452 (2021)
5. Michulke, D., Schiffel, S.: Distance features for general game playing agents. In Proceedings of the 4th International Conference on Agents and Artificial Intelligence, pp. 127–136 (2012)
6. Bontrager, P., Khalifa, A., Mendes, A., Togelius, J.: Matching games and algorithms for general video game playing. AIIDE $12(1)$, 122–128 (2016)
7. Mendes, A., Togelius, J., Nealen, A.: Hyper-heuristic general video game playing. In: 2016 IEEE Conference on Computational Intelligence and Games (CIG), pp. 94–101 (2016)
8. Horn, H., Volz, V., Pérez-Liébana, D., Preuss, M.: MCTS/EA hybrid GVGAI players and game difficulty estimation In: 2016 IEEE Conference on Computational Intelligence and Games (CIG). IEEE Press, pp. 459–466 (2016)
9. Kim, J., Wi, J., Jang, S., Kim, Y.: Sequential recommendations on board-game platforms, Symmetry. $12(2)$, 210 2020
10. Zalewski, J., Ganzha, M., Paprzycki, M.: Recommender system for board games In: 2019 23rd International Conference on System Theory, Control and Computing (ICSTCC), pp. 249–254 (2019)
11. Soemers, D.J.N.J., Mella, V., Piette, É., Stephenson, M: Browne, C., Teytaud, O.: Transfer of fully convolutional policy-value networks between games and game variants. https://arxiv.org/abs/2102.12375 (2021)
12. Stephenson, M., et al.: A continuous information gain measure to find the most discriminatory problems for AI benchmarking, In: IEEE Congress on Evolutionary Computation (CEC) **2020**, pp. 92–99 (2020)
13. Browne, C.: Modern techniques for ancient games, In: IEEE Conference on Computational Intelligence and Games. Maastricht: IEEE Press, pp. 490–497 (2018)
14. Webber, J.B.W.: A bi-symmetric log transformation for wide-range data. Meas. Sci. Technol. $24(2)$, 027001 (2012)
15. van der Maaten, L., Hinton, G.: Visualizing data using t-SNE. J. Mach. Learn. Res. $9(86)$, 2579–2605 (2008)

Decision Making in Games and Puzzles

Improving Computer Play in Skat with Hope Cards

Stefan Edelkamp[✉]

Faculty of Electrical Engineering, Czech Technical University in Prague, Prague, Czechia
edelkste@fel.cvut.cz

Abstract. Skat is a strategy-rich card game, posing several combinatorial questions to advanced computer play for improved cooperation and competition. In this paper we advance trick-taking play by introducing hope cards, namely cards that excel not in all, but in the set of winnable worlds. Besides winning rate and scoring, we evaluate the strength of computer engine mainly based on the proximity of its results to the outcome of the open-card solver. This way, the opponents' and the overall playing strength of a state-of-the-art automated Skat player has been upgraded significantly, while keeping the response time small for swift play. For the first time, we won an online tournament with 20 series against a top German Skat player.

1 Introduction

Many board games like Checkers [24], Nine-Men-Morris [11] have been solved, or, as in Chess, Shogi or Go, computers outperform humans. Therefore, research attention has shifted to card games. After some variants of Poker have also been solved to a satisfying degree [1], trick-taking games like Skat [2] or Bridge [3,20] have been identified as current AI game playing challenges. One obstacle is that —facing the larger number of tricks and degree of uncertainty— the application of deep and reinforcement learning appears to be less apparent than in perfect-information games [26].

We selected Skat [25] as a fascinating card game *drosophila*, posing many combinatorial search challenges such as cooperative and adversarial behaviors (among the players), randomness (in the deal), and partial knowledge (due to hidden cards). With three players and 32 cards it is more compact than Bridge, but with the additional uncertainty of two cards in the Skat full of subtleties. From a combinatorial perspective, Skat has $n = \binom{32}{10}\binom{22}{10}\binom{12}{10} \approx 2.8$ quadrillion possible deals. Following the well-known *birthday paradox*, the probability p that at least one deal is repeated in k deals is $p = 1 - (\prod_{i=0}^{k-1}(n-i)/n^k)$; and fixing $p \geq 50\%$ yields $k \geq 40$ million games.

Published results [2,6] were too optimistic for playing against top humans. The Seeger-Fabian score includes terms for good opponent play, but one can also increase it by weakening opponent play. Even though lost and turn-around games are awarded, solely maximizing this score value favors the declarer. Applying ELO ranking [7] to measure the strength of the three AIs playing each other does not help: it is linked to

This work has been supported by the project CZ.02.1.01/0.0./0.0./16_019/0000765.

C. Browne et al. (Eds.): CG 2022, LNCS 13865, pp. 133–145, 2023.
https://doi.org/10.1007/978-3-031-34017-8_12

the Seeger-Fabian score. Moreover, ELO points awarded to one player were deducted from the others, so that the sum stays the same and average gains over a longer series of games cancel out.

The main contribution of this paper are *hope cards*, that may not perform well in all states in the belief space, but in the winnable ones. We apply new criteria to evaluate the strength of the computer players.

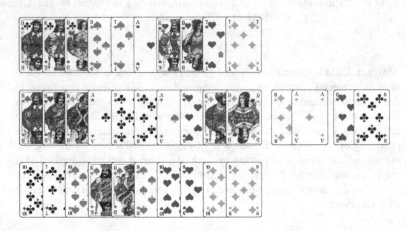

Fig. 1. Skat deal in a game of a human against two AIs, with $\diamond 8$ and $\diamond$ A in the skat, and the eights in $\heartsuit$ and $\clubsuit$ being discarded by the declarer in the middle.

2 Computer Skat

Skat[1] is a three-player imperfect information game played with 32 cards, a subset of the usual 52 cards Bridge deck. It shares similarities to Marias(ch) (played in Czech Republic and Slovakia) and Ulti (played in Hungary). The game of Skat is studied in many books [13–15, 17, 19, 21, 29]. The *double-dummy skat solver* (DDSS), a fast open card Skat game solver [18]. was extended to partial-observable game play using Monte-Carlo sampling. The lack of knowledge information exchange between the players has led to efforts to apply machine learning, e.g., in Skat [2, 10, 16, 22, 23, 27], Hearts [28], and Spades [4].

At the beginning of a game (see Fig 1), each player gets 10 cards, which are hidden to the other players. The remaining two cards, called the skat, are placed face down on the table.

After distributing the cards we have 4 stages of play:

bidding where the players are trying to become declarer by announcing lower bounds to the contract

---

[1] For the rules of Skat see www.pagat.com/schafk/skat.html.

game selection after taking the skat (optional) the winner of the bidding decides the game to be played

skat putting declarer discards two cards (if taken) and announces game to be played

trick-taking in clockwise order each player places a card on the table, and the winner of trick continues with next one.

Definition 1. *Let* $\mathcal{P} = \{p_0, p_1, p_2\}$ *be the players (p_0 is the declarer, p_1 and p_2 are the opponents). Let* $\mathcal{C} = \{c_0, \ldots, c_{31}\} = \{\clubsuit A, \ldots, \diamondsuit 7\}$ *be the set of all cards, and* $\mathcal{B}_p$ *be the belief space at the current moment of play with player p to move. Let the proposition* legal(p, s, c) *denote that a card* $c \in \mathcal{C}$ *is playable for player p in state* $s \in \mathcal{B}_p$, *proposition* knows(p, s) *denote that a state* $s \in \mathcal{B}_p$ *is consistent with the current knowledge of p, and* $\mathcal{K}_p = \{s \in \mathcal{B}_p \mid$ knows$(p, s)\}$ *be the set of consistent states.*

The knowledge is complex, it includes simpler aspects like cards being played, the eyes of tricks taken by the players, the cards being played but also if the player is certain whether or not a certain card is at the other player's hand or in the skat. It is updated with each card that is played.

3   Incomplete-Information Search

Random deals and hidden cards result in incomplete information and partial observations. In incomplete information search like in card games, we usually have many different *worlds* (alias states) in the belief space of the players. The number of possible worlds goes down with each card that is played and with each bit of information extracted from the tricks. There are two main search options for incomplete-information games, which —depending on the length of the play— are applicable mainly to endgame play. The core difference for two approaches for card selections put into quantifiers are as follows.

Open-Card Solvers: All Worlds – One Card $\forall_{s \in \mathcal{K}_p} \exists_{c \in \mathcal{C}}$ *legal*$(p, s, c) \wedge win(p, s, c)$ In this case, each individual world is evaluated, and different cards for different worlds may be proposed, so that there needs to be some fusion like a voting. In several cases the entire belief space is sampled, sometimes weighted with the probability of a card in a hand.

World Search: One Card – All Worlds $\exists_{c \in \mathcal{C}} \forall_{s \in \mathcal{K}_p}$ *legal*$(p, s, c) \Rightarrow win(p, s, c)$ This requires a play against all worlds in one search tree, branching on the location and selection of cards.

Both searches have their pros and cons, in term of the quality of the card recommendation, and the performance to calculate it, so that we have included both in our player.

All card playing software for trick-taking games like Bridge, Skat, Spades, etc. rely on a fast open-card game solver . The challenge is to cope with partial information due to the randomness in the deal and cards being hidden. Earlier approaches like *perfect-information Monte-Carlo sampling* (PIMC) [12] fuse the results of different calls to the open-card solver, as one card may be good in one world and a different card in another world. There are new developments on top of PIMC like *weighted Monte-Carlo sampling* [4] , which selects worlds within the belief space according to the deduced probabilities of players having a card.

Another recent suggestion is $\alpha\mu$ [3] that progress Pareto frontiers, attacking the fusion problem with dominance pruning of winning vectors over the chosen set of worlds. Still the apparent issue of information exchange among the opponent players remains, which is reflected also in bidding and playing conventions, and is hardly be met by open-card solvers, as they neither look nor progress the knowledge of the players.

In *complete belief-space enumeration* [5], *all* feasible worlds are evaluated for a open card analysis, which is feasible after a small number of tricks. Our voting system does not only feature won contracts, but includes points and additional bonus for higher contracts like Schneider and Schwarz.

Voting for Null games is a simple majority on the games that are won by the player to select a card. For trump games, we apply a slightly more complex voting, and let $score(s, c)$ be the game value for the score of the declarer in the open-card solver given s, *declarer-eyes*(s) the eyes collected by the declarer so far, and c the recommended cards that meet the optimal score. We selected the following voting scheme.

1. For $c \in C$ in s initialize $votes(c)$ with 0.
2. For each state s in the belief space $\mathcal{K}_p$ and legal card $c \in C$ to be played in s:
   opponent card Set $votes(c)$ by $120 - score(s, c)$, and
   - if $(score(s, c) \leq 60)$ then $votes(c) \leftarrow votes(c) + 10$.
   - if $(score(s, c) < 90)$ then $votes(c) \leftarrow votes(c) + 5$.
   - if $(declarer\text{-}eyes > 60 \wedge score(h, c) < 90)$ then $votes(c) \leftarrow votes(c) + 5$.
   declarer card increase $votes(c)$ by $score(s, c)$, and
   - if $(score(s, c) > 60)$ then $votes(c) \leftarrow votes(c) + 10$.
   - if $(score(s, c) \geq 90)$ then $votes(c) \leftarrow votes(c) + 20$.

Let $z = \Sigma_{c \in C}\, votes(c)$ and α some confidence threshold (e.g., $\alpha = 90\%$) As the voting recommendation we take $c^* = arg\, min_{c \in C}\, votes(c)$, but only for the case that $votes(c^*)/z \geq \alpha$. In case of large belief spaces we relaxed full enumeration to every k-th generated world. With $k = 5$ this lifted the size of the belief space considered for voting from 3 to 15 thousand states.

In *world search* (*Weltensuche*) only one card suggestion is extracted from searching a tree that branches on both a) the location (distribution of free cards into different hands and the skat) and b) the choice of cards to be played. The time spent for the analyses shows that it may be difficult to search the optimal scoring card on a full hand in a tournament, but it may become feasible to decide whether a game is won against all odds. We applied world search in smaller belief spaces, after some cards have been played already. This *worst-case* variant of *world search* was called *paranoia search* by [8,10] and is especially effective for the declarer, as s/he usually knows the skat, and has a significant information advantage over the two opponents, leading to a much smaller belief space, so that the search can also be invoked earlier in the search. The handling of the more complex knowledge in worst-case opponent worlds search is involved [8]. For both cases, knowledge inferred can be progressed down the tree, and restored on a backtrack. There is a compromise on the complexity of knowledge representation and reasoning and the speed for traversing the search tree.

We apply *move ordering* for traversing the search tree, as breaking ties can still be relevant to both the search tree size and the card recommendation. For example, the player may know that two cards are equally good, but the one hides some information better and may lead to inferior play of the opponents, maybe having less information. At first we applied heuristic guidelines like the length of a suit, then, we applied different ordering principles based on trump and suit play, as well as the current lead in the current trick. Breaking ties may also be relevant for following playing conventions among the opponent players e.g., to indicate which cards s/he does not have. Last but not least, we used the suggestion of the expert recommendation module as the first branch in the search tree. As some of these aspects are crucial to the performance of the system, we apply it only to the top levels of the search tree.

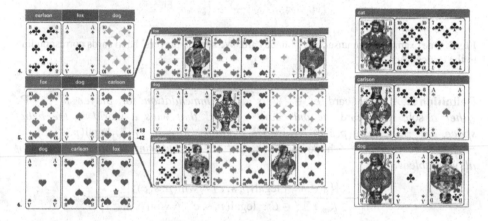

Fig. 2. Two examples of a successful and one example of an unsuccessful hope card. We see the players' hand cards corresponding to the critical trick. In the left example the context of played tricks and scores is provided with trick 5 being critical.

4   Hope Cards

Roughly speaking, a *hope card* may not win most possible worlds, but a large fraction of the winnable ones. The concept applies to many, if not all trick-taking games. Professional players interpret a hope card as a card, which is the only one that leads to victory and exploit the concept e.g. in issuing a *sharp 10*, which is played in the hope that the corresponding A is owned by the partner, and that the declarer has to obey the suit with a small card, see Fig. 4 (left, trump is clubs). For another example of a hope card, consider an endgame situation as shown in Fig. 4 (right). Assume three remaining cards for each player as shown, and that dog as the declarer has collected 40 points. Moreover, let ♠ A known to be in the hand of carlson and the location of the other cards being unclear. If cat issues ♣ 7 and carlson continues with ♣ K, then there is only one way that dog can win, if he plays ♣ Q, and tries to catch ♣ 10.

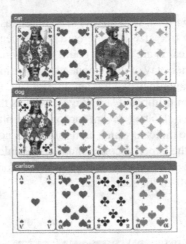

Fig. 3. One example of an unsuccessful hope card. We see the players' hand cards corresponding to the critical trick.

Definition 2. *A* hope card $c \in C$ *is a recommendation for player* $p \in P$; *either a* sole hope card *the only card* $c \in C$ *that wins a world in the belief space, i.e.,* $\exists_{s \in \mathcal{K}_p} \text{legal}(p, s, c) \wedge \text{win}(p, s, c)$, *and* $\forall_{s' \in \mathcal{K}_p} \forall_{c' \in \mathcal{C} \setminus \{c\}} \text{legal}(p, s', c') \Rightarrow \neg\text{win}(p, s', c')$; *or an* $f\%$ hope card *is a card* $c \in C$ *that wins at least fraction* f *of all winnable worlds:*

$$f \geq \frac{|\{s \in \mathcal{K}_p \mid \text{legal}(p, s, c) \wedge \text{win}(p, s, c)\}|}{|\{s \in \mathcal{K}_p \mid \exists c' \in \mathcal{C} : \text{legal}(p, s, c') \wedge \text{win}(p, s, c')\}|}$$

Instead of naively enumerating the states in the belief space, for hope cards we filter the ones that win. Hope cards are available for both declarer and opponent play in all three table positions (forehand, middle hand, rear hand). There are also hope cards for Schneider and Schwarz. Note the difference to *high-confidence cards* that have the highest vote, who also apply in worlds that do not win. An example of an unsuccessful hope card is presented in Fig. 4: $\diamondsuit$ 7 is correctly played by the declarer cat for game $\heartsuit$ at 52 eyes against 15, but, based on the unfortunate distribution 2:0 in $\diamondsuit$, it fails to succeed. The simple idea was to cut $\spadesuit$ and win the contract exceeding 60. Unfortunately, for the true distribution, the declarer makes no more tricks.

5   Evaluation

The player is written in C++, compiled with `gcc` version 9.3.0 (optimization level `-O2`). The AIs ran as fully independent programs on 1 core of an Intel Xeon Gold 6140 CPU @ 2.30GHz, which can play either on a server or replay games. In contrast to fully-observable games, sample sizes matter because of expected variance: even weak players beat top ones when provided a strong hand.

For Grand (after taking skat) $\spadesuit J, \heartsuit J, \heartsuit 10, \heartsuit Q, \heartsuit 9, \heartsuit 8, \clubsuit A, \clubsuit 10, \clubsuit 9,$ $\clubsuit 7, \heartsuit 7, \diamondsuit J$ world search finds the optimal declarer score of 61 in 5m5s (1m24s in the decision variant) by putting ♣7 and ♣9, and first issuing ♣A. If not cut, ♣10, followed by ♡7. One worst case play for the declarer is ♡8, ♡A, ♠A; ♡9, ♡A, ♠A; ♡10, ♣J, ♠10 with 59 eyes. The decision variant took 1m23s, also returning ♣A.

For hand ♣J, ♠J, ♡J, ♢J, ♣9, ♣8, ♣7, ♠9, ♠8, ♠7 with skat ♡7, ♢7 a game in clubs is won for the declarer in forehand position, but potentially lost in middle and in rear hand positions. Solving all three decision variants takes 16s in total and returns ♢J, ♠A, and ♠K, respectively. The best scores for the declarer are 63 (fore hand), 48 (middle hand), and 49 (rear hand). The ♢J was found less than 1s, the ♠A in 1m31s, and the ♠K in 3m15s.

Machine vs Machine Comparison We validated that the bidding strategy results in a plausible game choice compared to humans in the online server statistics: Table 1 shows that the AI plays more Grands and less Null Hand.

In replaying games, human bidding, game and skat selection can be compared to ones of the AI. To evaluate the strength of play, therefore, we took tens of thousands of human games and record the numbers of won and lost games for the human, open-card solver, and the computer.

Table 1. Distribution of all games and Null games: AI vs Human (latter statistics taken from our server on 180,948 games and 11,819 Null games being played).

Game	#Games AI	%	Human
Grand	22,447	31.09%	27.86%
Diamonds	6,948	9.62%	11.43%
Hearts	9,498	13.15%	14.66%
Spades	11,648	16.13%	17.15%
Clubs	15,871	21.98%	21.98%
Null	5,787	8.01%	6.86%

Game	#Games AI	%	Human
Null	2,843	49.12%	52.7%
Null Hand	376	.63%	2.1%
Null Ouvert	2,705	46.74%	40.6%
Null Hand Ouvert	202	3.49%	4.5%

Judging self-play of 3 identical players is demanding. Let $won(human, opencard, ai)$ be the numbers of games won in an experiment, with $human, opencard, ai \in \{0,1\}$, and $total = \sum_{(i,j,k)\in\{0,1\}^3} won(i,j,k)$. We use the following criteria to measure playing strength (*the higher the better*).

Win Rate the number of games won by the declarer divided by the number of played games (all but folded ones), i.e., Win-Rate $= (won(0,0,1) + won(0,1,1) + won(1,0,1) + won(1,1,1))/total$.

Accuracy Fraction of games matching the prediction of the open card solver (OCS), i.e., Acc $= (won(0,0,0) + won(0,1,1) + won(1,0,0) + won(1,1,1))/total$.

Combination Win Rate and Accuracy Optimizing the win rate leads to improvements of the declarer but not the opponents, which are better reflected with OCS accuracy. The closer the play is to the open-card solver, the better the opponent players communicate on their respective knowledge of the cards. To combine the two we use Combined $=$ (Win-Rate $+ 1 \cdot$ Acc)/2, Double $=$ (Win-Rate $+ 2 \cdot$ Acc)/3, Triple $=$ (Win-Rate $+ 3 \cdot$ Acc)/4, and Quadruple $=$ (Win-Rate $+ 4 \cdot$ Acc)/5.

Seeger-Fabian Officially (DSKV and ISPA) approved scoring of games, normalized to 36 games per series[2].

Initial Experiments with Base Player We use a database of 83,844 human expert games to evaluate our proposal. Initial self-playing results on human deals are shown in Table 2. We observer a Seeger-Fabian score of more than 1,000 together with a high win rate of more than 87%. The results at the first Skat Olympiad[3], however, finished with an overall value of only about 920, indicating that the Seeger-Fabian score obtained during self-play was not a perfect predictor of the computers' playing strength against top human players. The reason is a rather small open-card solver accuracy of 81.56% (highlighted in red), indicating weak opponent and overall play.

Table 2. Initial results in self-replaying 83,844 human deals (taken from [9]). The middle column shows the outcome of the open card solver. The left column refers to the human result.

Human wins	OCS wins	AI wins	# Games
0	0	0	4,021
0	0	1	4,184
0	1	0	302
0	1	1	4,770
1	0	0	5,132
1	0	1	9,567
1	1	0	1,048
1	1	1	52,876
68,623	58,996	71,397	81,900
N.d	n.d.	**1005.07**	Seeger-Fabian Score
83.78%	72.03%	**87.17%**	Win Rate
53,92	58,996	57,64	Win as in OCS
8,20	22,904	9,15	Lost as in OCS
62,121	81,900	66,79	Total as in OCS
75.85%	100.0%	81.56%	Acc

The Effect of Hope Cards Hope cards apply to all players in all table position, but they are more relevant for the improved play of the opponents, as more often they are at the edge of losing. We compared the play with and without hope cards. Table 3 shows that while the win rate and the Seeger-Fabian values increase without them, the open-card solver accuracy, our main criterion again is low. This manifests in the

---

[2] see https://second.wiki/wiki/skatabrechnung. ELO values for ranking players in Skat [7] dampen the effect of luck in the cards. It is based on series of games, that aligns with Seeger-Fabian. ELO is not applicable in self-playing one engine and but can generate highscore tables.

[3] https://32karten.de/forum/viewtopic.php?f=40&t=13063.

Table 3. Evaluating search with hope cards (world search at cards 7/10, endgame cards 13).

Setting	-Hope Card	+Hope Card
Time per Game	2.12 s	2.14 s
Seeger-Fabian	**986.67**	955.27
Acc	82.17%	**84.27%**
Winrate	**87.23%**	84.87%
Combined	**84.70%**	84.57%
Double	83.86%	**84.47%**
Triple	83.44%	**84.42%**
Quadruple	83.18%	**84.39%**

higher-order criteria, And indeed, the player utilizing hope cards is much stronger. The significant drop in the win rate is counter-balanced by playing closer to the open-card solver, leading to a considerable improvement of opponent and overall play. In order to compare the results with Table 2, in Table 4 we provide more detailed results of the new player. The open-card solver accuracy has improved.

Table 4. Replaying 83,844 human deals with three identical AIs. Computer bidding, game selection, and Skat putting, resulted in 81,673 games of various type (892 were folded). In the self play all kinds of hope cards were included. The central column refers to the outcome when analyzing the game with the open card solver (OCS). The left column refers to the original human result. World search started with cards 8 and 11, endgame (voting) with card 21.

Human wins	OCS wins	AI wins	# Games
0	0	0	4,848
0	0	1	3,356
0	1	0	340
0	1	1	4,676
1	0	0	6,015
1	0	1	7,998
1	1	0	1,152
1	1	1	53,288
68,453	59,457	69,436	81,673
918.18	N.d	**955.27**	Seeger-Fabian
83,8%	72,8%	**84,87%**	Win Rate
54,441	59,457	**5,796**	Win as in OCS
8,204	22,216	**1,086**	Lost as in OCS
62,645	81,673	**6,882**	Total as in OCS
76.7%	100.0%	84.27%	Acc

In a sensitivity analysis we varied the search parameters. Table 5 first looks at the effect of varying the voting endgame player, which includes hope card selection. As expected, if we start searching earlier on in the game, the time for the analysis increases. For the win rate and Seeger-Fabian value, we have a maximum at card 14, while for card 12 the combined value is largest. We judge the best compromise to start the endgame player at Card 13 (beginning of 5th trick).

Table 5. Varying card to start endgame with hope cards, world search card 8 (approximate World-Search-D(D)) 11 (World-Search-D(D)-opt).

End Game Card	14	13	12
Average Time per Game	1.87 s	2.14 s	3.6 s
Seeger-Fabian	**957.21**	955.27	956.40
Acc	83.95%	84.27%	84.21%
Winrate	**85.02%**	84.87%	84.95%
Combined	84.48%	84.57%	**84.58%**

In Table 6 we changed the card to start the worst-case world search for the declarer. Moving from the 7th to the 8th card, however, showed only a small change. Table 7 show our final results with further changes to bidding and trump play.

Table 6. Varying card to start world search with hope cards, endgame starts with Card 14.

World Search Card: 8/11	Time: 1.87 s per game
Seeger-Fabian	**957.21**
Acc	83.95%
Winrate	**85.02%**
Combined	84.48%
World Search Card: 7/10	Time: 4.9 s per game
Seeger-Fabian	955.10
Acc	84.26%
Winrate	84.86%
Combined	**84.56%**

Human-Machine Comparison In online play is crucial to have a transparent algorithm to generate a fair deal. We use the Mersenne-Twister from the std library to shuffle the cards, and validated that 10 million random deal match the the theoretical predictions implied by the hyper-geometrical distribution [13]. To our surprise the difference to the theory was smaller than by using overhand shuffling and real random numbers[4].

---

[4] taken from https://www.random.org.

Table 7. Final AI performance; Combined = **84.75%**.

Game	WonAI	LostAI	%Win	# Games
9	6,601	1,600	80.5%	10.04%
10	9,125	2,123	81.1%	13.77%
11	11,120	2,550	81.3%	16.74%
12	15,146	3,573	80.9%	22.92%
23	2,175	1,038	67.7%	3.93%
24	22,127	1,029	95.6%	28.35%
35	39	3	92.9%	0.05%
46	2,865	317	90.0%	3.90%
59	230	3	98.7%	0.29%
	69,428	12,236	**85.0%**	Winrate
Seeger-Fabian. **951.18**			Acc: 84.5%	

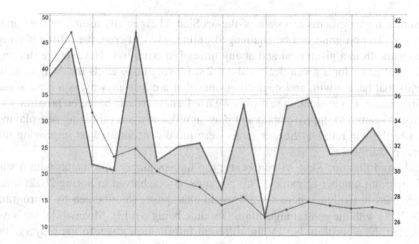

Fig. 4. Server statistics of top human Skat player playing a tournament against two (identical) AIs: 20 series were played over the period of one month: x axis is time, y-axis the Seeger-Fabian score (per series, green, and cumulative, red). The average Seeger score of was 24.2. (Color figure online)

Our AI played a online match of 20 series (a total of $19 \times 36 + 1 \times 6 = 690$ Games) in Feb/Mar 2022 against Rainer Gößl, a top Skat player from Germany. In international tournaments at least 10 series a 36 games are played. Kermit, a Skat engine by Michael Buro reported Seeger score of 1,200 on both sides playing Rainer Gößl [2]. With 49 individual games (as acknowledged by the author) the sample size was seemingly small. In the statistics displayed in Fig. 4 we see the human player's performance goes down, suggesting an increase of the program's playing strength during this time span.

About 28.4% of the games were taken on as declarer, 170 were won, and 26 lost, On average one game was folded per series, the average playing time per series was 21.2 min. In this series the AIs performed much better than Rainer Gößl with his score $24.82 \cdot 36 = 893.52$ in the Seeger-Fabian system, and the first engine where he scored less than 1,100 points. Even though the performance is remarkable, it has to be dealt with care. We are **not** claiming that the computer already plays Skat superior to Rainer Gößl, nor to other top human players. The number of games played is statistically more relevant than the experiment of Buro, but it is only one unofficial match against one human player. Even in 20 series, still there is a large factor of luck in the cards. In earlier matches, Rainer Gößl achieved better scores against our AIs and against human players. The match was played over a month and was also not controlled by an arbiter. Moreover, there is at least one other top player on our server, who maintains a positive comparison against the computer players.

6 Conclusion

We presented improvements to a state-of-the-art Skat AI especially useful for the opponent players. The program can be challenged online, and can continue offline playing a human game from a given deal and at any time of interruption. The average running time of a full game for a given deal is about 2 s. Playing hope cards that win most of the worlds that have a win, and neglecting ones that are lost anyway, is a natural but powerful concept. For evaluating self-play we used a new criteria based on proximity to the open-card games to improve opponent play significantly, as optimizing self-playing criteria like the win rate and Seeger score were more concentrated on improving the declarers' performance.

We showed that our Skat AI *can* beat a top human player in a match with a statistically relevant number of games. This advance, also achieved in Spring 2022, links to the progress in Bridge, where several world champions were beaten by a program called NOOK, with the central algorithmic module being $\alpha\mu$ [3]. Meanwhile, we have implemented the algorithm, but by the different information given to the players and scoring systems, we could not make it as effective for Skat.

Acknowledgements. We thank Rainer Gößl for his match against the Skat AIs, and Stefan Meinel for his insights when annotated his play against the AIs on the server. We also thank the players of the First International Skat Competition for their participation.

References

1. Bowling, M., Burch, N., Johanson, M., Tammelin, O.: Heads-up limit hold'em poker is solved. Commun. ACM **60**(11), 81–88 (2017)
2. Buro, M., Long, J.R., Furtak, T., Sturtevant, N.R.: Improving state evaluation, inference, and search in trick-based card games. In IJCAI, pp. 1407–1413 (2009)
3. Cazenave, T., Ventos, V.: The $\alpha\mu$ search algorithm for the game of bridge. CoRR, abs/1911.07960 (2019)
4. Cohensius, G., Meir, R., Oved, N., Stern, R.: Bidding in spades. In ECAI, pp. 387–394 (2020)

5. Edelkamp, S.: Challenging human supremacy in Skat. In: Proceedings of the 12th International Symposium on Combinatorial Search, SOCS 2019, Napa, California, pp. 52–60 (2019)
6. Edelkamp, S.: Representing and reducing uncertainty for enumerating the belief space to improve endgame play in Skat. In ECAI, pp. 395–402 (2020)
7. Edelkamp, S.: ELO system for Skat and other games of chance. CoRR, abs/2104.05422 (2021)
8. Edelkamp, S.: Knowledge-based paranoia search in trick-taking. CoRR, abs/2104.05423 (2021)
9. Edelkamp, S.: On the power of refined Skat selection. CoRR, abs/2104.02997 (2021)
10. Furtak, T.M.: Symmetries and Search in Trick-Taking Card Games. PhD thesis, University of Alberta (2013)
11. Gasser, R.: Harnessing Computational Resources for Efficient Exhaustive Search. PhD thesis, ETH Zürich (1995)
12. Ginsberg, M.: Step toward an expert-level Bridge-playing program. In IJCAI, pp. 584–589, (1999)
13. Gößl, R.: Der Skatfuchs - Gewinnen im Skatspiel mit Mathematische Methoden. Selfpublisher. Dämmig, Chemnitz, Available from the Author or via DSKV Altenburg (2019)
14. Grandmontagne, S.: Meisterhaft Skat spielen. Krüger Druck+Verlag, Selfpublisher (2005)
15. Harmel, S.: Skat-Zahlen. Klabautermann-Verlag, Pünderich (Mosel) (2016)
16. Keller, T., Kupferschmid, S.: Automatic bidding for the game of Skat. In KI, pp. 95–102 (2008)
17. Kinback, T.: Skat-Rätsel - 50 lehrreiche Skataufgaben mit Lösungen und Analysen. Books on Demand, Norderstedt (2007)
18. Kupferschmid, S., Helmert, M.: A Skat player based on Monte-Carlo simulation. In Computers and Games, pp. 135–147 (2006)
19. Lasker, E.: Strategie der Spiele - Skat. August Scherl Verlag, Berlin (1938)
20. Li, J., Zanuttini, B., Cazenave, T., Ventos, V.: Generalisation of alpha-beta search for AND-OR graphs with partially ordered values. In IJCAI, pp. 4769–4775. ijcai.org (2022)
21. Quambusch, M.: Gläserne Karten - Gewinnen beim Skat. Stomi Verlag, Schwerte Rau Verlag, Düsseldorf (1990)
22. Rebstock, D., Solinas, C., Buro, M.: Learning policies from human data for Skat. CoRR, abs/1905.10907 (2019)
23. Rebstock, D., Solinas, C., Buro, M., Sturtevant, N.R.: Policy based inference in trick-taking card games. CoRR, abs/1905.10911 (2019)
24. Schaeffer, J., et al.: Solving checkers. In IJCAI, pp. 292–297 (2005)
25. Schettler, F., Kirschbach, G.: Das große Skatvergnügen. Urania Verlag, Leipzig, Jena, Berlin (1988)
26. Silver, D., et al.: Mastering the game of Go with deep neural networks and tree search. Nature, 529, 484–489 (2016)
27. Solinas, C., Rebstock, D., Buro, M.: Improving search with supervised learning in trick-based card games. CoRR, abs/1903.09604 (2019)
28. Sturtevant, N.R., White, A.M.: Feature Construction for Reinforcement Learning in Hearts. In: van den Herik, H.J., Ciancarini, P., Donkers, H.H.L.M. (eds.) CG 2006. LNCS, vol. 4630, pp. 122–134. Springer, Heidelberg (2007). https://doi.org/10.1007/978-3-540-75538-8_11
29. Wergin, J.P.: Wergin on Skat and Sheepshead. Mc. Farland, USA, Wergin Distributing (1975)

Batch Monte Carlo Tree Search

Tristan Cazenave[✉]

LAMSADE, Université Paris Dauphine - PSL, CNRS, Paris, France
Tristan.Cazenave@dauphine.fr

Abstract. Making inferences with a deep neural network on a batch of states is much faster with a GPU than making inferences on one state after another. We build on this property to propose Monte Carlo Tree Search algorithms using batched inferences. Instead of using either a search tree or a transposition table we propose to use both in the same algorithm. The transposition table contains the results of the inferences while the search tree contains the statistics of Monte Carlo Tree Search. We also propose to analyze multiple heuristics that improve the search: the μ FPU, the Virtual Mean, the Last Iteration and the Second Move heuristics. They are evaluated for the game of Go using a MobileNet neural network.

1 Introduction

Monte Carlo Tree Search (MCTS) using a combined policy and value network is used for complex two-player perfect information games such as the game of Go [18]. MCTS is also used for many other games and problems [1]. We propose multiple optimizations of MCTS in the context of its combination with deep neural networks. With current hardware such as GPU or TPU it is much faster to batch the inferences of a deep neural network rather than to perform them sequentially. We give in this paper MCTS algorithms that make inferences in batches and some heuristics to improve them. The use of a transposition table to store evaluations in combination with a tree, the Virtual Mean, the Last Iteration and the Second Move heuristics are new. The search algorithms are evaluated for the game of Go.

The second section deals with existing work on MCTS for games. The third section presents our algorithms. The fourth section details experimental results.

2 Monte Carlo Tree Search

MCTS has its roots in computer Go [10]. A theoretically well founded algorithm is Upper Confidence Bounds for Trees (UCT) [13]. Dealing with transpositions in UCT was addressed with the UCD algorithm [16]. The authors tested various ways to deal with transpositions and gave results for multiple games in the context of General Game Playing (GGP).

The GRAVE algorithm [3] is successful in GGP. It uses a transposition table as the core of the tree search algorithm. Entries of the transposition table contain various kind of information such as the statistics on the moves as well as the generalized All Moves As First (AMAF) statistics. It does not use the UCB bandit anymore but an improvement of RAVE [12].

C. Browne et al. (Eds.): CG 2022, LNCS 13865, pp. 146–162, 2023.
https://doi.org/10.1007/978-3-031-34017-8_13

PUCT combines MCTS with neural networks [17]. The neural networks are used to evaluate states and to give probabilities to possible moves. PUCT is currently used in games such as Go [19] and Shogi [18]. It was used in the AlphaGo program [17] as well as in its descendants AlphaGo Zero [19] and Alpha Zero [18].

The PUCT bandit is:

$$V(s, a) = Q(s, a) + c \times P(s, a) \times \frac{\sqrt{N(s)}}{1 + N(s, a)}$$

Where $P(s, a)$ is the probability of move a to be the best move in state s given by the policy head of the neural network, $N(s)$ is the total number of descents performed in state s and $N(s, a)$ is the number of descents for move a in state s.

Many researchers have replicated the Alpha Zero experiments and also use the PUCT algorithm [6, 11, 15, 21, 23].

In this paper we improve the PUCT algorithm parallelizing the evaluation of a batch of leaves. We also propose modification to the search algorithm that improve its results.

2.1 Parallelization of MCTS

As we propose to improve PUCT parallelizing the inferences at the leaves of the search tree, we briefly recall previous works on the parallelization of MCTS.

Three different ways to parallelize MCTS were first proposed in 2007 [7]. They were further renamed Root Parallelization, Leaf Parallelization and Tree Parallelization [8, 9]. Root Parallelization simply performs multiple independent tree searches in parallel. Leaf Parallelization performs multiple playouts in parallel at each leaf. Tree Parallelization makes multiple threads descend a shared tree in parallel.

In this paper we do not use multiple CPUs to perform playouts in parallel as in previous work but we use tools such as the virtual loss that were designed for the parallelization of MCTS on CPUs.

2.2 The Virtual Loss

As we propose in this paper the Virtual Mean heuristic we describe the related works on the virtual loss heuristic as the Virtual Mean improves on the virtual loss.

The virtual loss enables to make multiple descents of the tree in parallel when the results of the evaluations at the leaves are not yet known and the tree has not yet been updated with these results. It is used in Tree Parallelization. The principle is very simple since it consists in adding a predefined number of visits to the moves that are played during the tree descent.

The virtual loss is used in most of the Go programs including AlphaGo [17] and ELF [21].

A related algorithm is the Watch the Unobserved heuristic [14]. It counts the number of playouts that have been initiated but not yet completed, named unobserved samples and includes them in the bandit. It gives good results on Atari games. It is quite different from our approach since it uses standard UCT when we use PUCT with neural networks and since the principle is to add unobserved samples to the number of simulations in the UCT bandit not to modify the Q value.

The virtual loss is also used in TDS-UCT [24] together with a message passing system that addresses load balancing. TDS-UCT was applied to molecular design with success.

2.3 Batched Inferences

Using batch forwards of the neural network to evaluate leaves of the search tree and find the associated priors given by the policy head is current practice in many game programs [6,11,15,21,23]. Usually a set of leaves is generated using multiple tree descents. The diversity of the leaves is obtained thanks to the virtual loss. The neural network is run on a single batch of leaves and the results are incorporated into the search tree, backing up the evaluations up to the root. This algorithm is much worse than sequential PUCT when using the same number of evaluations. However as it makes much more evaluations than sequential PUCT in the same time it recovers strength when given the same time.

We propose to improve on this algorithm simulating sequential PUCT with batched inferences. The idea is to first evaluate a set of heuristically chosen leaves, to put the evaluations in a transposition table, and then to use this transposition table in a sequential PUCT algorithm that uses a part of the leaves. It does not use for the sequential PUCT as many leaves as the algorithms used by the previous programs but it is much better because it simulates sequential PUCT and it is much faster than sequential PUCT.

2.4 First Play Urgency

In this paper we propose to evaluate different options for the First Play Urgency (FPU). We recall the previous works on the FPU.

Vanilla UCT begins by exploring each arm once before using UCB. This behavior was improved with the FPU [22]. A large FPU value ensures the exploration of each move once before further exploitation of any previously visited move. A small FPU ensures earlier exploitation if the first simulations lead to an urgency larger than the FPU.

In more recent MCTS programs using playouts, FPU was replaced by RAVE [12] which uses the AMAF heuristic so as to order moves before switching gradually to UCT. RAVE was later improved with GRAVE which has good results in GGP [2,20].

In AlphaGo [17], the FPU was revived and is set to zero when the evaluations are between -1 and 1. We name this kind of FPU the constant FPU. It has deficiencies. When the FPU is too high, all possible moves are tried at a node before going further below in the state space and this slows down the search and makes it shallow. When the FPU is too low, the moves after the best move are only tried after many simulations and the search does not explore enough. When the constant is in the middle of the range of values as in AlphaGo, both deficiencies can occur, either when the average of the evaluations is below the constant or is greater than the constant.

In other programs such as ELF [21] the FPU is set to the best mean of the already explored moves. This is better than using a constant FPU since the best mean is related to the mean of the other moves. It encourages exploration.

We propose another FPU the μ FPU which uses instead the average of all explored moves.

3   The Batch MCTS Algorithm

In this section we describe the Batch MCTS algorithm and its refinements. We first explain how we deal with trees and transposition table. We also give the main algorithm and the two ways to update statistics. We then detail the proposed heuristics: the μ FPU, the Virtual Mean, the Last Iteration and the Second Move.

3.1   Trees and Transposition Table

The principle of Batch MCTS is to simulate a sequential MCTS using batched evaluations. In order to do so it separates the states that have been evaluated from the search tree. We name the usual transposition table used in current program as the usual transposition table and the transposition table used in Batch MCTS as the value transposition table.

The value transposition table only contains the evaluations of the states. The search tree is developed as in usual sequential MCTS. When the algorithm reaches a leaf it looks up the state in the value transposition table. If it is present then it backpropagates the corresponding evaluation. If it is not in the value transposition table it sends back the Unknown value. The algorithm has two options: developing the tree or building the batch. When it develops the tree it stops the search as soon as it reaches a leaf which is not in the value transposition table and an Unknown value is returned. When it builds the batch it continues searching when a leaf is not in the value transposition table and an Unknown value is returned in order to fill the batch. In this case it adds the state associated to the leaf to the next batch of states, and updates statistics in a different way than when developing the tree (see Sect. 3.3).

Batch MCTS increases the number of tree descents for a given budget of inferences compared to usual MCTS with a usual transposition table in place of a tree. An entry in the value transposition table of Batch MCTS can serve as a leaf multiple times. Batch MCTS will redevelop a subtree multiple times with only a small increase in search time since the costly part of the algorithm is the evaluation of the states and since previous states evaluations are cached in the transposition table. Redeveloping shared subtrees makes the statistics of the moves not biased by reaching some already developed states from a different path. In this case usual MCTS with a usual transposition table will go directly to a leaf of the subtree instead of redeveloping it since the subtree is in the usual transposition table.

Batch MCTS uses one value transposition table and two trees. The value transposition table records for each state that has been given as input to the neural network the evaluation of the state and the priors for the moves of the state. The first tree records the statistics required to calculate the bandit and the children that have already been explored. The second tree is a copy of the first tree used to build the next batch of states that will be then given to the neural network.

Algorithm 1. The GetMove algorithm

1: Function GetMove (s, B)
2:      **for** $i \leftarrow 1$ to B **do**
3:          GetBatch(s)
4:          $out \leftarrow$ Forward $(batch)$
5:          PutBatch (s, out)
6:      **end for**
7:      $t \leftarrow tree.node(s)$
8:      **return** $argmax_m(t.p(s, m))$

3.2 The Main Algorithm

The main algorithm is the GetMove algorithm (Algorithm 1). It calls the GetBatch algorithm at line 3 (see Algorithm 2) that descends the second tree many times in order to fill the batch. In the GetBatch algorithm the BatchPUCT algorithm is called with the $True$ value (line 5 of GetBatch) since the goal is to build the batch. The next instruction in the GetMove algorithm is to run a forward pass of the neural network on the batch of states (line 4 of GetMove). The next algorithm called by the GetMove algorithm is the PutBatch algorithm (see Algorithm 3) that puts the results of the inferences in the transposition table and then updates the main tree. The BatchPUCT algorithm is called with the $False$ value in the PutBatch algorithm (lines 5 and 7) since the goal is to simulate sequential PUCT. GetBatch, forward and PutBatch are called B times. In the end the GetMove algorithm returns the most simulated move of the main tree.

Algorithm 2. The GetBatch algorithm

1: Function GetBatch (s)
2:      $treeBatch \leftarrow tree$
3:      $i \leftarrow 0$
4:      **while** batch is not filled **and** $i < N$ **do**
5:          BatchPUCT $(s, True)$
6:          $i \leftarrow i + 1$
7:      **end while**

Algorithm 2 gives the main algorithm to build the batch. In order to present the algorithm simply we assume a copy of the main tree to treeBatch which is then used and modified in order to build the batch. A more elaborate implementation is to separate inside a node the statistics of the main tree and the statistics made during the building of the batch. A global stamp can be used to perform a lazy reinitialization of the batch statistics at each new batch build.

Algorithm 3. The PutBatch algorithm

1: Function PutBatch (s, out)
2:     **for** $o \in out$ **do**
3:         add o to the Transposition Table
4:     **end for**
5:     $res \leftarrow$ BatchPUCT ($s, False$)
6:     **while** $res \neq Unknown$ **do**
7:         $res \leftarrow$ BatchPUCT ($s, False$)
8:     **end while**

Algorithm 4 gives the main PUCT search algorithm using a transposition table of evaluated states and the two trees. The GetBatch boolean is used to make the distinction between the first option to develop the tree and the second option to build the batch. The first tree is the main search tree while the second tree is only used to build the batch.

3.3   Updating the Statistics

Algorithm 5 gives the usual way of updating the statistics used for the main tree. Algorithm 6 gives the update of the statistics for the second tree. It updates the statistics as usual when an evaluation is backpropagated, but it updates the statistics differently when an Unknown value is backpropagated. In this case it can either use the usual virtual loss or the Virtual Mean that will be described later.

3.4   The μ FPU

The way we deal with the FPU is to set it to the average mean of the node (using the statistics of all the explored moves). We name this kind of FPU the μ FPU.

3.5   The Virtual Mean

Tree parallel MCTS uses a virtual loss to avoid exploring again and again the same moves when no new evaluation is available. We propose the Virtual Mean as an alternative to the virtual loss. The Virtual Mean increases the number of simulations of the move as in the virtual loss but it also adds the mean of the move times the virtual loss to the sum of the evaluations of the move in order to have more realistic statistics for the next descent.

Algorithm 6 gives the different ways of updating the statistics of a node. The vl variable is the number of virtual losses that are added to a move when it leads to an unknown leaf. A value greater than one will encourage more exploration and will avoid resampling again and again the same unknown leaf. The value is related to the maximum number of samples allowed in the GetBatch algorithm (the variable N in Algorithm 2). A low value of N will miss evaluations and will not completely fill the batch. A large value of N will better fill the batch but will take more time to do it. Increasing vl enables to fill the batch with more states for the same value of N. However a too large value of vl can overlook some states and decrease the number of visited nodes in

Algorithm 4. The BatchPUCT algorithm

1: Function BatchPUCT (s, $GetBatch$)
2:    **if** isTerminal (s) **then**
3:        **return** Evaluation (s)
4:    **end if**
5:    **if** $GetBatch$ **then**
6:        $t \leftarrow treeBatch$
7:    **else**
8:        $t \leftarrow tree$
9:    **end if**
10:   **if** $s \notin t$ **then**
11:      **if** $s \notin$ transposition table **then**
12:         **if** $GetBatch$ **then**
13:           add s to the batch
14:         **end if**
15:         **return** Unknown
16:      **else**
17:         add s to t
18:         **return** value (s)
19:      **end if**
20:   **end if**
21:   $bestScore \leftarrow -\infty$
22:   **for** $m \in$ legal moves of s **do**
23:      $\mu \leftarrow FPU$
24:      **if** $t.p(s,m) > 0$ **then**
25:         $\mu \leftarrow \frac{t.sum(s,m)}{t.p(s,m)}$
26:      **end if**
27:      $bandit \leftarrow \mu + c \times t.prior(s,m) \times \frac{\sqrt{t.p(s)}}{1+t.p(s,m)}$
28:      **if** $bandit > bestScore$ **then**
29:         $bestScore \leftarrow bandit$
30:         $bestMove \leftarrow m$
31:      **end if**
32:   **end for**
33:   $s_1 \leftarrow$ play (s, $bestMove$)
34:   $res \leftarrow$ BatchPUCT (s_1, $GetBatch$)
35:   **if** $GetBatch$ **then**
36:      UpdateStatisticsGet (res, $bestMove$, s, t)
37:   **else**
38:      UpdateStatistics (res, $bestMove$, s, t)
39:   **end if**
40:   **return** res

---

the main search tree. The res value is the evaluation returned by the tree descent, m is the move that has been tried in the descent, s is the state and t is the second tree.

When the Virtual Mean option is used, the sum of the evaluations of the move and the sum of the evaluations of the node are both increased by $vl \times \mu$ where μ is the average evaluation of the move. It will give a better insight of the real average of the move after the backpropagation than using the virtual loss alone.

Algorithm 5. The UpdateStatistics algorithm for the main tree

---

1: Function UpdateStatistics (res, m, s, t)
2:    **if** $res \neq Unknown$ **then**
3:       $t.p(s, m) \leftarrow t.p(s, m) + 1$
4:       $t.sum(s, m) \leftarrow t.sum(s, m) + res$
5:       $t.p(s) \leftarrow t.p(s) + 1$
6:       $t.sum(s) \leftarrow t.sum(s) + res$
7:    **end if**

Algorithm 6. The UpdateStatisticsGet algorithm

1: Function UpdateStatisticsGet (res, m, s, t)
2:    **if** $res = Unknown$ **then**
3:       $\mu \leftarrow \frac{t.sum(s,m)}{t.p(s,m)}$
4:       **if** $VirtualLoss = True$ **then**
5:          $t.p(s, m) \leftarrow t.p(s, m) + vl$
6:          $t.p(s) \leftarrow t.p(s) + vl$
7:       **else if** $VirtualMean = True$ **then**
8. $t.p(s, m) \leftarrow t.p(s, m) + vl$
9:          $t.sum(s, m) \leftarrow t.sum(s, m) + vl \times \mu$
10:         $t.p(s) \leftarrow t.p(s) + vl$
11:         $t.sum(s) \leftarrow t.sum(s) + vl \times \mu$
12:       **end if**
13:    **else**
14:       $t.p(s, m) \leftarrow t.p(s, m) + 1$
15:       $t.sum(s, m) \leftarrow t.sum(s, m) + res$
16:       $t.p(s) \leftarrow t.p(s) + 1$
17:       $t.sum(s) \leftarrow t.sum(s) + res$
18:    **end if**

Using the Virtual Mean is the equivalent for PUCT of Watch the Unobserved for the UCT tree policy [14].

3.6 The Last Iteration

At the end of the GetMove algorithm, many states are evaluated in the transposition table but have not been used in the tree. In order to gain more information it is possible to continue searching for unused state evaluations at the price of small inacurracies.

The principle is to call the BatchPUCT algorithm with GetBatch as True as long as the number of Unknown values sent back does not reach a threshold.

The descents that end with a state which is not in the transposition table do not change the statistics of the moves since they add the mean of the move using the Virtual Mean. The descents that end with an unused state of the transposition table modify the statistics of the moves and improve them as they include statistics on more states.

The Last Iteration algorithm is given in Algorithm 7. The U variable is the number of visited unknown states before the algorithm stops.

Algorithm 7. The GetMoveLastIteration algorithm

1: Function GetMoveLastIteration (s, B)
2:    **for** $i \leftarrow 1$ to B **do**
3:        GetBatch(s)
4:        $out \leftarrow$ Forward $(batch)$
5:        PutBatch (s, out)
6:    **end for**
7:    $nbUnknown \leftarrow 0$
8:    $treeBatch \leftarrow tree$
9:    **while** $nbUnknown < U$ **do**
10:       $res \leftarrow$ BatchPUCT $(s, True)$
11:       **if** $res = Unknown$ **then**
12:           $nbUnknown \leftarrow nbUnknown + 1$
13:       **end if**
14:    **end while**
15:    $t \leftarrow treeBatch.node(s)$
16:    **return** $argmax_m(t.p(s, m))$

Algorithm 8. The GetMoveSecondHeuristic algorithm

1: Function GetMoveSecondHeuristic (s, B)
2:    $b \leftarrow size(batch)$
3:    **for** $i \leftarrow 0$ to B **do**
4:        GetBatchSecond $(s, B \times b, i \times b)$
5:        $out \leftarrow$ Forward $(batch)$
6:        PutBatchSecond $(out, B \times b, i \times b)$
7:    **end for**
8:    $t \leftarrow tree$
9:    $best \leftarrow bestMove_m(t.p(s, m))$
10:   $\mu \leftarrow \frac{t.sum(s, best)}{t.p(s, best)}$
11:   $secondBest \leftarrow secondBestMove_m(t.p(s, m))$
12:   $\mu_1 \leftarrow \frac{t.sum(s, secondBest)}{t.p(s, secondBest)}$
13:   **if** $\mu_1 > \mu$ **then**
14:       **return** $secondBest$
15:   **else**
16:       **return** $best$
17:   **end if**

3.7   The Second Move Heuristic

Let n_1 be the number of playouts of the most simulated move at the root, n_2 the number of playouts of the second most simulated move, b the total budget and rb the remaining budget. If $n_1 > n_2 + rb$, it is useless to perform more playouts beginning with the most simulated move since the most simulated move cannot change with the remaining budget. When the most simulated move reaches this threshold it is more useful to completely allocate rb to the second most simulated move and to take as the best move the move with the best mean when all simulations are finished.

Algorithm 9. The BatchSecond algorithm

1: Function BatchSecond $(s, GetBatch, budget, i, root)$
2:    **if** isTerminal (s) **then**
3:        **return** Evaluation (s)
4:    **end if**
5:    **if** $GetBatch$ **then**
6:        $t \leftarrow treeBatch$
7:    **else**
8:        $t \leftarrow tree$
9:    **end if**
10:    **if** $s \notin t$ **then**
11:        **if** $s \notin$ transposition table **then**
12:            **if** $GetBatch$ **then**
13:                add s to the batch
14:            **end if**
15:            **return** Unknown
16:        **else**
17:            add s to t
18:            **return** value (s)
19:        **end if**
20:    **end if**
21:    $bestScore \leftarrow -\infty$
22:    **for** $m \in$ legal moves of s **do**
23:        $\mu \leftarrow FPU$
24:        **if** $t.p(s, m) > 0$ **then**
25:            $\mu \leftarrow \frac{t.sum(s,m)}{t.p(s,m)}$
26:        **end if**
27:        $bandit \leftarrow \mu + c \times t.prior(s, m) \times \frac{\sqrt{1+t.p(s)}}{1+t.p(s,m)}$
28:        **if** $bandit > bestScore$ **then**
29:            $bestScore \leftarrow bandit$
30:            $bestMove \leftarrow m$
31:        **end if**
32:    **end for**
33:    **if** root **then**
34:        $b \leftarrow highestValue_m(t.p(s, m))$
35:        $b_1 \leftarrow secondHighestValue_m(t.p(s, m))$
36:        **if** $b \geq b_1 + budget - i$ **then**
37:            $bestMove \leftarrow secondBestMove_m(t.p(s, m))$
38:        **end if**
39:    **end if**
40:    $s_1 \leftarrow$ play $(s, bestMove)$
41:    $res \leftarrow$ BatchSecond $(s_1, GetBatch, budget, i, False)$
42:    **if** $GetBatch$ **then**
43:        UpdateStatisticsGet $(res, bestMove, s, t)$
44:    **else**
45:        UpdateStatistics $(res, bestMove, s, t)$
46:    **end if**
47:    **return** res

The modifications of the search algorithm that implement the Second Move heuristic are given in Algorithm 9. Lines 33-39 modify the best move to try at the root when the most simulated move is unreachable. In this case the second most simulated move is preferred.

Algorithm 8 gives the modifications of the GetMove algorithm for using the Second Move heuristic. Lines 8-17 choose between the most simulated move and the second most simulated move according to their means.

4   Experimental Results

Experiments were performed using a MobileNet neural network which is an architecture well fitted for the game of Go [4,5]. The network has 16 blocks, a trunk of 64 and 384 planes in the inverted residual. It has been trained on the Katago dataset containing games played at a superhuman level.

4.1   The μ FPU

We test the constant FPU and the best mean FPU against the μ FPU. Table 1 gives the average winrate over 400 games of the different FPU for different numbers of playouts. For example, the first cell means that the constant FPU wins 13.00% of its games against the μ FPU when the search algorithms both use 32 playouts per move.

Table 1. Playing 400 games with the constant and the best mean FPUs and different numbers of evaluations against the μ FPU, $\frac{\sigma}{\sqrt{n}} < 0.0250$.

FPU	32	64	128	256	512
constant	0.1300	0.1300	0.0475	0.0175	
best	0.3775	0.3450	0.3275	0.3150	0.2725

It is clear that the μ FPU is the best option. In the remainder of the experiments we use the μ FPU.

4.2   Trees and Transposition Table

We now experiment with using a single tree associated to a transposition table. An entry in the transposition table only contains the evaluation and the prior. A node in the tree contains the children and the statistics of the state. We compare it to the PUCT algorithm with a transposition table that stores both the statistics, the evaluation and the priors. PUCT with a transposition table searches with a Directed Acyclic Graph while its opponent develops a single tree with transpositions only used to remember the evaluation of the states.

Table 2 gives the budget used by each algorithm (the number of forward of the neural network), the number of descents of the single tree algorithm using this budget and the ratio of the number of descents divided by the number of forwards and the win rate of the single tree algorithm. Both PUCT with a transposition table and the single tree algorithm are called with a batch of size one. The PUCT with a transposition table algorithm makes exactly as many descents as forwards when the single tree algorithm makes more descents than forwards. The ratio of the number of descents divided by the number of forwards increases with the budget. We can see that both algorithms have close performances with the single tree algorithm getting slightly better with an increased budget.

Table 2. Playing 400 games with a tree, a transposition table and a batch of size 1 against PUCT with a transposition table with a batch of size 1, $\frac{\sigma}{\sqrt{n}} < 0.0250$

Budget	Descents	Ratio	Winrate
256	273.08	1.067	0.4800
1024	1 172.21	1.145	0.4875
4096	5 234.01	1.278	0.5275

4.3   The Virtual Mean

In order to compare the virtual loss and the Virtual Mean we make them play against the sequential algorithm. They both use batch MCTS. The results are given in Table 3. The first column is the penalty used, the second column is the value of vl the number of visits to add for the penalty used. The third column is the number of batches and the fourth column the size of the batches. The fifth column is the average number of nodes of the tree. The sixth column is the average of the number of useful inferences made per batch. The number of inferences made can be smaller than the batch size since the batch is not always fully filled at each call of the GetBatch algorithm. The last column is the win rate against the sequential algorithm using 64 batches of size 1. All experiments are made with the maximum number of descents $N = 500$. It is normal that the number of inferences per batch is smaller than the batch size since for example the first batch only contains one state because the priors of the root are not yet known.

The best result for the Virtual Loss is with $vl = 3$ when using 8 batches. It scores 20.75% against sequential PUCT with 64 state evaluations. The Virtual Mean with 8 batches has better results as it scores 31.00% with $vl = 3$ against the same opponent.

We also tested the virtual loss and the Virtual Mean for a greater number of batches. For 32 batches of size 32 (i.e. inferences on a little less than 1024 states) the best result for the virtual loss is with $vl = 2$ with an average of 157.69 nodes in the tree and a percentage of 79.00% of wins against sequential PUCT with 64 state evaluations. The Virtual Mean with $vl = 1$ and the same number of batches is much better: it has on average 612.02 nodes in the tree and a percentage of wins of 97.00% of its games.

In the remaining experiments we use the Virtual Mean.

Table 3. Playing 400 games with the different penalties (VL = Virtual Loss, VM = Virtual Mean) against sequential PUCT with 64 state evaluations. $\frac{\sigma}{\sqrt{n}} < 0.0250$

P	vl	B	Batch	Nodes	Inference	Winrate
VL	1	8	32	24.47	23.17	0.1300
VL	2	8	32	24.37	24.46	0.1525
VL	3	8	32	24.11	25.16	**0.2075**
VL	4	8	32	23.87	25.53	0.2025
VL	5	8	32	23.91	25.72	0.1600
VL	1	32	32	166.09	28.08	0.7725
VL	2	32	32	157.69	28.25	**0.7900**
VL	3	32	32	151.02	28.30	0.7800
VL	4	32	32	144.45	28.19	0.7550
VM	1	8	32	46.45	20.22	0.2625
VM	2	8	32	43.75	21.64	0.3025
VM	3	8	32	41.63	22.10	**0.3100**
VM	4	8	32	40.41	22.53	0.2400
VM	1	32	32	612.02	26.63	**0.9700**
VM	2	32	32	619.07	27.83	0.9675
VM	3	32	32	593.91	28.20	0.9500

4.4   The Last Iteration

Table 4 gives the result of using the Last Iteration heuristic with different values for U. The column vll contains the value of vl used for the Last Iteration. We can see that the win rates are much better when using 8 batches than for Table 3 even for a small U. A large virtual loss (vll) of 3 makes more descents but it is less accurate. Using a virtual loss of 1 is safer and gives similar results.

When using 32 batches against 512 states evaluations the win rate increases from 62.75% for $U = 0$ to 68.00% for $U = 40$.

Table 4. Playing 400 games with the Last Iteration algorithm against sequential PUCT with P state evaluations. $\frac{\sigma}{\sqrt{n}} < 0.0250$.

U	vl	vll	B	Batch	P	Nodes	Winrate
10	3	3	8	32	64	109.02	0.4975
10	3	1	8	32	64	75.09	0.4450
40	3	3	8	32	64	232.09	0.5100
40	3	1	8	32	64	129.90	0.5275
0	1	1	32	32	512	729.41	0.6275
40	1	3	32	32	512	962.84	0.6650
40	1	1	32	32	512	835.07	0.6800

4.5 The Second Move Heuristic

Table 5 gives the winrate for different budgets when playing PUCT with the second move heuristic against vanilla PUCT. We can see that the Second Move heuristic consistently improves sequential PUCT.

Table 5. Playing 400 games with the second move heuristic used at the root of sequential PUCT against sequential PUCT. $\frac{\sigma}{\sqrt{n}} < 0.0250$.

Budget	Winrate
32	0.5925
64	0.6350
128	0.6425
256	0.5925
512	0.6250
1024	0.5600

4.6 Ablation Study

The PUCT constant $c = 0.2$ that we used in the previous experiments was fit to the sequential PUCT on a DAG with 512 inferences. In order to test the various improvements we propose to fit again the c constant with all improvements set on. The results of games against sequential PUCT for different constants is given in Table 6. The $c = 0.5$ constant seems best and will be used in the ablation study.

Table 6. Result of different constants for 32 batches of size 32 against sequential PUCT with 256 state evaluations and a constant of 0.2. $\frac{\sigma}{\sqrt{n}} < 0.0250$.

c	Winrate
0.2	0.7575
0.3	0.7925
0.4	0.8100
0.5	**0.8275**
0.6	0.7975
0.7	0.7700
0.8	0.7550
1.6	0.5900

Table 7. Playing 400 games with the different heuristics using 32 batches of size 32 against sequential PUCT with 512 state evaluations. $\frac{\sigma}{\sqrt{n}} < 0.0250$.

μ FPU	VM	LI	SM	Winrate
y	y	y	y	0.6800
n	y	y	y	0.4775
y	n	y	y	0.0475
y	n	n	y	0.2950
y	y	n	y	0.6275
y	y	y	n	0.5750

Table 7 is an ablation study. It gives the scores against sequential PUCT with 512 evaluations of the different algorithms using 32 batches with some heuristics removed.

Removing the Virtual Mean heuristic is done by replacing it with the virtual loss heuristic. However the virtual loss combined with the Last Iteration is catastrophic. So we also removed both the Virtual Mean and the Last Iteration heuristics in order to evaluate removing the Virtual Mean.

Removing the μ FPU was done replacing it by the best mean FPU. The Last Iteration uses $vll = 1$ and $U = 40$.

We can observe in Table 7 that all the heuristics contribute significantly to the strength of the algorithm. The Virtual Mean (VM) has the best increase in win rate, going from 29.50% for the virtual loss to 68.00% when replacing the virtual loss by the Virtual Mean. The Second Move heuristic (SM) also contributes to the strength of Batch MCTS. LI stands for the Last Iteration.

4.7   Inference Speed

Table 8 gives the number of batches per second and the number of inferences per second for each batch size. Choosing batches of size 32 enables to make 26 times more inferences than batches of size 1 while keeping the number of useful inferences per batch high enough.

Table 8. Number of batches per second according to the size of the batch with Tensorflow and a RTX 2080 Ti.

Size	Batches per second	Inferences per second
1	38.20	38
2	36.60	73
4	36.44	146
8	33.31	267
16	32.92	527
32	31.10	995
64	26.00	1664
128	18.32	2345

5 Conclusion

We have proposed to use a tree for the statistics and a transposition table for the results of the inferences in the context of batched inferences for Monte Carlo Tree Search. We found that using the μ FPU is what works best in our framework. We also proposed the Virtual Mean instead of the Virtual Loss and found that it improves much Batch MCTS. The Last Iteration heuristic also improves the level of play when combined with the Virtual Mean. Finally the Second Move heuristic makes a good use of the remaining budget of inferences when the most simulated move cannot be replaced by other moves.

Acknowledgment. Thanks to Rémi Coulom for fruitful discussions and for giving me the idea to simulate a sequential PUCT algorithm.

References

1. Browne, C., et al.: A survey of Monte Carlo tree search methods. IEEE Trans. Comput. Intell. AI Games **4**(1), 1–43 (2012)
2. Browne, C., Stephenson, M., Piette, É., Soemers, D.J.: A practical introduction to the ludii general game system. In: Cazenave, T., van den Herik, J., Saffidine, A., Wu, I.C. (eds.) Advances in Computer Games. ACG 2019. LNCS, vol. 12516. Springer, Cham (2019). https://doi.org/10.1007/978-3-030-65883-0_14
3. Cazenave, T.: Generalized rapid action value estimation. In: 24th International Joint Conference on Artificial Intelligence, pp. 754–760 (2015)
4. Cazenave, T.: Improving model and search for computer Go. In: IEEE Conference on Games (2021)
5. Cazenave, T.: Mobile networks for computer Go. IEEE Transactions on Games (2021)
6. Cazenave, T., et al.: Polygames: Improved zero learning. ICGA J. **42**(4), 244–256 (2020)
7. Cazenave, T., Jouandeau, N.: On the parallelization of UCT. In: proceedings of the Computer Games Workshop, pp. 93–101 (2007)
8. Cazenave, T., Jouandeau, N.: A parallel Monte-Carlo tree search algorithm. In: van den Herik, H.J., Xu, X., Ma, Z., Winands, M.H.M. (eds.) CG 2008. LNCS, vol. 5131, pp. 72–80. Springer, Heidelberg (2008). https://doi.org/10.1007/978-3-540-87608-3_7
9. Chaslot, G.M.J.-B., Winands, M.H.M., van den Herik, H.J.: Parallel Monte-Carlo tree search. In: van den Herik, H.J., Xu, X., Ma, Z., Winands, M.H.M. (eds.) CG 2008. LNCS, vol. 5131, pp. 60–71. Springer, Heidelberg (2008). https://doi.org/10.1007/978-3-540-87608-3_6
10. Coulom, R.: Efficient selectivity and backup operators in Monte-Carlo tree search. In: Computers and Games, 5th International Conference, CG 2006, Turin, Italy, 29–31 May 2006. Revised Papers, pp. 72–83 (2006)
11. Emslie, R.: Galvanise zero. https://github.com/richemslie/galvanise_zero (2019)
12. Gelly, S., Silver, D.: Monte-Carlo tree search and rapid action value estimation in computer Go. Artif. Intell. **175**(11), 1856–1875 (2011)
13. Kocsis, L., Szepesvári, C.: Bandit based Monte-Carlo planning. In: Fürnkranz, J., Scheffer, T., Spiliopoulou, M. (eds.) ECML 2006. LNCS (LNAI), vol. 4212, pp. 282–293. Springer, Heidelberg (2006). https://doi.org/10.1007/11871842_29
14. Liu, A., Chen, J., Yu, M., Zhai, Y., Zhou, X., Liu, J.: Watch the unobserved: a simple approach to parallelizing Monte Carlo tree search. arXiv preprint arXiv:1810.11755 (2018)
15. Pascutto, G.C.: Leela zero. https://github.com/leela-zero/leela-zero (2017)

16. Saffidine, A., Cazenave, T., Méhat, J.: UCD: upper confidence bound for rooted directed acyclic graphs. Knowl.-Based Syst. **34**, 26–33 (2011)
17. Silver, D., et al.: Mastering the game of Go with deep neural networks and tree search. Nature **529**(7587), 484–489 (2016). https://doi.org/10.1038/nature16961
18. Silver, D., et al.: A general reinforcement learning algorithm that masters chess, shogi, and go through self-play. Science **362**(6419), 1140–1144 (2018)
19. Silver, D., et al.: Mastering the game of go without human knowledge. Nature **550**(7676), 354–359 (2017)
20. Sironi, C.F.: Monte-Carlo tree search for artificial general intelligence in games, Ph. D. thesis, Maastricht University (2019)
21. Tian, Y., et al.: ELF OpenGo: an analysis and open reimplementation of AlphaZero. CoRR abs/1902.04522 (2019)
22. Wang, Y., Gelly, S.: Modifications of UCT and sequence-like simulations for Monte-Carlo go. In: 2007 IEEE Symposium on Computational Intelligence and Games, pp. 175–182. IEEE (2007)
23. Wu, D.J.: Accelerating self-play learning in go. CoRR abs/1902.10565 (2019)
24. Yang, X., Aasawat, T.K., Yoshizoe, K.: Practical massively parallel Monte-Carlo tree search applied to molecular design. arXiv preprint arXiv:2006.10504 (2020)

Towards Transparent Cheat Detection in Online Chess: An Application of Human and Computer Decision-Making Preferences

Thijs Laarhoven[1] and Aditya Ponukumati[2(✉)]

[1] TNO, Eindhoven, The Netherlands
mail@thijs.com
[2] Washington University, Saint Louis, MO, USA
aditya.ponukumati@wustl.edu

Abstract. Online game providers face the challenge of preventing malicious users (cheaters) from breaking the rules and winning games through illegal means. This issue in particular plagues the online chess scene, where the strongest algorithms have long surpassed the world's best players [4] – any cheater can beat the best human players through computer assistance. Moreover, recent developments in AI-based chess engines have opened the door to even more human-like engines [33], which are increasingly able to mimic legitimate human players. Unfortunately, because major chess websites do not discuss their cheat detection mechanisms publicly, there is limited scientific literature on how to tackle the pervasive problem of cheating in online chess. Certainly, there is no way to validate whether these mechanisms actually work.

We take a first step towards formalizing a proper cheat detection framework for online chess by leveraging a large-scale statistical examination of human and computer decision-making tendencies over millions of chess games played online. Although cheaters are not engines (computer players) but centaurs (computer-assisted human players), the insights into computer play serve as a useful guideline for finding the strongest indicators of cheating. We then demonstrate how these findings may distinguish legitimate human players from cheaters in an automated, rules-based manner. Additionally, we argue that the status quo of hiding cheat detection mechanisms from the public eye is dangerous to the integrity of the game, and that cheat detection is foremost a service to society instead of a competitive advantage for chess websites to attract more users. Consistent with Kerckhoffs' paradigm [24], we believe that the benefits of an open discussion on cheat detection far outweigh the potential drawbacks of cheaters learning about these methods.

Keywords: chess · cheat detection · decision-making

1 Introduction

Cheating in Online Games. In recent decades, the online gaming industry has developed rapidly into a multi-billion dollar industry. As the stakes have increased,

C. Browne et al. (Eds.): CG 2022, LNCS 13865, pp. 163–180, 2023.
https://doi.org/10.1007/978-3-031-34017-8_14

prizes for the top players have also increased, making it all the more profitable for malicious users to try to break the rules in these games to their advantage. Moreover, if games are plagued by wide-spread cheating, then players will lose interest in the game and move on to other games with better cheat detection. Robust cheat detection mechanisms are therefore becoming increasingly important in online gaming, to make sure that bad actors get banned before they do irreparable damage to the game [26, 50].

Cheating in Chess. A prime example of a popular game which has been around for centuries is the board game chess. For several decades, online chess servers have been able to operate both on a freeware and commercial level, with the popular chess servers FICS and ICC from the 1990s/2000s now being surpassed by Lichess and Chess.com in terms of popularity. Since chess computers have long eclipsed humans in terms of playing strength [4], and freely available chess software can easily beat the best human players [48], the illegal use of computer assistance (cheating) is a major issue in chess – both in physical tournaments [17, 47] and in online events [7, 18, 19]. As physical monitoring of players is much harder in online settings[1], advanced cheat detection methods are necessary to prevent cheaters from gaining an unfair advantage.

Cheat Detection in the Wild. As cheating in (online) chess is a widespread problem, many chess servers employ some form of cheat detection. Since chess servers conduct their cheat detection behind closed doors, their internal procedures are not verifiable. Perhaps the most transparent high-profile chess cheating case coverage comes from the Fair Play Team at Chess.com, where "Strength Scores" were used to defend their decision to remove Grandmaster Hans Niemann from their platform [16]. However, the algorithms behind Strength Score calculation are proprietary. Only Lichess provides public source code of some parts of their cheat detection software [13, 28] among minor subroutines for automatic cheat report generation on the main site. Even then, Lichess (intentionally) makes no effort to make the code or underlying concepts understandable to the public, proudly embracing the regime of "security via obfuscation" [29].

1.1 Ethical Considerations

As the problem of cheating is inherently a zero-sum cat-and-mouse game between the cheater and the game server, publicly discussing methods for cheat detection may indeed help cheaters understand these methods and avoid detection in the future. Security via obfuscation and other philosophies that denounce transparency maintain that the most effective way to stay ahead of cheaters in this arms race is to not tell them (or anyone) how players get caught, even denying explanations for publicly labeling players as cheaters.

---

[1] For high-stakes events [8], players often need to use cameras directed towards both their face and their computer screens. Although this may work for restricted events [9, 11], such a level of monitoring becomes impractical for e.g. the regular prize events held on Lichess [31] and Chess.com [12], with hundreds of participating players every week; let alone for the average online chess game played between two humans.

To counter these points, we observe that "security by obscurity" has long been condemned in various fields as the main means of deterring adversarial attacks [36,42]. Already in the 19th century, the cryptographer Kerckhoffs [24] stated that the security of a system should not rely on keeping the inner workings secret, as sooner or later they may fall into enemy hands. Sharing the inner workings further allows the system to receive public scrutiny, give third parties a chance to avoid "reinventing the wheel", and repair methodological flaws before bad actors exploit them in the shadows (or before good actors are wrongly punished). As aptly phrased by Hoepman and Jacobs [21]: "it may seem counter-intuitive, but going open all the way offers the most security."

Moreover, cheat detection systems serve a social role beyond being merely a security measure – at least in this case, they are the face of law and order in online chess. Under the current regime of obfuscation, veiled cheat detection systems cannot be validated, replicated, or publicly improved upon. In other words, chess websites do not trust chess players with the mechanisms that keep them safe. We believe that a culture grounded in distrust, even if it is widely accepted and tolerated, is surely detrimental to the game as a whole.

Analogous to ideas championed by the open-source and free software movements, we contend that it is not only foolhardy but also immoral to deny public access to cheat detection information. Accordingly, we believe that the only way to truly tackle the persistent problem of cheating in (online) chess is to collaborate and share knowledge, working together towards a solution in an open manner.

1.2   Related Work

Cheat Detection. Within the area of cheat detection, besides the aforementioned public libraries [13,28,32], there are some scientific works implicitly dealing with distinguishing humans from computers [3,20,38], and there are some papers explicitly treating cheat detection. Barnes and Hernandez-Castro [2] studied the effectiveness of trying to distinguish humans from computers from single games, concluding that false positives will be abundant as players will sometimes simply play excellent games. Patria et al. [37] attempted to use neural networks trained on game data to distinguish cheaters from legitimate players, but only achieved distinguishing rates slightly above 50%. As recent work in machine learning has famously allowed computers to overtake humans in the popular game of Go [44,45], some work has also started developing in the area of cheat detection there: Coquidé et al. [14] focused on local board configurations to distinguish computers from humans, while Egri-Nagy and Törmänen [15] focused on derived metrics – much like our proposed approach – to assess the quality of play and distinguish humans from cheaters.

Human and Computer Play in Chess. Some works have previously studied aspects of human and computer play in chess, most notably by research teams lead by Regan [3,20,38,39] and Anderson and Kleinberg [1,33–35]. Various papers have studied human behavior in chess, such as blunder rates [1,5], move accuracy [33,38], move time distributions [40,43], and other metrics measuring human skill in chess [20]. Other works have tried to emulate human play with a computer [33,34] or tried to classify humans based on their moves [23,35].

1.3 Contributions

With the combined goals of improving cheat detection in (online) chess and challenging the existing wide-spread opacity on this topic, we take a step towards formalizing a proper, robust framework for finding cheaters in chess. With millions of chess games played online everyday, artificial intelligence (AI) plays an increasingly important role in screening players. While high-performance, black-box machine learning techniques have been proposed to solve the constantly evolving cheat detection problem, they are often not explainable and have produced false positive detections. Accordingly, human validation of AI output, black-box or otherwise, is essential. Human validation requires a rigorous, theoretical, well-accepted, and publicly accessible foundation underpinning cheat detection decisions. Such a foundation does not yet exist for online chess.

One of the key differences between online and so-called "over-the-board" chess is that all of a player's online games are publicly archived. This means that we can rely less on circumstantial evidences (i.e. a player using the restroom too often, or the online analog of constantly switching browser tabs) and instead look for patterns in quantitative data. Similar to schemes that apply Benford's Law to detect falsified real-world data [25], we contend that there are second-order characteristics – underneath simply a player's in-game strength – that serve as "signatures" of legitimate chess: namely, a player's decision-making behavior. Consequently, we make an effort to understand the unique ways humans play chess using measurable in-game variables. In the spirit of explainable AI, we then develop simple "naive", rules-based binary classifiers to detect cheaters given our understanding of how decisions in chess are made. We approach this through the three-step process briefly outlined in the next section.

2   Data Sets and Metrics

Human Play. To analyze human behavior in online chess, we used the open database [30] of games played on Lichess, the second-largest online chess server. From this enormous data set of over 3B games, we selected only those games which (a) were played in 2021; (b) had readily-available engine analysis (Fishnet) results [27]; (c) did not have unequal starting clock times; (d) did not involve accounts permitted to use computer assistance; (e) were played at the $3 + 0$ or $10 + 0$ time control (each player having exactly three or ten minutes for the entire game); and (f) were played between players with roughly equal ratings (i.e., where $\lfloor r_1/200 \rfloor = \lfloor r_2/200 \rfloor$ for players with ratings r_1 and r_2). We note that we cannot use all games in the data set chiefly because parameters of the Fishnet engine are periodically updated. To respect the page limit, only $3 + 0$ data is presented, and the $3 + 0$ data set summarized in Table 1.

Table 1. Breakdown of the human $3+0$ data set. Ratings correspond to Lichess blitz ratings. Data sets in gray were not processed due to small sample size.

rating range	games	positions	users
$(-\infty, 599)$	–	–	–
(600, 799)	43.075	1.272.253	31.747
(800, 999)	217.697	6.135.940	111.604
(1000, 1199)	510.524	14.621.895	206.025
(1200, 1399)	775.876	22.753.336	260.294
(1400, 1599)	1.047.152	31.388.275	324.295
(1600, 1799)	1.224.679	37.518.430	267.679
(1800, 1999)	1.361.779	43.027.012	234.769
(2000, 2199)	1.143.017	37.258.477	157.008
(2200, 2399)	967.743	32.668.589	75.197
(2400, 2599)	900.573	31.343.983	25.391
(2600, 2799)	237.525	8.458.513	5.803
(2800, 2999)	10.922	400.859	607
(3000, 3199)	72	2.745	5
(3200, $+\infty$)	–	–	–
all	8.440.634	266.850.307	1.058.974

Computer Play. To analyze computer behavior we used two data sets that cover a broad range of search algorithms and play styles: games from the Chess.com Computer Chess Championship (CCCC) [10]; and games played by the human-like AI, Maia [33], on Lichess. The former data set focuses on world-class chess engines (using either alpha-beta or Monte Carlo tree search) playing at similar time controls ($2+1$ and $5+5$, initial two/five minutes per side plus one/five seconds per move); while the latter data set, still played at the $3+0/10+0$ time controls, surveys chess engines designed to emulate human play. To respect the page limit, these results are not shown but are still briefly discussed.

Cheat Detection. Finally, to evaluate our cheat detection framework, we used public information regarding user statuses obtained via the Lichess API. For the users with the most games in our filtered database, we stored whether the account is currently (a) open and unaffected by playbans; (b) publicly marked for a Terms of Service (ToS)-violation; or (c) closed. Our data set consists of 100K players with the most games in 2021. We calculated individual player metrics using their own games and compared them to their rating-appropriate benchmark using the following protocol: 1) buckets without data on the player's end are excluded from both the player and benchmark distributions; 2) the non-sparse distributions are normalized into unit vectors; and 3) Euclidean distance is calculated between these two unit vectors. We construct false positive vs false negative (FP/FN) profiles, which are essentially receiver operating characteristics (ROCs), for each metric's ability to differentiate between (un)labelled cheaters.

Metrics. In brief, we considered the following metrics for each move for all games and positions: (a) player response time (0–30 s w/ 1 s bins); (b) player clock time (0–180 s w/ 2 s bins); (c) computer evaluation of the position before the move (0–100% w/2% bins, measured as expected score by converting centipawns on a fitted logistic curve); (d) move accuracy (0–100% w/ 2% bins, measured as change in expected score); (e) legal move availability (1–60 moves w/ 1 move bins); and (f) total board material (20–78 points w/ 1 point bins, measured using the traditional chess piece weights). Because the start and end of many chess games tend to rely on routine or trivial decisions, only moves 11–30, inclusive, were analyzed in an attempt to survey complex positions occurring in the "middle game".

3   Human Play

Figures 1a–1f show distributions of human behavior for the $3+0$ time control. $10+0$ results are omitted to respect the page limit, but we note that the results are similar to those of $3+0$.

3.1   Move Accuracy Plots

Perhaps the most common and natural way to assess a player's chess behavior is to measure the accuracy of their moves. Below we compare how various factors influence the move accuracies exhibited by the players in our data set.

Move Accuracy vs. Position Evaluation (Fig. 1a). Apart from a higher move accuracy (lower evaluation loss) at roughly equal positions, there are two peaks of lowest move accuracy when positions are (a) better for the player to move at 80% winning odds (but not winning enough to be easy to play), or (b) worse for the player to move at 30% winning odds (but again not lost enough that all moves are equally good/bad). Stronger players play consistently better across all position evaluations, and the gaps are most apparent in these positions with small (dis)advantages for either side. In the $10+0$ data sets, we would observe that the shapes of the curves remain mostly the same, with move accuracy being slightly better than in the faster $3+0$ time control.

Note that if the expected score for the player to move is 0% (the left side of the graphs) it is impossible to play a "bad" move, as all moves will achieve an expected score of 0%. On the other hand, when the evaluation is close to 100%, it is still possible to commit errors. While severity of potential errors increases as a player's advantage increases, the odds of making such an error drops, leading to a "heart" shape graph. This may explain why evaluation loss is generally low when far above 90% expected score. Holdaway and Vul [22] might explain the asymmetry in this "heart" shape to the "house money" hypothesis (i.e. the tendency to take more risk when playing with "house money").

Move Accuracy vs. Remaining Board Material (Fig. 1b). Each game starts with a total board value of 78, and this value generally drops as the game progresses and pieces are captured/exchanged. More material generally implies

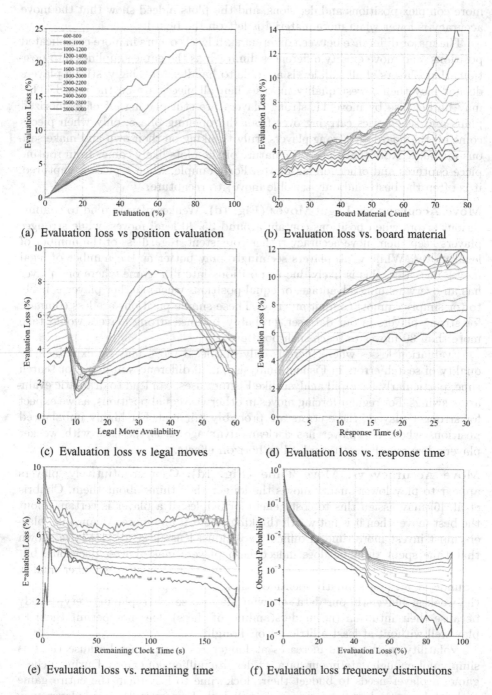

(a) Evaluation loss vs position evaluation

(b) Evaluation loss vs. board material

(c) Evaluation loss vs legal moves

(d) Evaluation loss vs. response time

(e) Evaluation loss vs. remaining time

(f) Evaluation loss frequency distributions

Fig. 1. Human evaluation loss metrics sorted by player strength $(3+0$ only$)$

more complex positions and decisions, and the plots indeed show that the move accuracy is lower when more material is left on the board.

The major difference between different skill levels occurs in more complicated positions, and move quality differences diminish as the game simplifies into positions that players of all skill levels are able to handle. Amusingly, strong players do not play their lowest quality moves when all pieces are on the board. This may be because by move 11, strong players are still playing off of memorized plans and schematics carrying over from the opening phase; only when pieces come off the board are strong players truly thinking on their own and make serious mistakes. Note that the erratic nature of the plots likely comes from routine piece captures and other forcing moves. For example, when a piece is captured, it is often the best (and only sensible move) to recapture.

Move Accuracy vs. Legal Moves (Fig. 1c). Weaker players tend to commit serious errors when positions contain around 35–40 legal moves, while stronger players keep their move accuracy rather consistent, regardless of the number of legal moves. While weak players seemingly play better as the number of legal moves increases, this is likely due to positions late in a game where one player has an overwhelming advantage, or equal positions where neither player is likely to (or simply cannot) commit an error. These simple positions are less common for strong players in our data set, probably because strong players would take more than 30 moves to reach such positions.

Evaluation losses where there is only one legal move may be explained by quality of search errors in Fishnet analysis; small differences in depth or search time, particularly for rapid analysis like Fishnet uses, can lead to dramatic evaluation swings. For regular forcing moves in otherwise equal positions, as we expect for stronger players, these errors are probably minimal. For highly imbalanced positions where one player has a clear advantage as is the case with weaker players, low search depth can lead to horizon effects.

Move Accuracy vs. Move Time (Fig. 1d). Counter-intuitively, players appear to play lower quality moves the longer they think about them. Chabris et al. [6] may assign this to cost-benefit principles: if a player is certain about the best move, then it is not worth thinking about it any more. Meanwhile, players must invest more time in difficult positions. Russek et al. [41] have shown that time spent thinking does indeed help players make better decisions, but our data suggest that, on aggregate, faster decisions are still of higher quality – Sunde et al. [46] similarly identified this. An exception to this rule is with the weakest players in our data set, who play worse when playing very quickly because their intuition (i.e. understanding of chess) does not permit them to play well without at least a little bit of thought.

Volatility in the plots increases at longer response times because there is simply not enough data in our data set despite millions of games. During a chess game, a player needs to budget their clock time to last them the entire game without knowing how long the game will last. Understandably, a player may often make a poorly thought-out decision to avoid "time pressure" later on.

Move Accuracy vs. Remaining Clock Times (Fig. 1e). The remaining time mostly starts to play a role once the time drops far below one minute, when players of all strengths start to perform worse. Move accuracy tends to be high during the early-middle game phase of the game, when there is ample time on the clock. However, even as we expect decisions to get simpler as pieces are exchanged, move quality rapidly deteriorates – even in simpler positions – as players have less time to confirm their decisions. We observe this for both $3+0$ and $10+0$, and for players of all strengths. This is consistent with previous observations [1,5,40,43].

Empirical Move Accuracy Distributions (Fig. 1f). As expected, players with higher ratings make more strong moves and fewer mistakes. We observe that the vast majority of moves, played at all skill levels, are high-quality decisions. This is in-line with a previous observation by McIlroy-Young et al. [34] who showed that humans already match computer best moves over 40% of the time given appropriate search depth. Notably, there is a peak at roughly 50% evaluation loss, likely corresponding to non-strategic mistakes that blunder a won position into an equal position or an equal position into a lost position. The peak is more intense for weaker players, who are more likely to commit such errors, partly due to skill and partly due to the nature of (imbalanced) positions played.

3.2 Move Time Plots

Another feature that characterizes how humans (and computers) play chess is clock time management. As discussed, each player has a limited time budget to make their moves, and humans at different skill levels may utilize their time budget differently.

Move Time vs. Position Evaluation (Fig. 2a). Overall, humans play fastest in equal and imbalanced but decided positions. They use the most time when they are slightly better or worse. This is loosely consistent with how evaluation loss scales with position evaluation: the positions where the player to move is slightly better/slightly worse are generally the positions with the lowest move accuracy, corresponding to the hardest choices, and therefore requiring the most time to reach a decision.

Unlike evaluation loss vs evaluation plots, however, move time vs evaluation plots are generally symmetric. A possible explanation for this is loss aversion: a player faces total loss in a losing position but only faces losing their advantage in a winning position.

Move Time vs. Remaining Board Material (Fig. 2b). Humans generally use the most time when there is more material on the board. We see the same choppy behavior as for the move accuracy against the board material: stronger players make routine chess decisions much faster than weak players. Further, stronger players are better able to limit their time usage when there is ample material on the board. This is potentially because faster moves in complex positions may loosely relate to the overall better time management of stronger play-

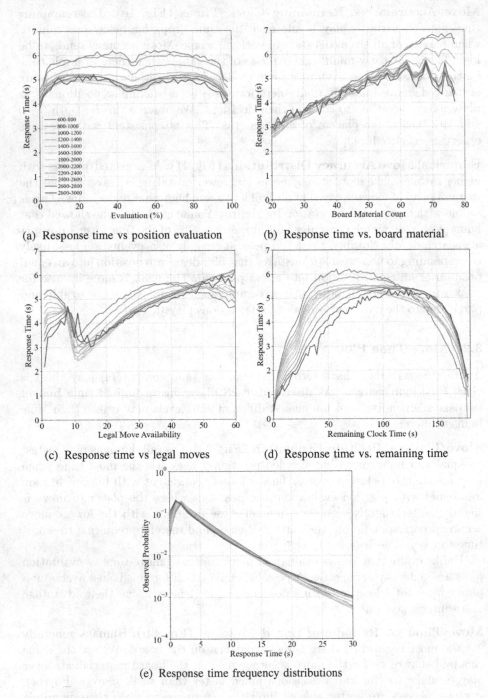

(a) Response time vs position evaluation

(b) Response time vs. board material

(c) Response time vs legal moves

(d) Response time vs. remaining time

(e) Response time frequency distributions

Fig. 2. Human response time metrics sorted by player strength (3 + 0 only)

ers, who understand when to settle for "good enough". Alternatively, stronger players are playing off of familiar themes carrying over from the opening phase.

Move Time vs. Legal Moves (Fig. 2c). As the number of options diminishes, players tend to use less time to reach a decision. This may be explained by the fact that positions with more legal moves have more attractive options as well as more opportunities to blunder, demanding more time invested. Response times decrease at the tail end of this distribution for weak players, again presumably because these positions are highly imbalanced and not actually complicated. Positions with fewer than 15 legal moves tend to be forcing in nature and often do not require significant time commitment.

Move Time vs. Remaining Time (Fig. 2d). Similar trends are observed as with other metrics. When a player's remaining time is close to their original starting time, the game has only just begun and players are still reciting opening moves from memory. As the remaining time decreases, this correlates with entering the complexity of middle games, which demand a greater time commitment. As players run short of time, this naturally demands an increase in pace regardless of a game's progress. Similar results were obtained by Russek et al. [41], though they did not exclude games with unequal starting times.

Notable is how player strength factors into time management. Stronger players are more likely to spend the bulk of their time early in the game and play quickly when their time is running low. The point at which strong players start thinking presumably arrives immediately after the opening phase, where strong players are making moves quickly. Weaker players, on the other hand, seemingly behave the opposite; they play quickly early on but think when short of time. Reasons for this are potentially twofold: 1) the weak player sample includes players who are irrational or inexperienced in their time management, and 2) weak players had already spent a significant fraction of their time before we collect data on move 11, which would mean that weak players simply have less time to manage over the observable game duration.

Amusingly, the time management profile changes when players of all skill levels have 30–60 s left. This may be attributable to the website issuing a warning sound at low clock times, which jolts players into making a move. It is subtle in Fig. 1e, but this jolting is also accompanied by lower quality moves.

Empirical Move Time Distributions (Fig. 2e). Presumably, chess players are making the majority of their moves quickly because most chess positions are forcing in nature. However, there is a minority of positions that demand particular attention (i.e. "critical moments"). Across both 3 + 0 and 10 + 0, strong players are playing forcing moves quickly and are more likely to spend time in critical moments, while weaker players do not know how to assess the relative importance of positions and thus have a tighter response time distribution where every position is equally challenging.

A player's thinking time can be summarized as the sum of decision-making time and the time it takes to physically move their mouse cursor and play the move. At least in online speed chess, the strongest players appear to have faster physical response times than the weakest players by 1 s, probably owing to playing experience. Further, they also play more moves in 0 s. These apparently instantaneous move times are attributable to so-called "pre-moves", where a strong player plans a (conditionally legal) move before it is their turn. Commonly, this occurs in very forcing positions where a skilled player's next move can be quickly determined even during the opponent's turn.

4   Computer Play

While CCCC and Maia metric plots are not presented to respect the page limit, the results broadly support the claim that humans and computers play chess differently. Unsurprisingly, the CCCC engines have super-human move accuracy and can be thought of as a limiting distribution of human play. Maia bots, on the other hand, more closely resembled human evaluation loss metrics expected of their skill level. While move quality, measured by evaluation loss, can potentially be a reasonable metric for distinguishing cheaters, the distinguishing ability has more to do with player skill than fundamental differences between humans and engines. As a result, we would expect cheaters to be able to dodge cheat detection by using weak engines like Maia bots – so long as they keep their skill level consistent across all measurable metrics.

The key qualitiative difference separating engine distributions from human distributions is that engine response times are generally agnostic of other variables (so-called "flat pacing" in the chess world) while human response time distributions are pegged to position complexity. One would expect response time-based cheat detection methods to have better predictive potential for cheat detection.

5   Cheat Detection

If we are to compute these metric distributions for individual chess players, our intuition is that cheaters will deviate further from their rating-appropriate human benchmark than normal human players. As a proof-of-concept that this can be levered for an automated cheat detection system, we created binary classifiers using an unbiased, uninformed (naive) heuristic: Euclidean distance between the player and human benchmark distribution. We computed ROC-like (FP/FN) curves for $3 + 0$ metric distances in Fig. 3, and results for $10 + 0$ are similar but not displayed. For comparison, a cheat detection model that relies on random chance will have a FP/FN profile spanning the line $y = 1 - x$.

5.1   Potential Biases and Limitations

One important observation is that many cheaters are likely children or lazy adults who are unaware of cheat detection mechanisms and who simply play the best engine moves (almost) all the time, after which Lichess can quickly detect them. Consequently, our mean-based classifiers would not be able to detect these players who only cheat (egregiously) in a small fraction of total games. This means

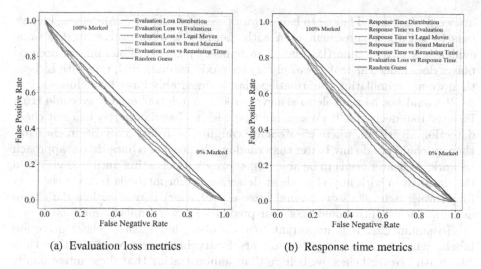

(a) Evaluation loss metrics   (b) Response time metrics

Fig. 3. False positive vs. false negative (FP/FN) curves for the binary classifiers based on evaluation loss and response time metrics (3 + 0 only).

that we will have a harder time solving even "easy" cheating cases. It is therefore important not to compare the results of our study with e.g. full sweeps of the data set that specialize in outlier game detection – those would be more "effective" from an FP/FN standpoint but operate on a different set of assumptions (i.e. in this case, that outlier games are sufficient to prove cheating).[2] Our method should be seen, if not as merely a proof of concept, then as a generalized approach that ought to work against all cheaters, especially those who do not fall prey to trivial detection methods.

A further limitation of our data set (and any publicly available data set for that matter) is that there is no way to verify whether a player actually cheated. The best we can do is compare to the user status on Lichess (accounts which to this date are open, accounts which have a public ToS-violation mark, and accounts which are closed), but we note that (1) an open account may just not be caught yet; (2) a ToS-violation mark is not limited to cheating (i.e. boosting, sandbagging, chat misbehavior, multi-accounting, or even cheating in a time control we are not screening); and (3) an account being closed could be due to the player's choice and not because Lichess closed it themselves. Because there are no proper data sets to our knowledge, the best we can do is compare against whether Lichess has marked this account or not.

We cannot fully trust Lichess' assessments because they are ultimately made by fallible humans (or their algorithms) amidst incomplete information and data handling biases. A 100% match with Lichess is not only unrealistic but also undesirable, as Lichess also makes systematic mistakes (i.e. incorrectly flagging

---

[2] To our knowledge, there are no similar models or ROC curves in the literature to which to compare our results, thanks to the opacity surrounding cheat detection.

innocent players and failing to ban certain classes of cheaters). Moreover, Lichess fails to get 100% agreement even with themselves when evaluating the same evidence a second time (i.e. their ban appeals process), assuming an accused player does indeed appeal. If we only try to maximize our match rate with Lichess, then we are stimulating confirmation bias on inevitably flawed conclusions.

It would not be possible to achieve a 100% match rate even if we could trust Lichess' ban decisions. If we suppose that Lichess has a perfectly efficient cheat detection algorithm, where cheaters are caught the instant they begin cheating, then we could not do any better than random chance. For a data-driven approach to work, a cheater needs to be able to get away with cheating until it is visible in the data. Even with imperfect cheat detection, other methods (i.e. via checking for browser extensions or unusual browser behavior) may need less data than our approach, which would make our predictive power similarly minimal.

To summarize, it is important to remember that Lichess' cheat detection labels, which we are comparing to, are faulty black box oracles rather than "the truth". Nevertheless, we believe that demonstrating that these intentionally naive classifiers have even a modest agreement with Lichess' independent conclusions would validate these metrics' utility for both automating the detection of potential cheaters, and for gathering distributional evidence of cheating.

5.2   Distinguishing Between Marked and Non-marked Players

It is immediately apparent that although these binary classifiers are better than random chance, the margin of outperformance is somewhat minimal. These metrics generally fared better in the (not-pictured) $10 + 0$ data set. This may be an indication that cheaters are better able to evade detection in longer games in part because they have more time to think about how to evade detection, which means the fraction of cheated moves is larger than in the $3 + 0$ data set.

Response time distributions were most effective at distinguishing cheaters in the $3 + 0$ data set by a large margin. Amusingly, they were most effective when constraining the FP rate to near zero. This may be an artefact of Lichess relying on related metrics for rapidly marking egregious cheaters. With only 3 min on the clock, a cheater may be forced to play at a chess engine's cadence for lack of time to fabricate their move times. To avoid this time crunch, a cheater might only consult a chess engine in certain situations, for example specifically in losing positions and without much regard to number of legal moves or other less apparent variables. This may explain why the evaluation loss vs evaluation metric was particularly effective for $3 + 0$.

Overall, the response time metrics may be slightly more effective at cheat detection than these evaluation loss metrics. Evaluation loss being used for cheat detection is intuitive and well-known: for instance, Ken Regan, who was a pioneer of using move quality metrics to catch cheaters, recently had his algorithms vetted by the U.S. Chess Federation [49]. But, if a cheater is not making a serious effort to avoid getting caught, they may be less likely to try to artificially match their response time benchmarks. Additionally, move quality may be a more volatile metric, which makes it harder to make high confidence cheat detection decisions. Players may not perfectly match their rating-appropriate evaluation loss benchmarks for a number of reasons, including opening preferences, play style, or their "form" on that day. But, presumably, if they are indeed human, they would not stray far from human response times.

5.3 Implications for Diagnostic Cheat Detection

While these metrics in their current, primitive implementation are probably not optimal for automated cheat detection, they do present some diagnostic ability. A natural improvement over these classifiers would be to identify qualitative differences in metric shape or using a weighted Euclidean distance that targets more important regimes of player metrics. For example, players may be more likely to cheat in losing positions, so data in losing positions might be overweighted.

Ultimately, cheat detection is a holistic endeavor and requires consideration of all evidence in tandem. This is contrary to the presented work, as it tackles cheat detection using one piece of evidence at a time. Therefore, it stands to reason that a sophisticated combination of these metrics would be likely to produce results better than the sum of the parts, but we do not present this because such an optimization approach strays from our goal of being as naive as possible.

6 Conclusions

This paper aims to take first steps towards describing a formal online chess cheat detection framework that serves as a basis for other researchers and the greater chess community to work collaboratively towards robust cheat detection systems. We believe that tackling cheat detection in an open manner does not jeopardize cheat detection's efficiency by revealing secrets to bad actors – even with all this knowledge in hand, it is not apparent to us how one would combine effective cheating with remaining fully undetected across all metrics, including those yet to be published. Further, by sharing cheat detection knowledge publicly, the validity of cheat detection frameworks can be scrutinized transparently, leading to improvement via the scientific method.

We contend that the fundamental idea driving cheat detection is that cheaters cannot mimic specific human behaviors in the long term. To assess exactly what human behaviors are, we consider a list of metrics that we believe measure a decision's complexity, including: move quality, response time, the number of available decisions, how many variables confound the decision-making process, and how much time is allotted to make a decision. On aggregate, humans exhibit concrete patterns that align with behavioral hypotheses. On the other hand, a selection of chess engines, including some designed to emulate human play, do not always follow these same trends. These behavioral differences can be leveraged for automated cheat detection. We find that there is some agreement between the predictions of naive binary classifiers grounded in behavioral hypotheses and Lichess' independent conclusions about which users are cheating. Overall, we hope that this paper promotes egalitarian dissemination of open chess cheat detection knowledge that has been long overdue.

References

1. Anderson, A., Kleinberg, J., Mullainathan, S.: Assessing human error against a benchmark of perfection. KDD 2016, New York, NY, USA, pp. 705–714. Association for Computing Machinery (2016). https://doi.org/10.1145/2939672.2939803
2. Barnes, D.J., Hernandez-Castro, J.: On the limits of engine analysis for cheating detection in chess. Computers & Security **48**, 58–73 (2015). https://doi.org/10.1016/j.cose.2014.10.002, https://www.sciencedirect.com/science/article/pii/S0167404814001485
3. Biswas, T., Regan, K.: Measuring level-k reasoning, satisficing, and human error in game-play data. In: 2015 IEEE 14th International Conference on Machine Learning and Applications (ICMLA), pp. 941–947 (2015). https://doi.org/10.1109/ICMLA.2015.233
4. Campbell, M., Hoane, A.J., Hsu, F.H.: Deep Blue. Artif. Intell. **134**(1), 57–83 (2002). https://doi.org/10.1016/S0004-3702(01)00129-1, https://www.sciencedirect.com/science/article/pii/S0004370201001291
5. Chabris, C.F., Hearst, E.S.: Visualization, pattern recognition, and forward search: effects of playing speed and sight of the position on grandmaster chess errors. Cogn. Sci. **27**(4), 637–648 (2003). https://doi.org/10.1207/s15516709cog2704_3, https://onlinelibrary.wiley.com/doi/abs/10.1207/s15516709cog2704_3
6. Chabris, C.F., Morris, C.L., Taubinsky, D., Laibson, D., Schuldt, J.P.: The allocation of time in decision-making. J. Eur. Econ. Assoc. **7**(2–3), 628–637 (2009). https://doi.org/10.1162/JEEA.2009.7.2-3.628
7. Chess24: Billionaire admits cheating against Anand in charity simul (2021). https://chess24.com/en/read/news/billionaire-admits-cheating-against-anand-in-charity-simul
8. Chess24: Meltwater Champions Chess Tour (2022). https://chess24.com/tour/
9. Chess.com: Bullet Chess Championship (2022). https://www.chess.com/article/view/bullet-chess-championship-2022
10. Chess.com: Computer Chess Championship (2022). https://www.chess.com/computer-chess-championship
11. Chess.com: Rapid Chess Championship (2022). https://www.chess.com/article/view/chesscom-rapid-chess-championship-2022
12. Chess.com: Titled Tuesday (2022). https://www.chess.com/article/view/titled-tuesday
13. Clarke, J.: Irwin - The protector of Lichess from all chess players villainous (2019). https://github.com/clarkerubber/irwin
14. Coquidé, C., Georgeot, B., Giraud, O.: Distinguishing humans from computers in the game of go: a complex network approach. EPL (Europhysics Letters) **119**(4), 48001 (2017). https://doi.org/10.1209/0295-5075/119/48001
15. Egri-Nagy, A., Tormanen, A.: Derived metrics for the game of Go - intrinsic network strength assessment and cheat-detection. In: 2020 Eighth International Symposium on Computing and Networking (CANDAR), Los Alamitos, CA, USA, pp. 9–18. IEEE Computer Society, November 2020. https://doi.org/10.1109/CANDAR51075.2020.00010, https://doi.ieeecomputersociety.org/10.1109/CANDAR51075.2020.00010
16. Fair Play Team at Chess.com: Hans niemann report (2022). https://drive.google.com/file/d/11IokKgTVSXdpYEzAuyViIleSZ_2wl0ag/view
17. FIDE - Fédération Internationale des Échecs: FIDE Ethics Commission announces the sanctions against Igor Rausis (2019). https://www.fide.com/news/246

18. FIDE - Fédération Internationale des Échecs: FIDE Statement on anti-cheating cases at Online Olympiad (2020). https://www.fide.com/news/674
19. FIDE - Fédération Internationale des Échecs: Statement regarding the FIDE World University Online Championships (2021). https://www.fide.com/news/1004
20. Haworth, G., Regan, K., Di Fatta, G.: Performance and prediction: Bayesian modelling of fallible choice in chess. In: van den Herik, H.J., Spronck, P. (eds.) ACG 2009. LNCS, vol. 6048, pp. 99–110. Springer, Heidelberg (2010). https://doi.org/10.1007/978-3-642-12993-3_10
21. Hoepman, J.H., Jacobs, B.: Increased security through open source. Commun. ACM **50**(1), 79–83 (2007). https://doi.org/10.1145/1188913.1188921
22. Holdaway, C., Vul, E.: Risk-taking in adversarial games: what can 1 billion online chess games tell us? Proc. Annual Meet. Cogn. Sci. Soc. **43**(43), 986–992 (2021)
23. Jayasekara, M.: Classification of chess games and players by styles using game data (2018). https://dl.ucsc.cmb.ac.lk/jspui/handle/123456789/4219
24. Kerckhoffs, A.: La cryptographie militaire. Journal des sciences militaires IX, 5–83 (1883)
25. Kossovsky, A.E.: Benford's law: theory, the general law of relative quantities, and forensic fraud detection applications., vol. 3. World Scientific (2014)
26. Laurens, P., Paige, R.F., Brooke, P.J., Chivers, H.: A novel approach to the detection of cheating in multiplayer online games. In: 12th IEEE International Conference on Engineering Complex Computer Systems (ICECCS 2007), pp. 97–106 (2007). https://doi.org/10.1109/ICECCS.2007.11
27. Lichess: Fishnet - Distributed Stockfish analysis for lichess.org (2022). https://github.com/lichess-org/fishnet
28. Lichess: Kaladin - Machine learning tool aimed at automating cheat detection using insights data (2022). https://github.com/lichess-org/kaladin
29. Lichess: Lichess Half-Year Update & New Feature Sneak Preview (2022). https://lichess.org/blog/YulPhhAAACAAvm1f/lichess-half-year-update-new-feature-sneak-preview
30. Lichess: Open Database (2022). https://database.lichess.org/
31. Lichess: Titled Arena Announcement(s) (2022). https://lichess.org/blog/YcY30BEAACIA38mp/titled-arena-announcements
32. M. Gleason: PGN-Spy - Chess game analyser for detection of cheating. https://github.com/MGleason1/PGN-Spy
33. McIlroy-Young, R., Sen, S., Kleinberg, J., Anderson, A.: Aligning superhuman AI with human behavior: chess as a model system. In: Proceedings of the 26th ACM SIGKDD International Conference on Knowledge Discovery and Data Mining, New York, NY, USA, pp. 1677–1687. Association for Computing Machinery (2020). https://doi.org/10.1145/3394486.3403219
34. McIlroy-Young, R., Wang, R., Sen, S., Kleinberg, J.M., Anderson, A.: Learning personalized models of human behavior in chess. CoRR abs/2008.10086 (2020). https://arxiv.org/abs/2008.10086
35. McIlroy-Young, R., Wang, Y., Sen, S., Kleinberg, J., Anderson, A.: Detecting individual decision-making style: exploring behavioral stylometry in chess. In: Ranzato, M., Beygelzimer, A., Dauphin, Y., Liang, P., Vaughan, J.W. (eds.) Advances in Neural Information Processing Systems. vol. 34, pp. 24482–24497. Curran Associates, Inc. (2021). https://proceedings.neurips.cc/paper/2021/file/ccf8111910291ba472b385e9c5f59099-Paper.pdf
36. Mercuri, R.T., Neumann, P.G.: Security by obscurity. Commun. ACM **46**(11), 160 (2003). https://doi.org/10.1145/948383.948413

37. Patria, R., Favian, S., Caturdewa, A., Suhartono, D.: Cheat detection on online chess games using convolutional and dense neural network. In: 2021 4th International Seminar on Research of Information Technology and Intelligent Systems (ISRITI), pp. 389–395 (2021). https://doi.org/10.1109/ISRITI54043.2021.9702792
38. Regan, K., Biswas, T., Zhou, J.: Human and computer preferences at chess (2014). https://www.aaai.org/ocs/index.php/WS/AAAIW14/paper/view/8859
39. Regan, K.W., Macieja, B., Haworth, G.M.C.: Understanding distributions of chess performances. In: van den Herik, H.J., Plaat, A. (eds.) ACG 2011. LNCS, vol. 7168, pp. 230–243. Springer, Heidelberg (2012). https://doi.org/10.1007/978-3-642-31866-5_20
40. Rheude, T.: Time management in chess with neural networks and human data (2021). https://ml-research.github.io/papers/rheude2021time.pdf
41. Russek, E., Acosta-Kane, D., van Opheusden, B., Mattar, M.G., Griffiths, T.: Time spent thinking in online chess reflects the value of computation. PsyArXiv (2022). https://doi.org/10.31234/osf.io/8j9zx
42. Schneier, B.: The nonsecurity of secrecy. Commun. ACM **47**(10), 120 (2004). https://doi.org/10.1145/1022594.1022629
43. Sigman, M., Etchemendy, P., Fernandez Slezak, D., Cecchi, G.: Response time distributions in rapid chess: A large-scale decision making experiment. Front. Neurosci. 4 (2010). https://doi.org/10.3389/fnins.2010.00060, https://www.frontiersin.org/article/10.3389/fnins.2010.00060
44. Silver, D., Huang, A., Maddison, C.J., Guez, A., Sifre, L., Van Den Driessche, G., Schrittwieser, J., Antonoglou, I., Panneershelvam, V., Lanctot, M., et al.: Mastering the game of Go with deep neural networks and tree search. Nature **529**(7587), 484–489 (2016)
45. Silver, D., et al.: Mastering the game of Go without human knowledge. Nature **550**(7676), 354–359 (2017)
46. Sunde, U., Zegners, D., Strittmatter, A.: Speed, quality, and the optimal timing of complex decisions: Field evidence. PsyArXiv (2022). https://doi.org/10.48550/arxiv.2201.10808
47. The New York Times: Three players suspended for conspiring to cheat (2012). https://www.nytimes.com/2012/08/12/crosswords/chess/chess-feller-hauchard-and-marzolo-are-suspended.html
48. The Stockfish team: Stockfish - Open Source Chess Engine (2022). https://stockfishchess.org/
49. US Chess: US Chess Endorses Dr. Kenneth Regan's Fair Play Methodology (2021). https://new.uschess.org/news/us-chess-endorses-dr-kenneth-regans-fair-play-methodology
50. Yan, J., Randell, B.: An investigation of cheating in online games. IEEE Secur. Privacy **7**(3), 37–44 (2009). https://doi.org/10.1109/MSP.2009.60

Procedural Generation of Rush Hour Levels

Gaspard de Batz de Trenquelleon[1,2], Ahmed Choukarah[1,3], Milo Roucairol[1],
Maël Addoum[4], and Tristan Cazenave[1(✉)]

[1] LAMSADE, Université Paris Dauphine - PSL, CNRS, Paris, France
Tristan.Cazenave@dauphine.fr
[2] École Polytechnique, Palaiseau, France
[3] École Normale Supérieure - PSL, Paris, France
[4] ISART Digital, Paris, France

Abstract. Procedural generation of puzzle games allows for more varied
and diverse levels, which provides a better gaming experience. However,
the generation based on deep-learning approaches is very challenging
with this genre of games due to their inherent complexity relative to
strict design rules and discrete components. In this work, we propose
a framework that is composed of three main modules: a solver and two
classifiers. Instances of *Rush Hour* are generated randomly and the solver
aims to assess the playability of the generated levels by classifying solvable and unsolvable levels and by evaluating the difficulty of solvable
levels. Two neural networks are used to improve the generation. One
network is trained to differentiate between solvable and unsolvable levels
and the other is trained to classify the difficulty of levels. The robustness
of the framework is examined on 6×6 and 7×7 grid dimensions. The
results obtained showed the effectiveness of our modules in generating
interesting and various levels with four degrees of difficulty for the *Rush
Hour* puzzle, where the classifier was able to quickly identify unsolvable
levels. Our framework could be easily adapted and extended for procedurally generating other game genres, such as Platformer or RogueLike.

Keywords: Procedural level generation · Deep Learning · Puzzle games

1 Introduction

Rush Hour is a puzzle game, initially not a video game, in which the player has
to unblock a red car from a crowded parking lot. In the initial version, it takes
place on a 6×6 grid with only movable cars, but variants exist on larger grids
or with unmovable blocks.

We explored different methods to generate levels of *Rush Hour* by trying to
maximize the interest of a level according to the number of moves needed to
complete it, as well as to detect unsolvable levels.

Using Generative Adversarial Network (GAN) architecture proved to be an
inadequate solution. Hence, we attempted to create a discriminator that would

quickly classify solvable and unsolvable levels to generate then random levels and ranking them according to their interesting degree.

In order to provide unsolvable levels for our training set, we used a solver and a random generator despite that is not the most efficient way. A neural network was trained to recognize solvable from unsolvable levels. Since the preliminary results are encouraging, the network is being examined to generate more complex and larger grids for which generation could be computationally expensive with the current solver.

The rest of the paper is structured as follows: Sect. 2 presents related work and Sect. 3 describes the application of a solver algorithm to classify solvable or unsolvable levels. Section 4 gives a more detailed insight into the neural network architecture used for the random generator. Section 5 concludes with our findings and proposes possible future work.

2   Related Work

PCG via Machine Learning (PCGML) is an emerging technology area that generates new game content using machine-learned models on existing content. Recently, GAN has produced significant results as a new approach for PCG in the computer vision field, such as video games.

2.1   PCG for Puzzles Games

Puzzle games are a specific type of game and there are several categories for puzzles such as Sokoban-type, Sliding, Tile-Matching, Mazes, Path-building, Physics-based and Narrative Puzzles [4]. PCGML techniques have mainly focused on Roguelike or Platformer game genres, because the generation of puzzles requires significant knowledge of specific design rules and constraints. Hence, most PCG approaches to generating puzzle levels have mostly focused on search-based methods or constructive algorithms such as the Markov chain. Sturtevant et al. used a large-scale best-first search-based approach for analysis and content generation for Fling! (2013), a puzzle of Sokoban-type and tile-matching [16]. Collette et al. generated hard configurations of the *Rush hour* puzzle using a constructive method based on symbolic technique with binary decision diagrams that allows to iteratively compute reachable configuration from a set of solvable initial levels for *Rush Hour* [2]. The constructive methods have shown their robustness for Narrative puzzle generation [3] [5] [6]. Recently, Monte Carlo Tree Search (MCTS) approach has been widely used to procedurally generate different game contents as an optimization problem. Kartal et al. used the MCTS approach to automatically generate *Sokoban* levels that are guaranteed to be solvable with varying sizes and difficulty [11].

2.2   GAN for PCG

The GANs have shown their ability for platformer and Roguelike game genres. Schubert et al. proposed TOAD-GAN (Token-based One-shot Arbitrary Dimension GAN) to generate *Super Mario Bros* 2D platform levels using a single original level for training [14]. This approach is inspired by SinGan architecture that allows learning from a single image [15]. Torrado et al. used a new GAN called Conditional Embedding Self-attention GAN architecture to condition their generation process and obtain the targeted token distributions in the generated levels [13]. Gutierrez et al. coupled GAN models to generate individual rooms of *The Legend of Zelda* with a graph grammar that combines these rooms into a dungeon [7]. GANs have also been applied to generate content for serious games, Park et al. used Deep Convolutional GAN (DCGAN) approach to automatically generate levels for educational games that incorporate the desired learning objectives with an adaptive gameplay [12]. A similar approach was used to generate game scenarios and context images while taking specific features into account to provide only plausible and enjoyable images for the game design [10]. Concerning board games, there is little research documenting the ability of the GAN approach to produce playable levels for puzzles. Hald et al. applied GAN to generate puzzle levels for Lily's Garden. While their GANs allow a good map-shape to be generated, they were not able to produce the targeted token distribution [8].

3 *Rush Hour* Solvers

Solving a *Rush Hour* grid is a non trivial problem as a single grid often has over 10 000 possible combinations, Fig. 1. The problem can be considered as a graph where the nodes are the states of the grid. Each two nodes are related if we can get from one to the other by moving a car one block away. We naively started with a Breadth-First search algorithm that solved the puzzle. This is a slow and inefficient algorithm as it explores irrelevant positions. It should be noted that the entire graph was explored because no appropriate criteria were identified to find the unsolvable levels. To improve our search, we use a heuristic that determines whether a grid is close to the solution or not, see Fig. 2. It is based on a score calculated by the Algorithm 1.

As shown in Fig. 2, the lower the score, the less the red car is blocked in the parking lot and therefore the better the grid is (a zero score represents a solved grid).

Using this score, the initial algorithm is modified into a Greedy-Best First Search Algorithm 2. This algorithm significantly improves the time required to solve the solvable puzzles. However, it did not considerably improve the complexity of the unsolvable puzzles, as the entire graph still to be explored.

Figures 3(a) and 3(b) show the times for solvable and unsolvable levels, respectively. Expect for one outlier, the GBFS algorithm is much faster than the breadth-first search algorithm, see Fig. 3(a). The time is directly correlated and similar since all states are explored, and are sufficiently large to expect a significant improvement using an AI discriminator, see Fig. 3(b).

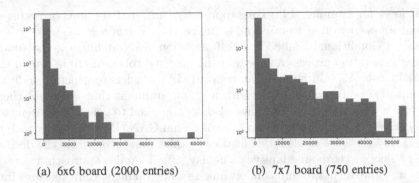

(a) 6x6 board (2000 entries)   (b) 7x7 board (750 entries)

Fig. 1. Distribution of state graph size

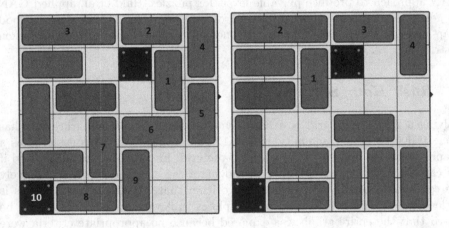

Fig. 2. Example of heuristic score evaluation

Algorithm 1. Heuristic score

1: $BlockingCars = []$
2: **for** each Car between RedCar and exit **do**
3:     $BlockingCars.add(Car)$
4: **end for**
5: **while** BlockingCars changes **do**
6:     **for** Car in BlockingCars **do**
7:         **for** OtherCar in Board **do**
8:             **if** OtherCar blocks Car and OtherCar not in BlockingCars **then**
9:                 $BlockingCars.add(OtherCar)$
10:            **end if**
11:        **end for**
12:    **end for**
13: **end while**
14: $Score = length(BlockingCars)$
15: $return\ Score$

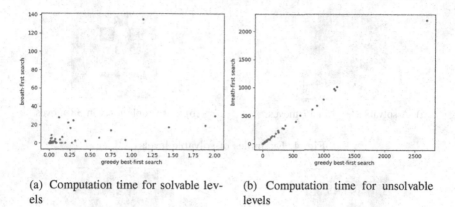

(a) Computation time for solvable levels

(b) Computation time for unsolvable levels

Fig. 3. comparison of the computational time for the two solving methods

---

Algorithm 2. Greedy best first search

```
    ToExplore = [InitialState]
 2: Explored = []
    function GBFS(ToExplore, Explored)
 4:    if ToExplore = [] then
          Return False
 6:    end if
       ToExplore.sort(HeuristicScore)
 8:    State = ToExplore.pop()
       Explored.add(State)
10:    if State is Solution then
          return True
12:    end if
       for Board in State.neighboors do
14:       if Board not in ToExplore and Board not in Explored then
             ToExplore.add(Board)
16:       end if
       end for
18:    return GBFS(ToExplore, Explored)
    end function
```

---

4   Accelerating the Generation Using Neural Networks

While, with sufficient time and computing power, the most solvable levels of the 6×6 *Rush Hour* grid can be found [1], any attempt to do so for bigger grids requires excessive amounts of computations.

Our approach was to use transfer learning to obtain an estimator on the solvability of random levels. To do so, we first used a database comprised of solvable levels (see Fig. 4) and unsolvable levels (see Fig. 5) generated randomly with a 50:50 distribution. We then use a Dense-Net [9] to learn to predict for the 6×6 grids if a setting is solvable or not.

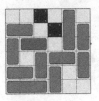

(a) A solvable level in 17 moves   (b) A solvable level in 38 moves

Fig. 4. Examples of solvable levels

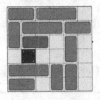
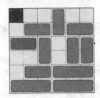

(a) An example of an unsolvable level   (b) Another example of an unsolvable level

Fig. 5. Examples of unsolvable levels

This specific network can have two different uses. It is known that the search algorithms become very computationally expensive as the grid sizes increase, especially for unsolvable levels. Our goal is to use transfer learning to avoid these scenarios and adapt the network to learn the solvability of higher dimension grids with few examples, as these tend to be very costly to generate. By using a neural network to dismiss all the unsolvable levels, we can speed up the generation process.

The other use for this network is to generate levels through a GAN's architecture, where our network would be the discriminator, but this still has to be explored.

4.1   Architecture Choice

After testing multiple architectures, it seemed that most deep networks had trouble with the task. We deduced that the added padding would dilute the information too much, as our grid size of 6×6 was too small. However, the Dense-net model allows that each layer receives a concatenation of every input each previous layer has received, thus leading for a constant flow of information and avoiding information loss between each layer.

4.2   Database

The number of solvable and unsolvable levels must be in the same order of magnitude. In our database, there are 2,577,412 puzzle obtained from the Fogleman database. Figures 4(a) and 4(b) represent two examples of solvable levels with 17 and 38 moves, respectively. However, no source for unsolvable levels was available. To address this issue, we synthesized a number of non solvable puzzles, both easy (Fig. 5(a)) and hard (Fig. 5(b)). We then randomly select from the solvable database to construct our final database.

4.3   Experimental Results

Solvability Tests - 6 × 6. Using the 6×6 database limited to 100 000 levels randomly selected from the initial database. This database is divided into 80% train and 20% test. For our hyperparameters, we have a learning rate of $5e^{-3}$, cosine scheduling and weight decay with a factor of $1e^{-3}$. The algorithm quickly converge towards a 100% accuracy on both train and test set. Moreover, our approach was tested with levels including black boxes, and the accuracy rate reaches 99.9% using the same parameters. Figure 6 shows three examples of generated levels.

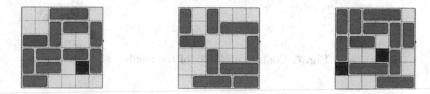

Fig. 6. Three examples of generated levels.

Solvability Tests - 7 × 7 - Transfer Learning. We do not have a real database of 7×7 levels, so we opted to generate a database of levels with the Heuristic methods. With that, we generated a total of about 2300 examples, with 1800 solvable and 500 unsolvable levels. Unfortunately, this database is unable to provide efficient training. Nevertheless, we can use our results from the 6×6 results using transfer learning as a support for the 7×7. Using this method with hyperparameters similar to the ones above, the results are obtained with 88.6% of accuracy rate.

Learning of Difficulty Levels 6 × 6. The created database of *Rush Hour* also included the minimum number of moves necessary to solve each level. This number is used as an indicator of difficulty for each level and train a model on 5 different categories of levels: Unsolvable - Easy - Medium - Hard - Very Hard.

The idea being to have better control over our generation, as most of the levels generated can be quite simplistic.

For similar hyperparameters, the obtained accuracy reaches 87.5%. This can be explained with the confusion matrix depicted in Fig. 7 where most of the misclassifications are edge cases, as difficulty can be a complicated concept to reduce to only four categories.

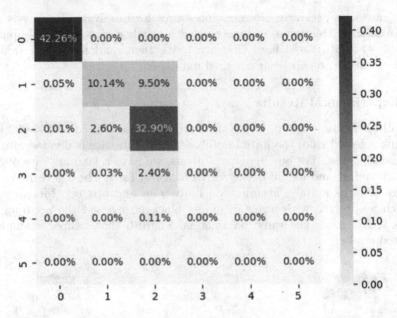

Fig. 7. Confusion Matrix of the results

4.4 Discussion

While we first tried approaches such as GAN, the network had difficulty grasping the importance of certain concepts in puzzles, such as puzzle complexity and form. Using our approach that is a more restricted concept gave us a better control over the generator, thus avoiding such issues. This approach also allows these results to be adapted to other games such as Sokoban, or other video games such as Angry Birds or Mario with a more restricted generation protocol. However, it is important to note that the availability of a complete database for the 6×6 and the ability to generate a small but sufficient one for 7×7 grid are what gave convincing results. Similarly, as grids become larger, computational power becomes a limiting factor for generating learning databases.

5   Conclusion

We defined a general approach to level generation that works well for the *Rush Hour* puzzle. We have designed a neural network able to discriminate very efficiently between solvable and unsolvable levels of *Rush Hour*. We have shown that a solver with Greedy Best First Search is considerably more efficient for solvable levels than a naive Breadth First Search, but that both algorithms take a lot of time to detect that a level is unsolvable. This property led us to design a neural network that detects unsolvable levels faster. Using a dense network trained on a dataset including unsolvable levels randomly generated and detected by our solver, we reached 100% accuracy on the detection of unsolvable levels for size 6×6. We also tested on size 7×7, and experimented with transfer learning and the automatic classification of the difficulty of generated levels.

The general intent of this research is to improve the gameplay by increasing the variability of the games using levels of varying difficulties. It is also to improve the reliability of the generating algorithm detecting unsolvable levels. It is important for the game industry since it provides a richer universe to the players.

Future work may include the use of our framework for other puzzles such as Sokoban, Angry Birds and Professor Layton and for video games such as platformers and roguelike.

References

1. https://www.michaelfogleman.com/rush/
2. Collette, S., Raskin, J.-F., Servais, F.: On the symbolic computation of the hardest configurations of the RUSH HOUR game. In: van den Herik, H.J., Ciancarini, P., Donkers, H.H.L.M.J. (eds.) CG 2006. LNCS, vol. 4630, pp. 220–233. Springer, Heidelberg (2007). https://doi.org/10.1007/978-3-540-75538-8_20
3. Dart, I., Nelson, M.J.: Smart terrain causality chains for adventure-game puzzle generation. In: 2012 IEEE Conference on Computational Intelligence and Games (CIG), pp. 328–334 (2012). https://doi.org/10.1109/CIG.2012.6374173
4. De Kegel, B., Haahr, M.: Procedural puzzle generation: a survey. IEEE Trans. Games **12**(1), 21–40 (2020). https://doi.org/10.1109/TG.2019.2917792
5. Doran, J., Parberry, I.: A prototype quest generator based on a structural analysis of quests from four mmorpgs. In: Proceedings of the 2nd International Workshop on Procedural Content Generation in Games. PCGames 2011, New York, NY, USA. Association for Computing Machinery (2011). https://doi.org/10.1145/2000919.2000920
6. Fernández-Vara, C., Thomson, A.: Procedural generation of narrative puzzles in adventure games: the puzzle-dice system. In: Proceedings of the The Third Workshop on Procedural Content Generation in Games. PCG 2012, New York, NY, USA, pp. 1–6. Association for Computing Machinery (2012). https://doi.org/10.1145/2538528.2538538
7. Gutierrez, J., Schrum, J.: Generative adversarial network rooms in generative graph grammar dungeons for the legend of Zelda. In: 2020 IEEE Congress on Evolutionary Computation (CEC), pp. 1–8 (2020). https://doi.org/10.1109/CEC48606.2020.9185631
8. Hald, A., Hansen, J.S., Kristensen, J., Burelli, P.: Procedural content generation of puzzle games using conditional generative adversarial networks. In: International Conference on the Foundations of Digital Games. FDG 2020, New York, NY, USA. Association for Computing Machinery (2020). https://doi.org/10.1145/3402942.3409601
9. Huang, G., Liu, Z., Weinberger, K.Q.: Densely connected convolutional networks. CoRR abs/1608.06993 (2016). http://arxiv.org/abs/1608.06993
10. Jiang, M., Zhang, L.: An interactive evolution strategy based deep convolutional generative adversarial network for 2d video game level procedural content generation. In: 2021 International Joint Conference on Neural Networks (IJCNN), pp. 1–6 (2021). https://doi.org/10.1109/IJCNN52387.2021.9533847

11. Kartal, B., Sohre, N., Guy, S.J.: Generating Sokoban puzzle game levels with monte Carlo tree search. In: The IJCAI-16 Workshop on General Game Playing, p. 47 (2016)
12. Park, K., Mott, B.W., Min, W., Boyer, K.E., Wiebe, E.N., Lester, J.C.: Generating educational game levels with multistep deep convolutional generative adversarial networks. In: 2019 IEEE Conference on Games (CoG), pp. 1–8 (2019). https://doi.org/10.1109/CIG.2019.8848085
13. Rodriguez Torrado, R., Khalifa, A., Cerny Green, M., Justesen, N., Risi, S., Togelius, J.: Bootstrapping conditional GANs for video game level generation. In: 2020 IEEE Conference on Games (CoG), pp. 41–48 (2020). https://doi.org/10.1109/CoG47356.2020.9231576
14. Schubert, F., Awiszus, M., Rosenhahn, B.: Toad-GAN: a flexible framework for few-shot level generation in token-based games. IEEE Trans. Games **14**(2), 284–293 (2022). https://doi.org/10.1109/TG.2021.3069833
15. Shaham, T.R., Dekel, T., Michaeli, T.: SINGAN: learning a generative model from a single natural image. In: 2019 IEEE/CVF International Conference on Computer Vision (ICCV), pp. 4569–4579 (2019). https://doi.org/10.1109/ICCV.2019.00467
16. Sturtevant, N.: An argument for large-scale breadth-first search for game design and content generation via a case study of fling! In: Proceedings of the AAAI Conference on Artificial Intelligence and Interactive Digital Entertainment, vol. 9, no. 3, pp.28–33 (2021). https://ojs.aaai.org/index.php/AIIDE/article/view/12594

Author Index

Printed in the United States
by Baker & Taylor Publisher Services